TABLE OF CONTENTS
A RUINOUS ROAD TWICE TAKEN: A COMPARISON OF THE 1920S WITH THE DECADE

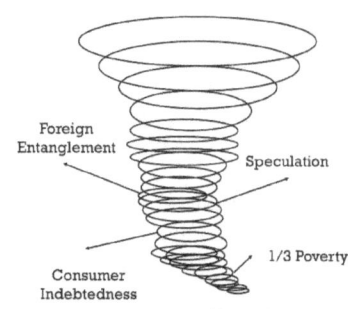

Franklin Shipman's:
A Ruinous Road Twice Taken
How the Past Decades of 2000 -2010
Closely Parallels the 1920's
[Document subtitle]
OF 2000-2010

Introduction: The Monetary Solution vs. The Disparities In Earnings Causation

Chapter One: The Economic Landscape of the 1920s and Its Lessons For Today: Pp. 3-60 This opening chapter sets forth the dominant economic characteristics of the 1920s. The determining economic factors leading to the Great Depression consisted of the following:

      1. Great disparities in earnings and wealth which consisted of at least one-third being in poverty.

      2. Attempt to compensate for inadequacy of earnings by extending somewhat easy consumer credit consisting of installment payments for the new durable goods. This credit was available to primary the middle class, upper middle class, and the wealthy.

      3. Improper and unwise banking practices consisting of call loans to brokers, investments in foreign nation's securities, overinvestment in real estate mortgages, and improper 'promotions' of investment securities by investment banks without regard to any due diligence as to the

      Franklin Shipman
      10-17-2014

soundness of the securities sold. Much of this banking practices was due to the lack of commercial banking opportunities for the banks who were confronted with capital being provided by stock options and retained earnings.

4. The attempts by the Federal Reserve Bank to satisfy demands imposed internationally by the Gold Standard and domestic demands presented by speculation and from 1929 on by declining consumption and investment. This proved to be unharmonious.

5. Due to their unwise extension of credit lending and investments, most banks were near insolvency. This meant that any infusion of cash by the Fed to the banks led to the banks buying federal securities to strengthen their balance sheets---not lending of the new cash reserves.

These conditions proved unresponsive to historical efforts by the Fed in their purchasing of treasury notes and window lending.

Chapter Two. Pp. 61-62 How Closely the Past Decade Resembles the 1920s. This chapter sets forth an outline of several parallels which exist between then and now.

Chapter Three. The Great Disparities in Earnings and Wealth. Parallel No. 1 Pp. 63-95 This chapter draws a comparison of the financial conditions of the middle class of the 1920s and their decline today. Featured are the decline of middle class jobs today and the result in scarcity of upper mobility which results. A comparison is made from the Lynd's Middletown- a book about Muncie Indiana in the late 1920s and early 1930s which cites the lack of upward mobility of most workers. In today's economy, only a dual working spouse household earnings provide a semblance of a middle class income -which is lowered by child care costs and work-related costs of the second earnings. The lack of opportunities for many college grads is cited in studies showing that many college grads work in jobs not requiring a college degree. Hindering any upward mobility for many college grads is the average college debt of $25,000, much of which is held by the students' middle class parents.

Chapter Four. Parallel Condition No. 2. Easy Credit Lending and The Lack of Commercial Lending by Banks. Pp 96-118 This chapter relates how loosely credit lending such as subprime mortgages (buyers lacking the three Cs of credit, cash, or collateral), securitization of mortgages made possible by the low interest rates and repeal of the Glass-Steagall Act which had prohibited commercial banks from operating investment banking also, and loose credit card debt extending for consumption. Following the lead of mortgage securitization, auto debt and variations of securitization occurred which resulted in an international banking system holding many insecure financial securities. The overall strategy of the Fed was that low interest lending would result in increased sales of real estate bolstered by equity lending and refinancing of mortgages. Continuing rise in the prices of homes created a 'wealth effect' consisting of increased value of homes. All of the above activities which were primarily in the financial industry were pursued without any regard for the decline of earnings in the middle class and the lack of earnings by the age group 25-35.

Chapter Five. Parallel Condition No. 3. Financing Beyond Borders and Lack of Regulation. Pp. 119-125 Summarizes the unsound and unethical banking and investment banking practices made possible by low interest rates and the securitization of securities.

Chapter Six. Parallel Condition No. 4 Opportunity Costs Caused by Speculation and an aversion to long-term capital investments. Pp. 125-142 This chapter shows how speculation and financial market trading denied the country capital investments in industries starving for capital and for any promising long-term industrial developments such as the drug penicillin .Speculation and other financial activities produced a scarcity of skilled jobs by the end of the 1920s to the extent that in the early 1930s any demand by industries for skilled workers could not be met due to the wide-spread existence of formerly skilled workers working in unskilled or unrelated skilled positions such as the city of Kokomo, Indiana experienced.

Chapter Seven: Parallel Condition No.5. Seeking Domestic Stabilization While Under the Coercion Of Foreign Financial Market Demands. Pp. 143-157 This chapter relates how the Fed's attempt to conform to gold standard mandates while also attempting to address domestic problems associated with excessive speculation and call loans by banks.

Chapter Eight. Parallel Condition No. 6. Confronting International Trading and The Fed's efforts at Corrections. Pp. 158-177. This chapter relates the history of the currency exchange ratio experience since 1945. It shows how the fixed ratio of the dollar's value to other foreign currencies was an effort to stabilize prices for business activities in international commerce. If an American grain dealer exports 200 tons at $10 per ton in March to be delivered in October after harvest, the dealer expects that he will still receive the $10 value in October and that dramatic currency exchange value for the dollar will not happen. A fixed currency exchange ratio guaranteed the dealer that his expected revenue will not be distorted or changed by other global economic trading. Given the stability and soundness of the U.S. dollar after WWII, this fixed ratio seemed sensible. However, maintaining a fixed ratio to the dollar impaired other nation's efforts at effective domestic policy. Say the franc had to maintain a currency exchange ratio to the dollar of 10 to 1. What if a sever recession hit France and its central bank increased the money supply of francs in order to establish low interest rates. With the supply of francs increased without a corresponding demand increase, the franc would abandon its fixed ratio as the increased supply (with international demand unchanged) could create a natural currency exchange value now of 13 francs to a dollar. If France tried to maintain the fixed ratio, it would be obligated to ignore any monetary domestic policy correction of its recession. After World War II, many economic transformations were occurring in Europe under the Marshall Plan and it lesser developed countries now recovering from a damaged past. The great economic expansions witnessed in Japan after the War and now China introduces new currencies which become more prominent in currency trading in financial markets and in goods and services. Even though President Nixon's taking the dollar off of the gold guarantee is often cited as the beginning of the floating currency exchange regime, his policy is only more public: other forces were by the early 1970s working their influences on the international financial and goods markets. As mentioned above, nations found an overriding need to ignore any fixed currency exchange ratio in order to deal effectively with their own domestic economic needs. Also, the Tifflin effect became more real where under its postulate the dollar becomes more unstable the more prevalent its global usage. With other nations having dollar reserves in great amounts, it became more difficult to achieve stability by mandating a fixed ratio to the dollar. Nevertheless, only a certain degree of departure from the original fixed ratio would be tolerated as central banks would intervene by buying dollars in order to increase the exchange value of the dollar or sell dollars in order to decrease its exchange value. Thus, if a cheap dollar threatened the export economy of Germany or Japan, central banks would intervene by buying dollar in order to restore a workable currency ratio. Burdening any policy corrections with respect to harmonizing foreign and domestic currency concerns was displacement of the real economy by speculators -particularly 'fast traders' using the internet buying and selling currencies and securities in milliseconds. The exposure to European banks and others to the securitized mortgages and others introduced new currency alignment difficulties. This chapter is an attempt to provide the historical background for understanding the next chapter.

Chapter Nine Confronting International Currency Trading: Identifying Causes and Effects To Determine Appropriate Policy Responses. Parallel No. 7 Pp. 179-242 This chapter attempts to show that any attempt by The Fed to harmonize international concerns and domestic mandates of monetary policies met with any difficulties concerning the exchange value of the dollar as it affects domestic conditions creates a policy at war with itself. Recent encounters with the Chinese exports whereby the Chinese are alleged to maintain a devalued yuan in order to give them an export advantage is of concern to many American businesses as it is to many Asian economies. Should the Fed make a special effort at the decline of the dollar with respect to the concern it poses in the fact that so many dollar-dominated treasury notes and other securities are held by the Chinese and the Japanese for example. How far a decline in the exchange value of the dollar can be tolerated? Or must the Fed work through solutions which our domestic economy presents while giving attention to the international market where it can be effectively integrated with domestic policies? The rise of the Chinese enormous economic growth and its demand for commodities and other natural resources effects the currency exchange values of almost every international player. Also described in this chapter is the interplay of interest rate increased by some national central banks upon the capital flow internationally. The main lesson to learn is how financial trading and speculation (in particular electronic trading) casts the real economy of goods and services into chaos.

Chapter Ten: The Credit Crunch Parallel No. 8 Pp 243-266
The lack of lending by financial institutions reflected their impaired capital condition which often bordered on insolvency. Attempts by the Federal Reserve Bank then and now to provide additional reserves has resulted in the banks efforts to improve their balance sheet conditions with the additional funds- not aggressive lending. In the past decade the Fed has resorted to buying stock of the endangered banks in addition to buying their troubled assets. Due to accumulated debt of consumers, the credit lending industry suffered from an impaired supply and unqualified demand side-borrowers who lacked the 3 Cs of cash, credit, and collateral. At least one-third of Americans lacked the three Cs in the early 1930s and therefore would not be eligible for any low interest loans. Only easy credit debt and subprime lending allowed the increased lending in the past decade. In addition to impaired supply and unqualified demand for credit is and was the distorting and weakening impact of the trading of the financial industry and its dominance in the GDP.

Chapter Eleven: Who Carried the Burden of Proof? The Monetarists that an increased money supply in 1930-31 would have spared the nation from the calamity of the Great Depression.? Pp 267-301 We return to the opening inquiry--Did the Fed miss an opportunity to prevent the Great Depression by failing to increase the money supply so as to restore consumption and lending. What does the reader believe now given the following economic conditions which prevailed then and somewhat today?

1. Great disparities in earnings which made it impossible for some to consume even necessities. Only through credit card debt and subprime lending were those not middle class able to buy. Others compensated for inadequate earnings by relying upon equity loans or refinancing of mortgages.

2. Consumption maintained primarily through unsustainable consumer debt.

3. Excessive speculation and improper investment banking. Most income generated was internal in the form of commissions and fees--not as a result of the investments promoted by the investment bankers.

4. The lack of substantial employment opportunities for college grads and skilled in middle income jobs. The lack of development of middle class jobs is due to the unbalanced industry structure created by speculation and low-risk investment. A nation cannot afford this type of 'opportunity costs' imposed by unwise capital usage--financial capital exceeding manufacturing capital.

5. The denial of upward mobility for most college grads and skilled workers. This condition existed in the late 1920s as reported by the Lynd's in their book Middletown about the city of Muncie Indiana.

6. A banking system which does not respond in aggressive lending despite an infusion of additional reserves by the Fed.

From the above economic landscape which fundamentally describes both the 1920s and the decade of 2000-2010, can one persuasively argue that low interest rates would ignite an economic recovery? Can low interest rate loans be expected to be available for essentially high risk borrowers? What does our recent experience tell us about the future for college grads that low interest rates made possible? Home buying? Continued consumption on income which remained the same or even diminished? Job opportunities open up by high tech borrowing?

What exists today which helps explain why we have yet to experience fully a great depression? Could it be the following entitlements available now but not in 1930-31 have served as stabilizers?

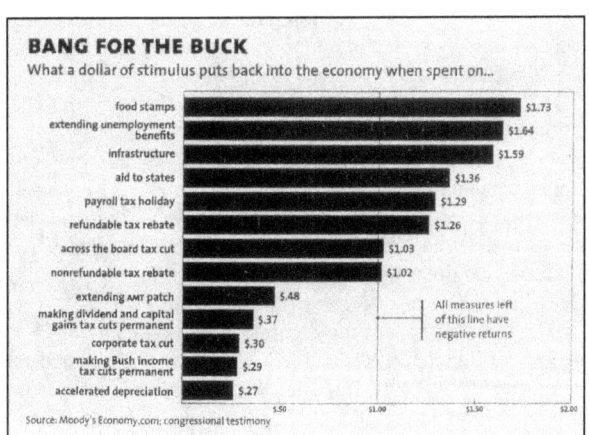

Chapter 12 Summing Up. What lessons we should gain from both experiences In seeking answers, the reader should ask himself/herself the following questions set forth below in the Preface:

Preface
A Reader's Challenge

To place oneself in today's economy compared to one similarly situated by age, occupation, or medical condition during the 1920s, consider the following:

1. In the late 1920s, most young adults sought immediate employment after graduating from high school and only those from the middle class or upper class families considered going to college. Most young workers remained at the same job and had little chance to move up to better jobs. These conditions were cited in the Lynds' book, Middletown, which was actually Muncie, Indiana in the late 1920. If the reader is in the age group of 25 to 35, ask yourself, if you have a college degree, are you presently employed in the field for which you received a degree or does your job even require a degree? What are your chances of upward mobility into a higher paying job and a job with more prestige? Have you experienced in today's economy the scarcity of professional or skilled trade opportunities to improve your finances and status?

2. If the reader is near the ages of 50 to 65 and you have recently lost a job at a manufacturing plant, what are the chances of you finding another job which pays a similar wage? Will you find a job which offers only part-time employment or maybe temporary employment at reduced pay? How does this compare with the chances of workers who were over 40 years of age and who had lost their jobs in the late 1920s

3. What if you are a boomer nearing retirement age of 65? Do you have adequate financial security for retirement in the form of a good retirement plan or have you suffered stock market losses in you 401(k) retirement plan? What about your wealth? Have you suffered a loss of equity in your home? Must you now depend upon a job instead of retiring? How do these conditions of bloomers compare with the financial security of the elderly in the 1920s? Does accumulated debt plague both in these decades?

4. Does today's declining middle class bear any comparison to that of the 1920s in that both suffered from declining job opportunities with little chance of upward mobility. Disparities in earnings reflect the decreasing number of middle class jobs in both decades. Also, both suffered from accumulated consumer debt to the point that they could not sustain consumption as before.

5. Do the recent scandals concerning banking practices in lending and in offering investments resemble the practices of banks in the 1920s to the point that both displaced investments in long term projects and instead pursued financial riches that involved more liquid commitments in asset holding. Does it matter that the emphasis in investment banking was to generate internal earnings without any real concern for the soundness of the investments which they sold?

6. As a result of the dominance of financial markets and their allied industries of real estate and insurance, do you feel that vital industries such as textiles, mining, clothing and shoes manufacturing and other durable goods industries suffered neglect?

7. Do you feel that the Fed gave excessive attention to the international value of the dollar to the neglect of domestic monetary needs?

8. Finally, what do you feel low interest rates accomplished during the period 2000-2010? Would they have helped during the period of 1930-32? What kind of relief was sought immediately by the national government--assistance to the poor and unemployed or rescuing the banks. Did the banks respond to the added reserves given them by making aggressive lending to consumers and business in both periods? What kind of interest rates are demanded for high risk lending--low interest rates or high interest rates? What does that tell you about the likelihood that low interest rates would have prevented the Great Depression? Does the fact that low interest rates promoted a boom in home sales and significant increases in the prices and values of existing homes made equity lending and mortgage refinancing possible. This so-called 'wealth effect' was the Fed's only immediate strategy for recovery even though this would assume that the housing industry business cycle would be repealed.(prices would never decline.)

Today's Economy by Franklin Shipman

Chapter 1

A RUINOUS ROAD TWICE TAKEN

COMPARING ECONOMIC DISTURBANCES OF THE 1920s and THE DECADE OF 2000-2010:

The Monetarists:

The Milton Friedman/Schwartz View:

From their book <u>A Monetary History of the United States</u>

"The drastic decline in the quantity of money during those years and the occurrence of a banking panic of unprecedented severity were not the inevitable consequences of other economic changes. They did not reflect the absence of power on the part of the Federal Reserve System to prevent them. Throughout the contraction the system had ample powers to cut short the tragic process of monetary deflation and banking collapse. Had it used these powers effectively in late1930 or even in early to mid-1931…… such action would have eased the severity of the contraction and very likely would have brought it to an end at a much earlier date."

The Income Distribution View

(2) Opposed to the Friedman/Schwartz view

Is a more fundamental cause--the great disparities of income distribution during the 1920s. David Kennedy, for example, in his <u>Freedom From Fear</u>, stated, "without broadly distributed purchasing power, the engine of mass production would have no outlet and would eventually fall idle". p.22

Or as offered by Robert S. McElvaine in The Great Depression: In dismissing exports as a correction for overproduction of goods, he states, "The basic macroeconomic problem growing out of mal-distribution (of income) was that those with the means to buy more of the products of mass production industry could satisfy their needs and desires by spending only a small fraction of their incomes, while those whose needs and desires were not satisfied had no money. One obvious temporary solution was to let those who wanted goods to buy them without the money. Thus the installment plan arose for the first time on a massive scale. By the second half of the decade, it was possible to purchase cars, appliances, radios, furniture, and other expensive items on 'easy monthly (or weekly) payments." p. 40

CHAPTER ONE – THE ECONOMIC LANDSCAPE OF THE 1920s AND ITS LESSONS FOR TODAY

A. THE CENTRAL CHARACTERISTIC OF THE 1920s ECONOMY: A DECADE OF MASS PRODUCTION FOR CONSUMPTION

How did corporate America establish the following dramatic increases in durable goods for consumption by the masses?

Production in early 1920s   Production in 1928-29

Autos[1] *Daily Life in the United States, 1920-1940.*#	sold 1.9 million in 1920	4.5 million sold in 1929
	Or as reported in Economic Boom, page 88	
	2.2 million sold in 1920	5.3 million sold in 1929
Trucks[2]	118, 520 registered in 1921	3,120,000 registered in 1928
Radios[3]	Sold 2.7 million in 1925	Sold 12 million in 1930
Household Furniture[4]	$466.6 million sales in 1921	$600.4 million sales in 1929
Electrical household appliances and supplies[5]	$63.2 million in sales in 1921	$176.7 million in sales in 1929
Heating and cooking apparatus	$186.5 million in 1921	$347.3 million in 1929
Shoes – men's	$69.5 million in 1921	$94.8 million in sales in 1929
Shoes – women's	$101.5 million in 1921	$131.3 million in sales in 1929# *Historical Abstract*, op. cit. page 693[6]

What economic factors permitted this great leap in productive output?

1. Achieving economies of scale. This results in many products being produced in a facility

whose features permit mass production at a level of output in which costs per unit of output decrease continuously until a certain level of output is reached, normally called 'practical capacity. The following management practices produced this outcome:

a. Mass assembly achieved through making routine, tasks to be performed mainly by unskilled workers doing one task at a time. This work environment has been described as such:

"The manufacturing of other new large-volume consumer goods – vacuum cleaners, washing machines, radios, and low-pressure balloon automobile tires, to name only the most common-employed fabrication and assembly-line innovations similar to those of the automobile industry. Likewise, attention was constantly paid to ways in which the production process could be made more rapid, efficient, and inexpensive. In all varieties of manufacturing, a premium was placed on quick, nimble movements done over and over. Young men under thirty-five years of age were therefore the most highly sought industrial workers. Once they began slowing down, however, their days were numbered. In Muncie, Indiana, where auto parts manufacturing was a large source of employment, few factory workers held on to their positions far into their forties, and once laid off they found it very difficult, if not impossible, to find another factory job.[7] The work was not done entirely by unskilled workers on the line. "Roughly 30 percent of the workforce practiced skill trades. Painters, upholsterers, carpenters, welders, and mechanics were all needed."[8]

b. Taylorism – Frederic Taylor is credited with introducing 'scientific management' whereby each task performed by workers is measured for time and motion needed to accomplish the individual task. This resulted in an industrial engineering system in which each worker was required to perform his individual task so many times within a certain period. Some credit for making 'Taylorism' a reality through actual trial and error efforts in his auto plants, even though Ford never read Taylor's book.

Some criticize this method of demand performance for its lack of effective sustainability by the workers – often resulting in workers leaving the job either voluntarily or involuntarily.

c. The introduction of new machine tools and equipment plus the increased availability of electricity enabled this Fordism to be pursued. The ability to avoid needing to add great numbers of workers to accomplish mass production was possible through automation. This reflected in the fact that there was essentially the same number of workers in manufacturing in 1921 as in 1929.

d. The financing of expansion – Major manufacturers were able to obtain funds for their operations through the sale of corporate stocks and bonds through the offerings of investment bankers. The surge in the value of stocks in the latter 1920s facilitated the sale of corporate stocks and bonds. Supreme Court rulings favoring 'capital gains' as taxable income added to investors preferring to buy and sell stock on an interim basis rather than hold the stock over a long period and being satisfied with dividends and the final cash-out of stock 15-20 years later. Raising funds through the sale of its stock, rather than bonds or loans from banks allowed corporations to avoid current expenses of paying interest and principle on any loans or any current payments required by their bonds. In not having to pay any debt-related expenses which occurred every year, companies' cash flow was not reduced each year by these expenses. On the other hand, dividends were not legally obligated, but so long as stock values soared, stockholders were more likely to seek instant riches through the sale of their stock, rather than be content with any declared dividends. This financial arrangement encouraged expansion, but also was deceptive in the 'tail end' of business, i.e. finance would begin to dictate the course of business practices. Easy financing produced excess retained earnings from the sale of their stock which could not be applied to capital expenditures by 1928. By that time, it was apparent that output exceeded consumer demand across the board of industry.

2. Despite the waning of mass production by 1927-28, it had been sustained during the 1920s by mass consumption made possible to a great extent by installment or credit purchases. Since much of the consumption occurred through credit-lending during the 1920s and therefore low interest rates would seemingly be an incentive for consumers to continue to buy durable goods, does this experience of the 1920s translate into 1930-31 conditions as proof of Milton Freidman's postulate that had the Fed lowered interest rates further in 1930-31, the Great Depression would have been avoided? Or is the economy of the 1920s based on a false bottom as some would argue was the economy of 2000-2008 in that consumption was sustained by an unnatural relationship between annual debt and annual disposable income? Even beyond that relationship, was consumption needed to sustain mass production fated by the great disparities in the distribution of income in the 1920s? Could families/workers be eligible for bank loans in 1930-31 if they had been ineligible for loans before the Crash of 1929? Would the Crash suddenly qualify those

who were ineligible for loans before 1929? Let's examine the extent of mass consumption during the 1920s and its components, product by product and source of loans.

B. THE DEPENDENCY UPON MASS CONSUMPTION: LIVING BEYOND ONE'S MEANS

The 1920s "witnessed the dramatic upturn in consumer credit spending. Prior to World War I, most goods had been purchased with cash, and even homes were financed with modest mortgages. But beginning around 1923, the concept of 'buy now, pay later' became popular as the advertising industry whetted appetites for products of every description. Easy credit convinced the middle class that there was no reason to defer the good life, or at least occasional gratification: by 1927, more than 85 percent of the furniture, 80 percent of the phonographs, 75 percent of the washing machines, 70 percent of the new and used cars, and more than half of the radios, pianos, sewing machines, vacuum cleaners and refrigerators sold to Americans were purchased through installment plans."[9] "Between 1925 and 1929, the amount of installment credit outstanding in the United States more than doubled, from $1.38 billion to $3 billion."[10]

Generally speaking, this is how buying on credit impacted family budgets:

"Many families live on the brink of danger all the time. They are car-poor. Saving is impossible. The joy of security in the future is sacrificed for the pleasure of the moment. And with the pleasure of the moment is mingled the constant anxiety entailed by living beyond one's means."[11]

"Customers would pay a percentage of the item's cost in cash as a down payment on purchase. Such payments' percentages depended upon the total cost of the merchandise. In 1925, down payments on radios and phonographs were typically 25 percent, and appliances such as sewing machines and washing machines required ten percent down. The highest down payments were demanded for automobiles, with percentages ranging from 30 to 40 percent depending upon whether the auto was new or used."[12]

1. Buying by the Working Class. The above cited facts may suggest a rather comprehensive usage of installment buying by almost all American families. This would be misleading, as installment buying was essentially confined to the middle and upper classes. As will become apparent, when the working class is excluded from extensive installment buying, as are textile workers, miners, farmers, sharecroppers, tenant farmers and the elderly and disabled, over one-third to forty percent of Americans were non-participants in mass consumption, which was (and is) so vital for the sustainability of mass producing economies. In examining the buying habits of workers in the 1920s, in particular Chicago workers, the overstated citing of mass consumption through installment buying is exposed by a breakdown of the buying powers of the workers and others who were mentioned above as excluded from this purchasing plan. Two studies provide evidence of working class limitations with respect to buying on credit.

    a. "While industrial workers were responsible for the construction of the plethora of new consumer items available during the 1920s, their lack of purchasing power constrained their ability to purchase the fruits of their labor. For a working-class family, there simply was not enough extra income after paying for necessities. Economist Emma Winslow calculated that 95 percent of a working-class family's monthly income went to food, clothing, housing, and utilities. This left a scant 5 percent for education, health, recreation, and luxury items."[13] While Winslow noted that "such a lifestyle left no money for savings," the following study, *Making a New Deal,* offers contradictory evidence that working class in Chicago was able to save. According to the Winslow study, "Blue-collar Americans had to make do with less costly 'major' purchases, such as radios and irons."[14]

b. A rather intensive examination of working-class buying habits in Chicago during the 1920s is provided by *Making a New Deal.* The author, Elizabeth Cohen, offers the following findings on the purchasing habits of those industrial workers.

> i. Only small 'major purchases, such as phonographs, radios, or washing machines were bought on credit (page 104).
>
> ii. For most of the 1920s, inner city working-class bought necessities from the local grocery, often an ethnic-flavored store. Few working-class purchases were from the emerging chain stores, even by 1929. "As late as 1929, the industrial workers of Cicero found chain management in only five percent of this industrial town's 819 retail stores and in 11 percent of its groceries," (page 109).
>
> iii. With 90 percent of a worker's income going for necessities, "those with low incomes automatically had less to put toward the purchase of automobiles. Automobiles by far accounted for the greatest proportion of the nation's installment debt outstanding at any given time, more than 50 percent, (page 103).
>
> iv. Contrary to general belief by most, Chicago workers, for instance, were savers, providing for a 'rainy day' caused by illness, layoffs, or

firings (page 103). "More than half of the privileged, 'fully employed,' unskilled and semiskilled manufacturing workers interviewed by Leila Houghteling in 1924 found themselves out of work, most for more than a month per year, because of seasonal layoffs or illnesses," (page 102).

v. Interrupted employment necessitated that other family members find work, even children (page 102).

vi. The cumulative effect of the above conditions resulted in that only three percent of the unskilled and semiskilled workers interviewed by Houghteling in 1924 had cars. At the end of the decade, in "the less urbanized environment of nearby Joliet, only 24 percent of the lower income families owned an automobile, according to a Chicago Tribune survey (page 102).

The above findings disclose that the mass-producing machine of industry was sustained in a very limited way by its own workers' inability to buy on credit such high-priced products as cars.

c. The Middle Class and its buying habits. If normal household items and emerging 'necessities' such as cars were to be sold on a scale which would support the economies of scale present in the large factories, durable goods must be sold in large quantities to a middle class as well as to the rich. All available studies show that companies were successful to selling to the middle class. This was made possible through installment buying. "The few contemporary studies that probed consumer credit experience suggest that it was middle-income people, not workers, who made installment buying such a rage during the 1920s, particularly the salaried and well-off classes who anticipated larger incomes in the future."[15] A later study revealed that despite the doubling of national installment credit between 1929 and 1940, by the end of that period, middle-income people were still the most likely to buy on installment."[16] This suggests that it is still income which drives the availability of credit – not interest rates.

Increased disposable income and shorter work weeks made it possible for the growing middle class to pursue leisure and shopping more. "By 1927, Americans purchased 15 percent of all goods sold on credit. Consumers had racked up $3 billion in personal debt. This bloated figure led the National Association of Credit Men, an organization that represented manufacturers and retailers, to issue a call for curbing the 'explosiveness of credit' . . . for undoubtedly in a credit pinch this condition would prove a very disturbing factor."[17]

Was it reasonable to expect consumption on the level sustained through installment buying to continue into the 1930s? We have reliably excluded most of the working class from extensive installment buying. Now add to this sizable part of the population the following low-income classes. The national government estimated that nearly one-third of Americans were in poverty during the 1920s. Brookings Institute placed nearly 40 percent living in poverty. Neither figure is reassuring.

d. Textile workers. Recall how limited factory workers were by their income in seeking installment buying of durable goods. Only purchases of small products, such as radios, phonographs, or perhaps washing machines were permitted by their disposable income after buying necessities. Compare the working and financial circumstances of textile workers -- were they in a worse financial position to buy on credit those durable products upon which the economy of the 1920s thrived?

    i. In judging the purchasing power of an income class, you examine the extent in which they are able to buy those products which increasingly define a middle class quality of life. If a segment of the working class lives in abject poverty, ask yourself – did they embrace poverty willingly out of ignorance or lack of ambition? Or was their source of employment one in which the market economy disfavored, placing employer and employee in a contentious relationship? Was installment credit available to this important working segment of America?

    ii.   The following is persuasive that the plight of textile workers was attributed to many factors – an industry in decline and in intense competition for market share, a culture that intimidated any effort for change with respect to working conditions and earnings, and a surplus of labor which permitted employment abuse.

    iii.   In anticipation of one of the central questions of this work, ask yourself would lower interest rates in 1930-31 have resulted in bank loans to textile workers to the extent of permitting them to buy durable goods on credit?

iv. David Kennedy describes the general plight of textile workers in the 1920s and 1930s in an industry that "had become ferociously competitive, chronically beset by excess capacity, price-gouging, and the by now familiar tribulations visited upon labor." He notes that "textile workers had long been a harshly abused lot. The greatest attraction of the South for investors had in fact not been proximity to the cotton fields, but proximity to an abundance of low-wage, non-unionized labor."[18] However, it was not just low wages which kept these inefficient firms afloat, but the abject economic bondage in which the workers and their families were held. Kennedy provides a stark vision of this 'hillbilly heaven':

"Whole families, including children as young as seven, worked grueling hours. Sometimes they toiled through the night amid the whirling spindles and clouds of lint, earning subsistence wages, often paid in scrip only good at the company store. Like their cousins who had stayed in the hills to dig coal, the 'lintheads,' long oppressed by the dependency, want, and fear, saw their lives go from unspeakably bad to unimaginably worse as the Depression deepened. Wages sank to as low as five dollars for a fifty-five hour week. Thousands of mill workers were laid off altogether. Those who remained on the job submitted resentfully to the hated 'stretch-out,' the mill hands' term for the practice of forcing fewer and fewer workers to tend more and more of the spindles clattering in their relentless ranks on the shop floor."[19]

Another author gives this description of the 'stretch-out':

"Guided by 'efficiency experts' and 'time-study men,' textile manufacturers began a massive restructuring of the workplace through mechanization, speedup, and increased supervisory discipline.". . . . . Some of the changes implemented by mill owners included changing worker quotas from 30 to 36 looms to 90 to 110 looms. Other mill owners simply instituted the speedup in which "overseers switched workers from hourly wages to piece rates, timed them by newly installed timepieces on each machine, and told them they had to keep up a faster pace if they wanted to keep their job."[20]

This changed workplace assignments are described by one of the mill workers in stark terms:

"Zelleree Donnahoo, a retired mill hand, describes the weeding-out of workers at her mill in Inman, South Carolina. 'The mill had about thirty weavers. They'd lay 'em off, stretch 'em out, lay 'em off, till they did have but twelve.' Zelleree's sister-in-law filled batteries, 'and she had about 180-something batteries to fill. They used to have, oh, about twelve or thirteen battery hands. And then, [by the time] they took these looms out, they didn't have but about five or six hands."[21]

This rapid-fire change of pace in the workplace imposed unemployment of some workers unrelated to market conditions of the mills.

"Those over the age of thirty were particularly vulnerable to dismissal because they were not nimble enough to work at the speed required by the new machines or the new work rules. Even if workers weren't fired, 'exhaustion and nervous stress' would push them out of their jobs. Their work was speeded up so fast that 'you was always in a hole, trying to catch up."[22]

Another mill hand provided this description of the hardship imposed by the new work rules:

"My husband and I go to the mill at seven. He's a stripper in the cardin' room and gets $12.85 a week . . . The put this stretch-out system on him shore enough. You know he's runnin' four jobs ever since they put this stretch-out system on him and he ain't getting' any more than he used to get for one. Where'd they put the other three men? – why, they laid 'em off and they give him the same $12.85 he got before."[23] The impact upon mill family security and welfare was destructive, as one mother related how she had lost four of her five children to whooping cough because there had been no time for her to care for them and no money for medicine or doctors. "I asked the super to put me on day shift so's I could tend them
. . . but he wouldn't. I don't know why. So I had to quit my job and then there wasn't any money for medicine, so they just died. I never could do anything for my children, not even to keep 'em alive, it seems."[24]

Finally, the following summary of the financial conditions of textile workers serves to refute any notion that lower interest rates in 1930-31 would have made these workers consumers of durable goods:

"The South had many more potential workers than the mills could absorb, creating a chronic surplus. The tenants and the mountaineers shared a common deprivation from a poverty-stricken agriculture. In 1927, for example, average gross agricultural income in ten southern states was only $609 as contrasted with $1611 in the rest of the nation. The mill was an attractive alternative, 500 families in Gaston County, North Carolina, studied in 1926-27, had an average income of $1313. 'The factory held out a promise,' in Harry M. Douty's words, 'that the land had not fulfilled.'"[25]

Any housing and other amenities provided to workers by the mill owners tended to impose more disadvantages than benefits. As Tom Tipper reported:
"He owns the community and he regulates the life that goes on there after the day's work is over at his mill. He has the power to discharge the worker at the mill, to refuse him credit at his store, to dump a worker's furniture out of a house, to have him expelled from church, to bar his children from school, and to withhold the services of a doctor or hospital," (The Lean Years, page 7).

The availability of credit at the 'company store' was often times a 'bad deal' for workers as related by a former mill child as he described the usage of gold coins provided by the mill-owners:

"Company money like Maggie's gold was never greatly appreciated by workers living in company towns. The only place it could be legitimately spent was in the company store, and workers everywhere sensed that the cost of every item they purchased there was higher than in other stores where they paid hard cash. Their perception of higher prices was more often than not justified; the elevated prices in company stores made it possible for mill owners to recapture a portion of the wages they had paid workers as profits on goods sold in their stores. Starkly put, the stores subtly reduced the wages of workers, who often had no alternatives but to trade in these stores. Like their counterparts in other mills throughout the South, many mill hands at the Bladenboro Cotton Mills resented Maggie's gold because they instinctively sensed that its use short-changed their wages. Nevertheless, the use of the coins made it possible for many of them to feed and clothe their families, albeit sometimes inadequately."[26]

This summarized description of the plight of textile workers in the 1920s and 1930s serves to dispel any notion that they would suddenly become eligible for bank loans at any rate of interest during 1930-31. They had job insecurity and no assets as collateral which a bank would require, especially after the scare of 1929. Add the number of textile workers to the factory workers initially covered and a significant number of Americans were not qualified borrowers before the Crash and definitely not after the Crash. To these numbers we will now add the coal miners of the 1920s.

e. Coal miners. What lending opportunities lurked in coal mining territories – even with the much lower interest rates urged by Milton Freidman? Does the following described region and its workers seem an area worthy of credit-risking or does it resemble a people so in need of help that their very desperation disqualified them for a bank loan under the best of economic times as the Roaring Twenties presumed to be? David Kennedy recites the findings of Eleanor Roosevelt and her companion journalist Hickok as they inspected the conditions of coal mining towns and the outlying areas:

"'In the whole range of the Depression,' said Gifford Pinchot, 'there is nothing worse than the condition of the soft coal miners.' Soft, or bituminous, coal had been for nearly two centuries the basic fuel that powered the global industrial revolution, but even before World War I the coal burning era was everywhere on the wane. Diesel engines had replaced coal-fired boilers in steamships and locomotives. Coal bins were disappearing from basements as Americans abandoned smudgy coal furnaces for clean-burning gas or oil or smokeless electric heating systems," (op, cit. page 169).

An industry in such dire condition and in retreat from new competing sources of fuel and heat is hardly a candidate for a low-interest loan during 1930-31, as were their workers. David Kennedy (op, cit. page 169) describes the economic landscape in which coal mines struggled to compete and what measures were imposed in order to keep the mines afloat after 1929:

1. "It had all the symptoms of a sick industry: shrinking demand, excess supply, chaotic disorganization, cutthroat competition, and hellish punishment for workers."
2. "At one point some of them begged the government to buy the mines 'at any price. . . anything so we can get out of it." (Sounds more like a government bail-out rather than a candidate for a bank loan.)
3. "Coal that had fetched up to $4 a ton in the mid-1920s sold for $1.13 a ton in 1932."
4. "Miners who had earned seven dollars a day before the Crash now begged the pit-boss for the

chance to squirm into thirty-inch coal seams for as little as one dollar."

5. "Men who had once loaded tons of coal per day grubbed around the base of the tipple for a few lumps of fuel to heat a meager supper -- often nothing more than 'bulldog gravy' made of flour, water and lard."

Consider the following findings and ask yourself if these workers and families would be qualified borrowers at banks in 1930-31:

"A social worker who in 1931 toured coal-rich Franklin County, Illinois uncovered numerous cases of starvation. Hundreds of children had not had a balanced meal in two years. James Myers of the Federal Council of Churches, who visited the mining camps of Kentucky and West Virginia in late 1931, reported 'alarming need.' Frank Bane of the American Association of Public Welfare Officials on December 29, 1931 gave the Senate Manufactures Subcommittee a state-by-state summary of unemployment. 'The coal states were severely disabled . . .' Others reported, 'Hunger stalked the mining camps.' Early in 1932, a teacher asked a miner's little girl if she were sick. 'No,' the child replied, 'I'm all right, only I'm hungry. 'When the teacher suggested that she go home to get something to eat, she replied, 'It won't do any good . . . because this is sister's day to eat. Entering West Virginia in 1931, the Quakers weighed the children in the schools and automatically chose for feeding those who were at least ten percent underweight.'"[27]

The above unimaginable conditions in coal-mining towns were confirmed also by Eleanor Roosevelt and her companion Hickok. Hickok noted that "some of them have been starving for eight years" in her report to Hopkins. "I was told there are children in

West Virginia who have never tasted milk! I visited one group of 45 blacklisted miners and their families, who had been living in tents two years . . . Most of the women you see in the camps are going without shoes or stockings . . . It's fairly common to see children entirely naked." The ravages of tuberculosis, 'black lung' disease, and asthma, as well as typhoid, diphtheria, pellagra, and severe malnutrition were everywhere apparent. Some miners' families,' said Hickok, 'had been living for days on green corn and string beans – and precious little of that.' She reported that 'at the Continental Hotel in Pineville, [Kentucky], I was told that five babies up one of those creeks had died of starvation in the last ten days. 'Dysentery is so common that nobody says much about it. We began losing our babies with dysentery in September,' one of Hickok's informants casually remarked."[28]

In as much miners, like textile workers, owned no home of any value and had great job insecurity, they would not qualify for bank loans before or after the Crash.

f. Sharecroppers, tenant farmers, family farmers, and rural America in 1920s. The general deplorable conditions of rural America can be described as follows:

"Rural poverty was most acute. Tenant farmers and sharecroppers, mainly in the South, came to symbolize how poverty crushed the human spirit. Eight and a half million people, three million of them black, crowded into two and three room cabins, lacking screens or even doors, without plumbing, electricity, running water, or sanitary wells. They subsisted – just barely, on salt pork, cornmeal, molasses, beans, peas, and whatever they could hunt or fish. All the diseases of dietary and vitamin deficiencies wracked them. When economist John Maynard Keynes was asked whether anything like this degradation had existed before, he replied, 'Yes, it was called the Dark Ages and it lasted four hundred years.'"[29]

Consider the following findings by investigators as they examined rural America:

"In Morton County, North Dakota, Hickok came out of a meeting in a 'shabby little country church' to find several denim-clad farmers wearing all the clothes they owned, huddled inside her car for warmth. As winter closed its grip over the northern plains, farmers were burning cow manure ('buffalo chips') and rushes cut from dried lake beds for fuel. Even the animals suffered. 'The plight of the livestock,' Hickok wrote, 'is pitiable.' Milk cows were drying up for lack of feed. Farmers eligible for relief road work did not have teams healthy enough to pull road scrapers. 'Half-starved horses have dropped in the harness,' Hickok related, 'right on the road job . . . they've even harvested Russian thistle to feed their horses and cattle. Russian thistle, for your information,' she explained to Hopkins, 'is a thistle plant with shallow roots that dries up in the fall and is blown across the prairies like rolls of barbed wire. The effect on the digestive apparatus of an animal would be, I imagine, much the same as though it had eaten barbed wire.' In neighboring South Dakota several days later, she found farm wives feeding Russian thistle soup to their children."[30]

David Kennedy continues Hickok's findings:

"'South Dakota,' she reported to Hopkins, 'is the Siberia of the United States. A more hopeless place I never say. Half of the people – the farmers particularly – are scared to death . . . the rest of the people are apathetic.' She poured out her feelings to Eleanor Roosevelt: 'Oh, these poor confused people, living their dreary little lives . . . And . . . my God, what families! I went to see a woman today who has ten children and is about to have another. She had so many that she didn't call them by their names, but referred to them as this 'little girl' and that 'little boy.' Far out on the wind-scoured prairie, Hickok visited 'what had once been a house. No repairs have been made in years. The kitchen floor was all patch up with pieces of tin . . . great patches of plaster had fallen from the walls. Newspapers had been stuffed in the cracks about the windows. And in that house two small boys . . . were running about without a stitch on save some ragged overalls. No shoes or stockings. Their feet were purple with cold.'"[31]

Farmers' conditions in particular can be summarized in the manner below:

"The failure of farmers to achieve relief from the federal government and the consolidation of agricultural wealth into large corporate farms caused a downward spiral in the standard of living for those involved in agricultural work. The increasingly marginal status of American farmers can be seen in the rise of farm tenancy during the 1920s. Although farm tenancy rates had steadily risen since the 1880s, the rate spike dropped dramatically during the Republican Decade. By the end of the 1920s, 40 percent of all farmers rented the land they worked. The nature of the tenancy also changed as the percentage of renters rose. In the past, farm tenancy (for white agricultural workers) often served as a rung on the ladder toward independent ownership of the land for young farmers

... By the 1920s, tenancy had become part of a descent toward landless farm laborer. Tenant farmers faced dramatic reductions in both social status and living conditions. Nationally, houses on rented farms had lower values than those owned by their residents. Landlords routinely allowed rented farm houses to go unpainted, unrepaired, and unelectrified in order to maximize profits..."[32]

>Sharecroppers and Southern tenant farmers were in worst financial and social shape than the prairie tenant farmers described above. "Migrant laborers were less commonly employed in the Deep South. There, tenancy and sharecropping were the most common means landowners used to control their property and have it worked with minimal investment. Each year landowners advanced their tenants money for seeds and other supplies. The tenant or sharecropper had to raise a crop, harvest it, and bring it in for weighing or other measuring in order to repay the debt, creating a virtual serfdom that bound families to the land. Because many black and white sharecroppers were illiterate, and landowners kept the books and had all the legal advantages, it was difficult to break out of the cycle. The tenant's small farmsteads often did not provide enough income for a family to survive, so many worked at other jobs – either as laborers on other farms or in local industry."[33]

This 'virtual serfdom' produced the following incomes and quality of life for sharecroppers and tenant farmers in the South:

>"The writer, Erskine Caldwell, no stranger to the harsh grindstone of southern tenant life, recorded scenes of almost unimaginable degradation. Visiting a

Georgia sharecropper's cabin that held three families jammed in two rooms, he saw a gaunt six-year-old boy licking the wrappings of a meat package, while 'on the floor before an open fire lay two babies, neither a year old, sucking the dry teats of a mongrel bitch.'"[34]

Two other observers labeled the conditions as worse or even worse than those under which European peasants lived.[35] Would tenant farmers or sharecroppers qualify for bank loans before or after the Crash regardless of how low interest rates were? Consider the uncertainty of their incomes and their lack of collateral as noted below:

"At the least profitable end of the scale, however, where tenant farmers without financial resources had to pledge a share of the crop they expected to harvest for land, rent and supplies, 59 percent were black. The value of the land and buildings of all American farms averaged $10,284, but on a sharecropper's farm, the average was $2,633. While U.S. farms on the whole averaged 148 acres, tenant farms averaged only 108 acres and thus had a correspondingly reduced profit potential. Sharecropped farms were even worse off: they averaged only 40 acres and were dismally poor."[36]

Even without developing a more fuller picture of the deplorable conditions of tenant farmers and sharecroppers, one can surmise from the information above that neither could qualify for bank loans under either income or collateral requirements during the 1920s or 1930-31.

To Hickok, her observations told her that the miserable conditions which she saw on the Dakota prairies, the mining towns of Illinois, West Virginia, and Kentucky, and in the rural South were not of recent causes, but reflected at least a decade long period of deprivation. "As her travels progressed, she gradually came to acknowledge the sobering reality that for many Americans the Great Depression brought times only a little harder than usual. She discovered, in short, what historian James Paterson has called the 'old poverty' that was endemic in America before the Depression hit. By his estimate, even in the midst of the storied prosperity of the 1920s some forty million Americans, including virtually all nonwhites, most of the elderly, and much of the rural population, were eking out unrelieved precarious lives that were scarcely visible and practically unimaginable to their more financially secure countrymen. . ."[37]

Summarizing the possibilities for loans to American workers, farmers, sharecroppers, tenant farmers, textile workers, and miners with interest rates reduced through Federal Reserve policies as advocated by Milton Freidman:

Remembering that living above the poverty line required a family income of around $2000 a year and that bank loans required the borrower to have job security and/or collateral which the bank could sell in the event the loan is not repaid, would these workers qualify for a loan in 1930-31 under their circumstances described above?

1. A typical worker in the South goes to a bank in North Carolina in 1930-31 and asks for a loan for

500 dollars at four percent annual interest for a period of five years. The loan officer asks the following questions to which the worker responds:

a. Loan officer: "What is your present job and your annual earnings?"

Textile worker: "I made five dollars for a fifty-five hour week last year, 1929-30."

Loan officer: "Did you work every week?"

Worker: "I did, but others could not keep up with the new work rules requiring each worker to do more than before at a quicker pace. Since I have been able to keep up due to my youth, I have been able to work the entire year."

Loan officer: "So, at $5 per week times 52 weeks, your total earnings amounted to $260 last year, is that right?"

Worker: "Yes, but my employer provides housing and I am able to shop at the company store, using company script as money."

Loan officer: "If your housing and necessities are available through your employer, why do you need a loan?"

Worker: "Due to the rapid speed and increased quantities that I am required to accomplish, I often suffer exhaustion, difficulty sleeping, and inadequate diet. Our family lacks adequate medical care. We lost three children in the last two years due to whooping cough. We need cash, not the company script, to go to doctors for care and treatment."

Loan Officer: "Given the employment history of the mills under their new work rules, many employees are unable to sustain working under this severe, stressful environment. Either they become disabled, too old to continue this pace of work, or get fired for failing to keep up with the new work rules. Moreover, your annual income, even with the availability of company stores and housing, is below the poverty line. Our bank requires at the minimum an above poverty income and a job which is not subject to uncertainties. Also, since you rent from your employer, you have no collateral to offer as a guarantee for payment of the loan."

Synopsis of this loan application: This is an effort by the worker to get a loan needed to rescue his family from disease and malnutrition, not to buy a home, car, appliance, radio -- all of which would be somewhat a secure transaction. Any failure to pay the loan would result in the bank repossessing the product – this would permit some recovery of the loan. Medical care and food would not provide any security for the lender, as both are consumed by their usage. For low interest rates to serve the purpose of economic recovery through increased consumption, they must be available to qualified buyers who intend to buy durable goods in industries which have produced too many products. In recent years, 2000-2008, bank lending to borrowers who were really unqualified by income and assets proved to be a 'false' stimulus as the borrowers were unable to maintain monthly payments which exceeded their monthly disposable income. These subprime loans were premised on the idea that the real estate purchased through these loans would continue to increase in value and therefore represented sufficient collateral to the subprime borrowers. In both cases, it is the absence of decent jobs which defeated the loans.

2. Miners seeking loans in 1930-31.
a. Loan officer to miner: "What is your annual pay in the mines?"

Miner: "Before the Crash, I made $7 a day; now I'm lucky to get a dollar a day."

Loan officer: "How do you feed your family on that meager income?"

Miner: "We go looking for a few lumps of coal to heat our meals. Our meals are mostly 'bulldog gravy' made of flour, water, and lard."

Loan officer: "How about clothes for your family and your work clothes? Are those necessities available to you and your family?"

Miner: "Usually my children go without shoes and have very little underwear for the winter. I go to work often with no underwear. Many times, our children have to take turns eating with one child having a meal on one day and the others on other days."

Loan officer: "How does this affect the quality of life of your family and you?

Miner: "Dysentery is common among mining families. Some have lost babies because of it. This is so common among us that nobody takes notice of it. Starvation has occurred among us. That is why I need cash to get medical treatment and necessities, such as shoes, clothes and food for my family. The company store is too expensive and eats up most of my pay with me ending up being in debt and still without clothes and shoes for my family."

Loan officer: "Do you own a home?"

Miner: "No, we live in a company-owned home."

Synopsis: Do you feel that a loan will be extended to this miner, who is typical of most miners? Is his income steady and sufficient to permit him to continue to buy necessities (made possible by the loan) and make monthly payments on the bank loan? What collateral does the miner have to offer to guarantee payment on the loan? Will this miner likely be able to use the loan to buy a car, an appliance, a radio, or even a home – all industries in need of revival in 1930.

3. Sharecroppers, tenant farmers, and family farmers seeking bank loans.

Loan officer to sharecropper or tenant farmer in the South: "What is your annual income for 1929-1931?"

Sharecroppers and tenant farmer: "In 1927, our income averaged about $609 per year. Since then, we have usually ended up owing money to the landowner for the advances he made to us for seed and supplies and for rent for the land and house. We aren't really sure what we actually earned since the landowners keep the books. We have to work at other jobs as laborers on farms or local industry for our families to survive."

Loan officer: "Do you own the land that you farm? And what is the size of your farm?

Sharecroppers/tenant farmers: "We do not own the farm land or our homes. We heard that the average value of a sharecropper's farm was $2633 (compared to the national average of $10,284). Housing is poor and not well maintained. Some of us live in cabins that hold three families jammed into two rooms. The owner rarely makes improvements or repairs on the property. Our neighbor, a tenant farmer, has 108 acres (compared to the national average of 148 acres), but we have only 40 acres as a sharecropper."

Loan officer: "Is your family in good health and will pose no problem for you to continue to maintain present spending of your income without having to divert some pay for medical expenses or loss of pay due to illnesses?

Sharecropper/tenant farmer: "That is why we need a loan. Our children have inadequate meals, clothes, and medical care."

Synopsis: Is this loan a plea for welfare-type relief -- the lack of necessities due to inadequate pay? If the loan is granted, will the farmers be able to maintain monthly payments on the bank loan, use the loan to buy necessities, and pay any debts owed to the landowner – all on unchanged disposable income earned as sharecroppers or tenant farmers? What property is owned to be offered as collateral for the loan?

4. Family farmers in the Plains and Prairies.

Midwest bank loan officers looking for potential borrowers in 1930-31 (assuming very low interest rates are available under Freidman's formula for recovery).

Loan officer examining property values of farms in Midwest – valuable property would represent good collateral and also be an indicator that the owner is financially stable.

1. North and South Dakota farms: A general description of property was found to be too often farms which had 'no repairs for years,' a patched-up kitchen floor with pieces of tin, great patches of plaster fallen from the walls, and newspapers stuffed as insulation from the cold in the cracks about the windows.
2. Across the Midwest, too many farmers have been reduced to tenant farmers. This resulted in less income for the farmers and a much reduced property value of the farm due to "the landowners allowing the farm houses to go unpainted, unrepaired, and unelectrified." This tenant farming has become too large a segment of agriculture in the reduced farm income and farm property values. It reached 40 percent of all farms by the end of the 1920s.
3. Farm income has suffered throughout the 1920s and its profits are not reassuring as a justification for loans to farmers.
4. Foreclosures of farms have created a 'distressed market' for such properties and would represent a risk that while the buyer/lender would make a bargain, given the depressed price, the continuing ability of farmers to pay for a mortgage could be jeopardized by the continued descent of farm prices and farm property values. Recent history suggests that any lending for distressed farm property would be too optimistic given the amount of recent foreclosures with indicate the inability of present farmers to make mortgage payments. This seems to be an industry pattern which will not be contained within the immediate future under a pure market-driven economy.

Synopsis: Bank lending in agriculture in 1930-31 would really anticipate the subprime lending of the 2000s without any possibility of increasing land values. This would be contrary to the commercial culture of the late 1920s into 1930-31.

5. Factory workers:
   1. *Bank loan officers seeking customers in the working class of Chicago or Detroit.* The officer must ask after their present job security and annual income.
   2. *Job security of factory workers in 1929-31.* The officer found that despite the apparent well-being of many factory workers, given their reported wage earnings per week, many still suffered layoffs or missed work. "More than half of the privileged, fully employed, unskilled and semiskilled manufacturing workers in 1924 found themselves out of work, most for more than a month per year, because of seasonal layoffs or illnesses."[38]
   3. Ninety-five percent of their income goes for food, clothing, housing, and utilities, leaving only five percent for discretionary spending. Any loans for the buying of durable goods, such as cars (requiring down payments of 30 to 40 percent), of radios or phonographs (requiring down payments of 25 percent), or appliances (requiring down payments of ten percent) would stretch the ability of the worker to use the loans for these purchases and still make timely monthly payments on bank loans.
   4. Also, potential customers are limited by age in the working class as the harshness of the manufacturing workplace generally caused those over 35 to be fired or leave due to physical reasons.
   5. Finally, most workers did not go to banks for loans during the 1920s, but instead relied upon

their ethnic associations or credit unions for loans. The fact that many of these financial lending institutions fell on hard times in 1929-30 reflects upon the deterioration of the working class financial well-being. Accordingly, many who could not make payments to 'friendly' lenders would not be reliable customers for state or national loan offices.

Synopsis: Workers were very limited buyers of durable goods in the 1920s as cited in the above pages. Their installment buying was somewhat limited, depending upon which employer for which they worked (many employers provided installment credit to their workers to buy their products). No recovery is likely by credit purchases from this segment of the population, given their limited participation in the 1920s. Low interest rates to many factory workers in 1930-31 would resemble subprime lending of the 2008-2008 period: borrowing which is not supported by the borrower's disposable income.

With an above-poverty income of between $2000-$2500 per year being required, one can surmise from the above descriptions of various workers' conditions as to qualifications for loans and from the summary of various earnings listed below as to whether a very low interest rate in 1930-31 would have resulted in the increased consumption needed to justify resumed full production by auto manufacturers, appliance manufacturers, a restored textile and clothing industry, a restored agribusiness in canned food and other food products, and any stimulus to other industries which would have resulted from resumed full production above.

1. Earnings for nonfarm workers in the Northeast were $1000 per person and $366 per year for farm workers there.
2. Earnings for nonfarm workers in the Midwest equaled $854 per year and $262 per year for farm

workers there.

3. Earnings for nonfarm workers in the Far West equaled $953 per year and $818 per year for farm workers. Not enough by itself to provide above-poverty income, but probably too much to get welfare assistance.
4. Earnings for nonfarm workers in the Northwest was $703 and $426 for farm workers.
5. Earnings for nonfarm workers in the Southwest was $683 annually, while farm workers earned $366 per year.
6. The Deep South of sharecroppers and tenant farmers' earnings were meager and most lived in abject poverty, whose very disheveled appearance would impose immediate disqualifications.

> It is persuasive that the above disqualifications for loans represent the following: a failure to revive the economy from a demand side activated by low interest loans for consumers. This leaves the possibility that low interest rate loans would provide incentives for business capital loans for equipment, plants, and expansion.

C. Could economic recovery in 1931 come from lending to corporate America under very low interest rate loans?

1. *The nature of bank commercial lending.* Banks are concerned primarily with having any loan repaid. This invites rather cautious banking attitude towards any corporate notion of product development, expansion, or other risk taking. However, this cautious attitude can interfere with bank profits. This poses a dilemma for banks : how to make conservative, safe loans, yet still earn good profits from lending. Robert Guttman provides an historical take on how banks tend to reconcile these opposing demands:

"The Fed only controls the monetary base, and, as such, the banks' ability to create new money out of available excess reserves. Yet it controls neither the banks' willingness to lend out these excess reserves nor the public's demand for bank loans, the other two determinants in the creation of private bank money. At times, especially during downturn periods, banks may prefer to keep more excess reserves as a safety cushion rather than lending them out to possibly shaky borrowers. Moreover, credit demand may be low due to depressed activity. Under such conditions, monetary stimulation tends to be quite ineffective. A similar problem, albeit in the opposite direction, may occur during boom periods. To the extent that banks manage to meet high loan demands by attracting funds other than regulated deposit liabilities, they can bypass the Fed's tightening efforts. The ability of the central bank to intervene against the dynamics of the business cycle is therefore limited at best. It cannot eliminate cyclical fluctuations of our economy, but it may reduce their amplitude."[39]

Guttmann gets to the heart of the banking dilemma, especially when applied to the economy of 1930-31:

"More generally, the problem is that the issue of credit-money is determined by the private profit motive of the issuing banks and their borrowing clients. In their risk-return calculations, banks face a direct trade-off between safety and profitability. Safety-oriented strategies, such as holding larger reserves, increasing capital base, or investing in low-risk assets, all come at the expense of profits. Conversely, more profitable investment strategies are inherently riskier."[40]

Guttmann explains the normal methods of banks in reconciling these opposing demands:

"Bank executives tend to manage this trade-off in distinctly procyclical fashion. During recovery periods, banks share the optimistic expectations of the public and, in the face of competitive pressures, eagerly seek to expand their assets in response to strong credit demand. The search for higher returns encourages investments that under less euphoric circumstances would have been rejected as too risky. Industry's overproduction tendency is thereby exacerbated by overextension of credit . . . that situation, characterized by emerging signs of excess capacity, declining profits, and the burst of speculative bubbles, prompts expectations to turn sour. Mounting losses and risks then force banks into a sudden emphasis on safety, with most of them insisting on tougher credit terms and/or cutting back on their loan supplies. Bank lending therefore engenders its own credit-cycle dynamic. Because money creation is directly tied to bank lending, the supply of private money tends to fluctuate in procyclical fashion as well."[41]

Given the alternative economic conditions of boom and bust under which bank lending accommodates the cycle by extending credit or restricting credit respectively, what banking attitude would prevail in 1930-31 given the following financial conditions of the auto industry during that period:

"In the beginning of 1930, no one was sure if the industry only had a flat tire or if the wheels were coming off. Sales were down considerably from the previous year, but many thought this might just be a 'breather' from the relentless upward push of production and sales in the last few years."[42] It didn't take long before the true nature of the 'slump' was apparent. "Sales were diving all over the place. Popular makes such as Hudson and Willys had seen their deliveries plummet from 1929's 300,000 and 257,000 respectively to 113,000 and 80,000 in 1930 ... By 1931, Hudson volume was cut in half again, to 58,6000 and Willys Overland sales collapsed by more than two-thirds to 26,444. On top of a $7.5 million loss in 1930, Willys dropped a sickening $14.6 million the following year and only had $1 million in the bank by year's end. Even Ford, with his volume cut nearly in half in 1931, went from a $42 million profit in 1930 to a $37 million loss, by far the biggest in the industry."[43]

Some companies still made profits in 1931. In addition to Chrysler, Nash and Studebaker, Auburn made its highest profits ever in 1931, but then suffered similar fates as other car companies' decline.[44] GM was the profit leader with $94.6 million, down 50 percent from 1930, but with only a decline of 10 percent in volume sales.[45] How could any auto profits be attained during this period? What price/quantity mix permitted the maintaining of profitable operations by GM, Chrysler, Ford and others during 1930-32? Do you raise prices and settle for less volume? Do you lower prices, seeking higher volume than 1930? Do you place emphasis upon reducing labor costs, material handling and parts costs, or reduce usage of electricity?

The following summarize efforts by most to maintain and increase profits:

    Nash, Packard and Studebaker raised prices in 1930.

    Chevrolet knocked of $30 from its coupe.

Willys cut $50 from each car price.

Chrysler reduced its Plymouth by $70, giving a unit price of $590 per car. The Plymouth now cost just $25 more than the Chevy in an effort to make it a competitive, low-price, high volume car.[46]

Chrysler added a "62-horsepower Chrysler Six, ranging in price from just $795 to $845, competing directly with the Desoto Six and slightly above the price of the Dodge Six. Both featured the introduction of a new eight-cylinder car."[47]

These managerial efforts had a mixed outcome in terms of sales and profits:

Despite the reduced price of the Plymouth, its sales sank to 67,000 units and with the sales of its other cars, Chrysler made the following earnings:

1. First quarter earnings of only $200,000, an $8 million reduction from 1929.
2. Chrysler earned only $34,000 during the rest of 1930 on a volume of only 60 percent of its output in 1929.[48]

While car output dropped in volume from $4.8 million in 1929 to $3 million in 1930, GM, Ford, Nash and Packard "still made hefty profits on the year."

How did car companies do in 1931? Did lower prices, cost reduction strategies, and retooling produce better profits?

Perhaps Chrysler represented the greatest example of inventive business management. It introduced a new styled, engineered Plymouth, the 'Floating Power,' on July 5, 1931. It featured the Model PA and possessed great advances in comfort, reliability, and safety. Walter Chrysler defied economic and financial logic by "spending $2.5 million in the face of declining sales and worsening business climate to give his customers a car value so special that they couldn't say no to it."[49] What was the result in sales and profits? "And the customers came. Plymouth sales rose from 67,000 in 1930 to 94,000 in 1931. In the teeth of the Depression. True, this figure didn't come anywhere near Chevrolet's 623,000 or Ford's 541,000. But Chevrolet was off by more than 25 percent and Ford was off by more than 50 percent from 1930, while Plymouth was up by 40 percent in this very bad year for the auto business."[50] These profit levels could not be maintained in 1932 as the Depression imposed its economic logic on the economy. Despite Chrysler's and other car companies' re-engineering efforts and cost cutting, 1932 proved that even great car engineering and management could not reverse economic dynamics opposed to recovery.

"But no matter how good the cars, nothing above the low-price level was selling. Dodge moved about 30,000 cars in 1932. DeSoto about 27,000 and Chrysler roughly 25,000. Even those glorious Imperials, with CH prices cut by $1000, or more than 35 percent below 1931 levels, saw sales plunge by 50 percent to 1,622.

Everybody else was in the same boat, with sales sinking to levels little more than half that of

1931, already a severely depressed year. From 2,038,000 cars in 1931, the industry turned out only 1,170,000 cars in 1932. It was now selling about 25 percent of what it had sold in 1929."[51] (As Vincent Curcio noted, "This was a great pity, for the industry was making much better cars in 1932, at prices that averaged $100 less than they had in 1929. With price cuts, manufacturers competing with Ford were actually selling their cars at the same level as his for the first time. Fords, Chevrolets, Plymouths and Terraplanes could all be bought for under $500."[52])

Curcio provided the reason for declining sales and profits despite lower cars and better engineered cars. "But the customers had disappeared from the marketplace, no matter what the price of the goods. Nonfarm workers had only 60 percent of the income they had had in 1929, and farmers did even worse, at only 44 percent of already depressed 1929 levels. All told, Americans were earning $26 billion less than in 1929, with 25 percent of all workers unemployed. Per capita income had been cut in half, from $600 to $300, so that a family of four earning $2,400 in 1929 had to get by on $1,200 in 1932 . . ."[53] He cites possible consumers of the 1920s. Add to the above diminished income the lack of income of sharecroppers, miners, textile workers, tenant farmers, seasonal unemployed workers, etc. and you arrived at a consumer market consisting of only the well-to-do with respect to the buying of durable goods. Any profits which GM, Chrysler, and other car companies made had to depend, one must surmise, from the selling of the higher-priced, lower volume luxury cars to the wealthy. This assumption is made from the following observation by Curcio in his Chrysler:

"Volume wasn't everything, however. General Motors, on much greater volume than Ford's in 1927 and 1928, and even on similar volume in 1929, made a great deal more money than Ford, owing to the fact that around a third of its cars sold in much higher and more profitable price categories. Selling 250,000 Buicks was worth as much to GM as selling two to three times as many Chevrolets, which in any case were more expensive and more profitable than Fords."[54]

Thus for GM, Chrysler, DeSoto, and other styled cars, price reductions did not produce increased volumes of sales. Why? Remember, buying a car on installment credit in the 1920s required at least a 20 percent down payment. With the reduced national income noted above and with the continued plight of sharecroppers, miners, textile workers, farmers, tenant farmers, the consumer was not responsive to price reductions. In the lingo of economics, cars did not have price elasticity. In fact, studies in the 1960s ad 1970s showed that car buying was more responsive to changes in income, not prices.

What about the 'leader of the pack' – Henry Ford? His path of recovery is more jagged than the others' efforts. Ford's refusal to restyle his Model T so as to regain market share lost to GM contributed to his decline.

"In 1931, the company went into the red by over $37 million, and since the traditional Ford clientele was concentrated at the lower end of the income scale that had been most hit by the Depression, future prospects were not promising . . ."[55] "In 1931, Ford vehicle sales dropped a million to less than 500,000. This represented a loss of market share to Chrysler's Plymouth and to the top seller, Chevrolet."[56] "The Model A, scheduled for a ten year run, suffered as being just another utility vehicle among several. Even other utility vehicle models were changed from year to year, making the Model A an even more 'static model.'"[57]

Ford re-engineered his car in 1930-31, but he did not seek bank loans. He sought to bring out a Model B "with a pepped-up A engine. The V-8 power unit would go into the new streamlined body, so effectively, you could buy the car with four cylinders or with eight."[58] The estimated additional investment in the V-8 was about $50 million.[59] Ford told Sorenson, "Charlie, we have too much money in the bank."[60] This re-engineering of his car involved buying a new "spectacular pouring furnace which could hold two tons of molten metal."[61] Other expenditures included electrical furnace equipment.[62] Despite a deepening depression, Ford received one hundred thousand advanced orders for his new B and V-8 cars, and within a few days of March 31st, 1932, the orders were doubled.[63]

The success of the Ford V-8 car is mixed. It suffered from a sullied reputation in its 1932 engine performance. While Ford made a recovery in 1933 with an improved V-8 in generating needed sales, it would fall behind Chrysler in overall sales with GM leading all in sales.[64] It would eventually not be offered by Ford after 1934. Ford would have to compete in the car industry on a managerial level posed by GM, Chrysler, and others.[65]

Does the description of the financial condition of the auto companies and their efforts to revamp their company during 1930-32 invite an aggressive willingness of banks to lend to these companies which were representative of most corporate giants in the 1930s effort to recover? Above we noted that banks are willing to pursue risky loans in boom times, but very reluctant during recessionary or depression times. Lending by banks for commercial purposes should be a 'boring business,' according to Joseph Stiglitz in his *Free Fall*. The auto industry's effort at reinventing itself with re-engineering, restyling, all to recover market share do not represent the financial conditions which banks welcome during difficult economic times almost of an unprecedented nature.

Bank loans do not, by their nature, invite or approve daring business undertakings. And any efforts by the auto companies would have to be of a daring nature, one not requiring marginal adjustments which the banks could tolerate as a part of doing business. The banks during the 1920s had lost much of their commercial lending business due to the corporate reliance upon the sale of their stocks and bonds for needed funds. Corporate financing through the offerings of its stocks and bonds anticipates aggressive corporate pursuit of profits and market shares. That is how the price of corporate stock rises on Wall Street.

To seek bank loans in order to finance 'Fordism' in manufacturing would impose bank controls over even any temporary reduction in profits or market share. This was not the game to be played in the 1920s and would not have any tolerance for bank restrictions or restraints imposed as a condition of bank loans. Commercial lending for plant expansion and equipment installation greatly declined in the face of corporate reliance upon the sale of their securities. Moreover, "once the stock market started its upward trend in 1925, firms could afford to lower dividends payouts without triggering a decline in the price of their equity. They were thus able to increase internal financing of investment outlays through retained earnings. Larger reinvestment of profits also boosted expectations of future gains, which in turn made stocks more attractive to investors. With the bull market thus starting to feed itself by late 1926, it became easier for large companies to issue new shares as another means of financing large-scale investment projects."[66]

As we have seen, auto companies did not seek help from bank loans in their efforts to restore profitability. They relied upon stock sales (Chrysler), retained earnings (Ford and GM) and cost reductions(probably all -- included reduced labor costs). Why would they seek a bank loan which would acknowledge their dire conditions? As noted above, in difficult times, banks seek to protect their reserves, capital, and equity. The cautious tendency of banks to ensure that the borrower can maintain an ability to make loan payments as they become due trumps any desire of extraordinary returns during uncertain economic times. GM, in particular, could remember how the restrictions imposed upon it during its formative years by bank trustees. Any significant lending to companies in transition during the 1930-31 period would invite similar controls by the lending banks.

Would banks be persuaded to lend millions of dollars for the reinventing of Chrysler, GM, or Ford as described above? Would DeSoto and Willys be likely candidates for commercial loans from banks during 1930-31 to be used to restyle or reengineer their cars? Since even lowering prices per car for many during the 1930-32 period did not achieve revival for many auto companies, banks would have been correct not to loan to these car companies for the purpose of designing new cars and for, say, additional automation through Taylorism to achieve lower labor costs. Although very laudable in many ways, these corporate efforts at the reconstructing of their firms did not restore full capacity operations as occurred during many years of the 1920s.

Anyway, were banks in a position to accommodate any lower interest rate which the Fed provided through its open-market operations? Would any infusion of funds/ additional reserves to the banks made possible by the Fed create an optimistic view by banks for lending or would they more likely use the additional reserves to secure their capital and equity by maintaining surplus reserves which the Fed had made possible? What did the economic times dictate to the banks: be aggressive, or be cautious and protect their solvency? Guttmann provided the standard policy sought by banks as shown before. To restate the bare-bones principle: "At times, especially during downturn periods, banks may prefer to keep more excess reserves as a safety cushion rather than lending them out to possibly shaky borrowers. Moreover, credit demand may be low due to depressed activity. Under such conditions, monetary stimulation tends to be quite ineffective."[67]

With these restrictions in mind, consider the general financial well-being of many banks in 1929 and beyond as they cope with the Crash of 1929.

1. As noted before, banks began to lose commercial customers in the mid 1920s as companies were able to raise desired funds through the offering of their stocks and bonds by investment bankers. "The loss of traditional corporate customers and the consequently shrinking asset base caught banks unprepared. Many of them were further weakened by intensifying competition over funds, especially time deposits, which increased from $12.2 billion in 1921 to nearly $20 billion in 1929 (compared to the slower expansion of demand deposits, from $18 billion to $22.7 billion)."[68]

2. With banks having to pay higher interest for time deposits, they were compelled to seek lending or investment returns which were higher than the interest they paid on their time deposits. In seeking higher returns to compensate for the high interest they paid on time deposits and for the

loss of commercial lending, banks began to concentrate their lending and investments in the following, which because they were riskier and/or had longer maturities, made banks less liquid:

a. Real estate loans grew from $2.1 billion in 1921 to $5 billion in 1929.[69]
b. Bank investments in stocks and bonds rose from $8.4 billion in 1921 to $13.4 billion in 1929.[70]
c. In 1927, banks held $3 billion in home mortgages.[71]
d. Banks held $1.5 billion in German and Austrian bonds in 1930.[72]
e. New York banks purchased over $1 billion per year of foreign bonds.[73]
f. The passage of the McGadden-Pepper bill in 1927 which provided limited authority for national banks to buy real estate bonds to an extent they increased from one-third of time deposits to one-half. This was permitted under the bill so long as they did not exceed 25 percent of capital and surplus.[74]
g. The authorization under the McGadden-Pepper bill resulted in "loans on real estate at national banks expanded more than 50 percent between 1927 and 1932 whereas real estate loans at state chartered banks expanded by only three percent. Real estate lending more than doubled at mutual savings banks, their share in the total having increased from 32 percent in 1927 to nearly 60 percent in 1932."[75] Real estate loans "'as a percentage of capital and surplus' increased from 24 percent in 1926 to 40 percent in 1927 to 57 percent by the end of 1932."[76]
h. The above 'switch from business loans to longer-term and higher yielding assets also made banks less liquid.[77] Eventually, it became an important cause of the "general illiquidity of national banks."[78]
i. The risk of illiquidity (not having sufficient reserves to make loans) and even insolvency (where liabilities – customers' deposits exceed a bank's assets and reserves and thereby endangers its capital account or net worth) became very apparent in 1929 and beyond as evidenced by the

following chronically listed foreclosures:[79]

1926	68,000 foreclosures
1930	154,000 foreclosures
1931	200,000 foreclosures
1932	250,000 foreclosures

3. The great vulnerability of banks to illiquidity or even insolvency which the above noted investments exposed them probably paled compared to the risks which call loans to brokers presented to banks. These were loans to brokers who then used the money to allow stock speculators to buy stock on the margin with the broker extending the remaining balance of the price of stock. Say you wanted to buy RCA stock for $30 a share and you would buy 20 shares, making a total price of $300 for the ten shares. A broker would get a 'call loan' from the bank for $270 in order to pay this amount for the $300 total cost of RCA stock. The buyer of the stock would pay only, say, ten percent of the cost of the RCA stock, or $30. The broker keeps the RCA stock as collateral in case the value of the stock goes below the $270 the broker extended to the buyer. If the RCA stock goes below the $270, the buyer must pay the broker the amount of $270 which he borrowed from the broker for the remaining amount of the stock price. If the buyer cannot pay the $270 in cash, he must allow the broker to sell the stock in order to get as much as he can to cover the loan which he made to the buyer. If the broker cannot recover the entire $270, his ability to repay the bank for his call loan is jeopardized. Thus, even though banks were

prohibited from speculating in stocks and bonds or even participating in the stock market with depositors accounts, banks were still vulnerable under call loans as if they had speculated, since the broker's collateral, RCA stock, is essentially the bank's collateral. By the end of 1928, call loans of $8 billion were outstanding, mainly on bank balance sheets as assets. Over half of call loans in 1929 were made by corporations, as banks had exhausted their ability to borrow through the Fed 'discount window.'[80] The banks' ability to circumvent federal prohibitions on stock market activities by banks was accomplished in the following ways:

a. Banks were permitted to offer trust services to their customers. In providing trust services, banks could trade in stocks on behalf of their wealthy clients.[81]

b. Commercial banks greatly expanded their investment banking subsidiaries by underwriting the selling of corporate stocks and bonds for a fee/commission. "By 1929, investment affiliates of commercial banks had taken a 41 percent share of the underwriting business, compared to only a ten percent share in 1921."[82]

c. And, as mentioned above, concerning call loans to brokers, "the banks also found a way to manipulate the speculative demand for stocks by increasing broker loans (from $800 million in 1921 to $2.6 billion in 1929)."[83]

d. As Guttman insightfully notes, "The combination of trust accounts, stock underwriting, and broker loans allowed banks to affect both sides of the market. Their active funding of margin credit fed speculative demand for stocks. This, in turn, helped their trust departments to boost trading volumes and commissions. The bull market also made it easier for their investment-bank subsidiaries to expand underwriting activities and to resell new issues at a larger profit. New shares, which did not fetch a sufficiently profitable market price, were often placed in trust accounts. This practice not only transferred price risks to their clients, but also acted to support a higher price level by restricting the supply of new stocks."[84]

Given the above listing of most bank loans and investments, including their commission earnings from their investment bank subsidiaries, what condition were most banks in 1929-1932 as the consequences of the Crash unfolded? Were most sufficiently liquid so as to be capable of lending on a level sufficient to provide economic stimulus for recovery? Or were many bordering on insolvency – their losses on foreign bonds, call loans, and real estate accumulated as to exceed their capital and thereby depriving them of net worth?

A question which anticipates a future chapter – did the banking system focus upon generating income within the banking system as opposed to earning income in supporting consumption and commercial investment in equipment and plants? George Stiglitz in his *Free Fall* makes this insightful point about our present banking system with its use of securitization of mortgages, credit card debt, and other debt securities.

Some scholars are convinced that the initial banking crisis was very localized in places like St. Louis, Chicago, and Philadelphia. In some of these banking crises, the cause was mainly mortgage foreclosures and consequences from the failure of a Tennessee financial institution, Caldwell and Company.[85] Wicker's listing of the portfolio changes for Federal Reserve Bank members and those of non-members between 1921 and 1929 would suggest that member banks were much more stable and that the initial banking crisis was mainly lodged and contained in small towns and cities, such as Chicago. The following summary of those portfolios reflect member banks holding more government securities than non-member banks. This is significant in that banks that held Treasury notes were eligible for Fed relief through the open market purchasing of those Treasury notes held by banks. In return, the banks would be given credit for the cash in their Reserve account. This would increase their reserves and their ability to loan.

The banking situation in the United States, 1921–33

Table 1.7 *Percentage change in select balance sheet items all member and nonmember banks between June 30, 1921–June 30, 1929 and June 30, 1929 and June 30, 1932*

	Percentage change June 30, 1921–June 30, 1929		Percentage change June 30, 1929 – June 30, 1932	
	Member*	Nonmember*	Member*	Nonmember*
Loans	42	27	−35	−48
Investments	68	70	14	−21
Government Securities	62	−5	36	−25
Other securities	71	116	−2	−20
Time deposits	54	37	−22	−42
Capital accounts	54	NA	−11	NA

Wicker, op. cit. page 14.

Were enough member banks stable enough to respond to Fed open-market buying of their government securities by renewing credit to businesses? The record suggests that the banks had some 'window of opportunity' to renew credit in 1930-31 in response to Federal Reserve policy actions. Instead, they chose mainly the posture which we mentioned earlier: in difficult and uncertain times, banks would prefer to protect their cushion of excess reserves, their capital and their equity by avoiding risky lending. That is what most banks did in 1930, squandering any assistance which the Fed and later the Reconstruction Finance Corporation (RFC) provided them. This point will be developed further in later chapters, but the following are highly persuasive that even lower interest rates would not persuade banks to renew lending on a scale sufficient to trigger economic capital spending and/or consumption.

Consider the following and ask yourself which policy did banks pursue: one of conservative safe-guarding their capital and equity, or one of using newly added reserves for the lending they were supposed to permit? If they chose to secure their capital, does this reflect a shortage of money to lend or does it reflect a fear that insolvency may be at risk? If it reflects a shortage of reserves for lending, the Fed's open market activity in buying bank-held government securities should have had some impact in preventing a credit freeze. But if despite receiving funds for selling to the Fed their government securities the banks refused to lend, then one must ask if the banks were simply being rescued by the Fed. If so, this would be contrary to the rule of a central bank lending only to solvent banks to restore liquidity.

1. In an unprecedented manner, the Fed purchased $1.1 billion of government securities from the end of February to the end of July, raising its holdings to $1.8 billion.[86] The Fed had also responded immediately in late 1929 with a similar effort at buying government securities. Despite the effort of the Fed in 1932 as cited above, total bank reserves rose only by $212 million, while the total money supply fell by $3 billion.[87] The reasons are clear for this anomaly:

- Depositors began to desire to hold Treasury notes rather than demand deposit accounts.
- Foreigners demanded gold instead of holding dollars, which could have been spent domestically.
- Banks refused to lend out their new reserves fully "with excess reserves rising to ten percent of total reserves by mid-year."[88]
- The Fed's increasing the money supply and thereby making interest rates very low (two percent at the window of the Fed), banks had no incentive to lend at such low returns for purposes that were mostly risky during this period of 1931-32.

2. Reconstruction Finance Corporation's efforts at loosening credit lending:

"Although the RFC helped shore up railroads on the verge of bankruptcy and cut down, at least for a time, bank closings, it did nothing to get the economy rolling again. Bankers viewed the RFC not as a way to expand the volume of credit, but as a means of preserving their own and other institutions from bankruptcy. The RFC virtually ignored its role as a public works agency; it moved with exasperating slowness in spending the public works and relief appropriations . . ."[89]

Summarizing the Economic Landscape

In addition to the disclosures above on the financial conditions of textile workers, miners, tenant farmers, family farmers, sharecroppers, laid off workers, seasonally or for physical reasons. And the disclosures as to the path of recovery pursued by GM, Chrysler, Ford, and others which seemingly disdained any effort at borrowing from banks, and finally the apparent exposure to illiquidity or insolvency of banks from their involvement in call lending, overreliance upon long-term assets, such as real estate mortgages, risky investments in foreign bonds, and their lack of real connection to the everyday economy of making goods and providing services as a result of their reliance upon their investment bank subsidiaries promotion of stocks and bonds which were not for capital or commercial purposes of buying equipment or expanding business facilities. Now add the following features of the 1920s economy and ask if easy credit could rescue this economy:

1. Great disparities in income and wealth distribution to the point that "if America's 27.5 million

families were divided into five equal-sized groups, the bottom fifth would have annual incomes below $1000, the next group $1000 to $1500, the third $1500 to $2000, the fourth $2000 to $3000, and the top 20 percent all those over $3000. In nearly one-third of families, income was produced by more than one person . . ."[90] Edward Kennedy observed that "the creation of wealth was proceeding so much more rapidly than the distribution of wealth that the output of the producer was becoming too great for the income of the purchaser."[91]

2. Even the celebrated workers' rise to consumerism was restrained. "A 1927 report from the National Industrial Conference showed that in New York City, the weekly budget of an urban manual laborer was $36, while the white-collar worker typically could afford to spend $40 per week. Out of each week's pay, a white collar worker in Brooklyn owed 'ten dollars to the landlord, fifteen to the grocer, butcher and milkman, five to the clothing stores and nine to all his other creditors.' That left the white-collar worker with one dollar per week in discretionary income. A factory worker in Queens spent a bit less to attain roughly the same standard of living—and because a manual laborer's budget was smaller, he, too, had little leeway for unexpected expenses."[92]

3. Factor in those who were in dire need as the 1930s unfolded and ask yourself what jobs these people are going to get under any economic recovery to the point that they become buyers of durable goods.

"'The typical unemployed urban worker on relief,' Hickok found, 'was a white man, thirty-eight years of age and the head of a household . . . [H]e had been more often than not an unskilled or semi-skilled worker in the manufacturing or mechanical industries. He had had some ten years' experience at what he considered to be his usual occupation. He had not finished elementary school. He had been out of any kind of job lasting one month or more for two years, and had not been working at his usual occupation for over two and a half years.' Hopkins stressed particularly the problems of the elderly, who, he concluded, 'through hardship, discouragement and sickness, as well as advancing years, [have] gone into an occupational oblivion from which they will never be rescued by private industry.'

In a summary report to Hopkins on New Years' Day 1935, Hickok rehearsed her worries about a 'stranded generation': men over forty with half-grown families, people who might never get their jobs back. 'Through loss of skill, through mental and physical deterioration due to long enforced idleness, the relief clients, the people who have been longest without work, are gradually being forced into the class of unemployables – rusty tools, abandoned, not worth using any more . . . And so they go on – the gaunt, ragged legion of the industrially damned. Bewildered, apathetic, many of them terrifyingly patient.'

For the great majority of workers, who lacked any pension coverage whatsoever, the very thought of 'retirement' was unthinkable. Most elderly laborers worked until they dropped or were fired, then threw themselves either on the mercy of their families or on the decidedly less tender mercies of a local welfare agency. Tens of thousands of elderly persons passed their final days in the 1920s in the nearly thirteen hundred city and county-supported 'old age homes.' Of the eight percent of the population who were over the age of sixty-five in 1935 – a proportion that had more than doubled since the turn of the century and would rise to more than 12 percent by the century's end – nearly half were on some form of relief."[93]

4. Many factory workers in cities such as Chicago, Philadelphia and New York relied upon their local ethnic savings and loans associations or banks and upon their local grocery store for credit – not upon the state and national banks. This limited their accessibility to these banks during the 1930s.

As we continue through this effort, the above description of th1920s economy speaks to us in our present economic crisis. It asks if low interest rates could rescue today's economy or if the great disparities in income distribution are fatal for any monetary solutions. Are financial bubbles and bursts just localized affairs, touching only a few wealthy families and businesses? Or do they impact in hidden ways in distorting the economy as to impose 'opportunity costs' which work to deprive Americans of opportunities to pursue talents and abilities in jobs which the speculation and emphasis upon housing and financial markets serves to deny us? Are there any parallels between the 1920s and today which would help us understand how to exit our present situation with paths to a more balanced economy offers? What is the proper role of the Federal Reserve Bank and can concern over the value of the dollar on the currency exchange distract the Fed from its primary responsibilities? One thing which absorbs our attention and informed judgment is the importance of consumer consumption of goods and services in our economy as a percent of GDP. During recent decades, it has become 70 percent of GDP. Recently, many experts insist that Americans begin to save more, maybe as much as ten percent of disposable income. If we do, can the GDP withstand, say, consumption becoming only 60 to 65 percent of GDP? Can the growing percent of annual consumer debt of annual disposable income be sustained and if not, what adjustments must we make in order to ensure a growing economy which offers real human resource opportunities to our workers?

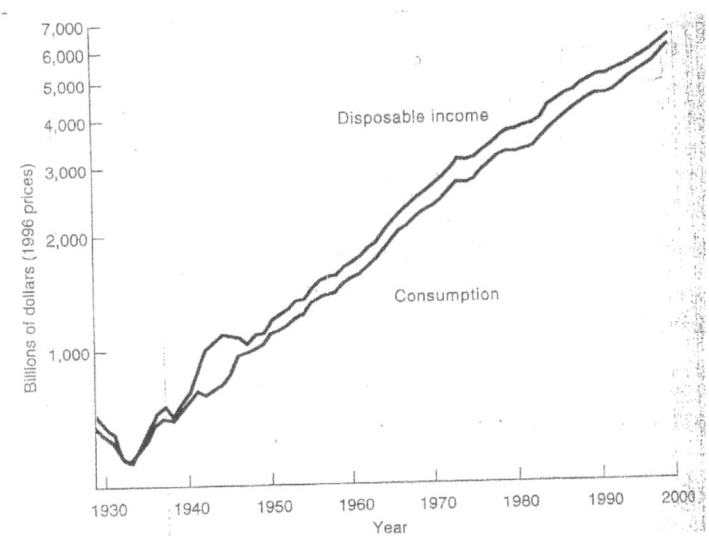

Paul A. Samuelson and William D. Nordhaus, *Economics*, 17th Ed. (McGraw-Hill, 2001, NY), page 464.

Chapter One Notes

1. *David Kyvig ,Daily Life in the United States, 1920-1940.*(Chicago: Ivan Dee, 2002)
2. *Historical Abstract of the United States: From Colonial Times to 1970.* Page 700
3. *Historical Abstract of the United States: From Colonial Times to 1970,* Ibid. p. 700
4. Ibid, page 700.
5. Ibid, page 700.
6. *Historical Abstract*, op. cit. page 693.
7. *David Kyvia op. cit. pp. 37-38*
8. Ibid., pages 37-38.
9. *Douglas Brinkley, A History of the United States*, page 400-401. See also *The Great Depression*, McElvaine, page 41.
10. Ibid, page 41. See also Linda Watts and Alice George Social History of the United States: The 1920s,(Santa Barbara: ABC CLIO, 2009) pages 73-74.
11. Ibid, pages 72., 73 citing Olney 1991, 113.
12. *Ibid,* page 349.
13. *Ibid,*. page 349.
14. *Elizabeth Cohen, Making a New Deal*(. page 104.
15. Ibid. page 104.and *,Linda Watts and Alice George* op .cit. page 344.
16. *David Kennedy, Freedom from Fear,* (New York: Oxford Press, 1999) page 198.
17. Ibid. page 181.
18. Janet Irons, *The General Textile Strike of 1934 in the American South,* University of Illinois Press, Urban, 2000, pages 22-23.
19. Ibid. page 23.
20. Ibid, page 23.
21. *The Hungry Years: A Narrative History of the Great Depression in America* (New York, Henry Holt & Co. 1999) pages 194-195.
22. Ibid. 193.
23. Irving Berstein, *The Lean Years*, (New York, A Da Capo Paperback, 1963) page 4.
24. *The Lost World*, page 26.

25. Bernstein, op. cit. page 363.

26. Kennedy. op. cit. pages 169-170.

27. History Text, page 611-612.

28. Kennedy. op. cit. page 192.

29. Ibid. page 191.

30. *Linda Watts and Alice George, op. cit.*, page 347.

31. Harvey Green, *The Uncertainty of Everyday Life*,(New York, Harper Collins, 1993) pages 48-49.

32. Kennedy, op. cit. page 208.

33. Ibid. page 208.

34. David Kyvig, *Daily Life in the United States,1920-1940* (Chicago, Ivan Dee, 2002) page 16.

35. Kennedy, op. cit. page 168.

36. Elizabeth Cohen, *op. cit.l*, page 102.

37. Robert Guttmann, *How Credit-Money Shapes the Economy: The United States in a Global System*, (New York, Oxford University Press, 2000) page 91.

38. Ibid, page 91.

39. Ibid, page 91.

40. Vincent Curcio, *Chrysler: The Life and Times of an Automobile Genius* (New York, Oxford Press, 2000), page 472.

41. Ibid, page 486.

42. Ibid, page 486.

43. Ibid, page 486.

44. Ibid, page 473.

45. Ibid, page 474.

46. Ibid, page 474.

47. Ibid, page 481.

48. Ibid, page 482.

49. Ibid, page 491.

50. Ibid, page 491.

51. Ibid, page 491.

52. Ibid, page 486.

53. Robert Lacy, *Ford, The Man, and The Machine* (Boston, Little Brown, 1986) page 306.

54. Douglas Brinkley, *Wheels of the World* (New York, Viking Press, 2003) page 385.

55. Ibid, page 385.

56. Lacy, op. cit. page 310.

57. Ibid, page 310.

58. Ibid, page 310.

59. Ibid, page 310.

60. Ibid, page 310.

61. Ibid, page 310.

62. Brinkley, op. cit. pages 420-421.

63. Ibid, pages 421-422.

64. Guttmann, op. cit. page 80.

65. Guttmann, op. cit. page 91.

66. Ibid, page 80.

67. Guttmann, page 81.

68. Ibid, page 81.

69. Benjamin Anderson, *Economics and the General Welfare*,(Indianapolis: Liberty Press, 1979) page 182.

70. Kennedy, op .cit. page 77.

71. Jeffrey Frieden, *Global Capitalism* (New York, W.W. Norton, 2006), page 141.

72. Elmus Wicker, *The Banking Panics of the Great Depression*,( ) page.

73. Ibid, page.

74. Ibid, page .

75. Guttmann, op. cit. page 81.

76. Wicker, op .cit. page .

77. Harvey Green, op .cit. page 76-77 (where he cites that one-half of all home mortgages were in default by the end of 1933.

78. Kennedy, op. cit. pages 36-37.

79. Guttmann, op .cit. page 81.

80. Ibid, page 81.

81. Ibid, page 82.

82. Ibid, page 82.

83. Wicker, op .cit.

84. *A History of Money and Banking in the United States: The Colonial Era to World War II*, page 294.

85. Ibid, page 294.

86. Ibid, page 294.

87. William E. Leuchtenburg, *The Perils of Prosperity 1914-32*. (Chicago, University of Chicago Press, 1958), page 258.

88. David Kyvig, op. cit. page 211.

89.

90. *Linda Watts and Alice George op. cit.* pages 135-136.

91. Kennedy, op. cit. pages 165, 215, 261.

CHAPTER TWO

HOW CLOSELY DOES THE 1920S RESEMBLE TODAY'S ECONOMY FROM THE PAST DECADE OF 2000-2010?

Chapter one presented the landscape of the 1920s economy. Can we draw close parallels between the major characteristics of the 1920s and those of today? Do these parallels between the two decades bear more than just a superficial meaning and relationship insofar as most households then and now are/were effective financially? Did the fact that consumerism was assisted too greatly by easy and unwise credit-lending? Does the easy lending of the 1920s through installment purchases of durable goods and balloon payment home mortgages in the 1920s represent the same economic peril as today's excessive equity loans, refinancing of mortgages, and subprime mortgage lending in that the gross disparities in incomes and wealth of both decades prohibited a sustained consumption of great proportions so vital to economic growth? Did the huge accumulated consumer debt of the 1920s present the same economic peril as did the great gap between household annual disposable income and annual consumer debt? Can we expect similar economic results under both parallel conditions? The central determination of this effort is to decide whether or not--"Easy credit terms extended broadly to the public can compensate for existing great disparities in earnings among American households". Chapter Three addresses the question of great disparities in earnings among Americans particularly during the past decade as Chapter One has set forth in detail the various earnings of American households during the 1920s. Chapter Four addresses the lending practices of the past decade as they affected adversely the natural economy of goods and services. Comparison between the 1920s and the past decade are drawn insofar as the lending practices of banks and other financial institutions produced the same economic results. Chapter Five focuses specifically upon unsound or unethical banking practices of the past decade and how they resemble those of the 1920s. Chapter Six concerns 'opportunity costs' which financial dealings of the 1920s and today imposed on the economy in denying more viable and useful capital investments in plants, equipment, and research and development. Chapter Seven concerns a problem common to the 1920s and during the past decade--how to address the domestic needs of the nation while maintaining international financial stability through monetary policies of the Fed. Chapter Eight carries the discussion in Chapter Seven further as it discusses the Fed's concern over any distortions or disequilibrium which international currency trading could or does cause. Chapter Nine concerns "Confronting International Currency Trading and Identifying Causes and Effects of Domestic and Foreign Disequilibrium and Seeking Appropriate Policy Responses." Chapter Ten deals with the most visible and immediate consequence of all the disturbing parallels--the credit crunch of the 1929-1932 and recently. Chapter 11 recites the numerous responses of the Fed to the financial crisis. A final chapter will attempt to place both decades in a proper perspective insofar as effective policies needed to correct the economic disaster.

CHAPTER THREE:

DISPARITIES IN INCOMES AND WEATLTH:-PARALLEL NO. 1

A. General Conditions Affecting Both Working Class and Middle Class in the 1920s and Today.

Are there any economic adversities which are common to the working class and the middle class in the 1920s and the past decade of 2000-2010? Were the middle class households of the 1920s and are today's middle class households, both, so indifferent and unaffected by those economic and financial practices which impoverished perhaps as much as one-third to 40 percent of Americans? Was the middle class of the 1920s and is today's so secure as to remain a stable source of consumption in 1930-32 and 2008-2010 and therefore provided economic stability sufficient to maintain an economy capable of growth? Or did parallel conditions of the 1920s and the past decade result in many middle class households becoming more like the households of the working class (those working nonstandard jobs of less than 40 hour weeks, below poverty wages, and an uninterrupted work schedule which full time work provides.)

First, what distinguished a middle class from a working class in the 1920s and what distinguishes the middle class today from those near poverty caused by non-standard jobs? What jobs predominated in the late 1920s and in 2001-2008-2009?
Did both decades feature jobs for working and middle class which provided a living wage and stable security with little job interruption? Did most jobs offer opportunities for advancing one's skills or knowledge with the promise of upward mobility to better positions?

Obviously, the working class of the 1920s lived differently than did the middle class. Much of the differences in life style came from the middle class' ability to buy durable goods and the auto on credit. The Lynds in their work, Middletown, defined the working class and the middle class or business class in this manner based on their observations of the conduct of commerce in Muncie, Indiana.

"The Lynds' study of Munice detailed the complex personal and social implications of those employment patterns. The principle factor that distinguished the 'working class' from the 'business class', they found, was insecurity of employment with its consequent disturbance in the rhythms of life. The business class, they noted, "are virtually never subject to interruptions of this kind," while among the working class "the 'shut-down' or 'lay-off' is a recurrent phenomenon." Indeed, they suggested that interruption in employment, even more than occupational category or income, was the chief defining characteristic for membership in the social group they called the 'working class'. Those members of the community who enjoyed a measure of job security were not, virtually by definition, 'the workers'. They had careers, not jobs. Their very conception of time was different, as were their life chances. They planned with confidence for their futures, and for their children's futures. They took annual vacations. They aspired to a better way of life."[1]

The Lynds' description of the working class basically corresponds with that of other authors. Recall from Chapter One the working and living circumstances of the 'working class' in Chicago. (See pages 4-5 above.) In Detroit similar financial constraints faced the working class as they were compelled to save for those periods of lay-offs at Ford and other factories. In Chapter One, the portray of other workers, coal miners, textile workers, sharecroppers and others revealed 'workers' who had even less financial security than many urban factory workers.

In the 1920s, the working class lived on the edge, having earnings barely enough for necessities and often ended up in debt.

"Also, by 1929, only about 20 percent of American families could be considered middle class. Some three-fourths of the nation's families lived below middle-class status. Although the generally accepted minimum working-class budget for a family of four was $2,000 per year, the average industrial wage only reached the $1300 per year mark shortly before the economic downturn of 1929. While the Great Depression created economic dislocations of unprecedented levels, many Americans faced dire circumstances before it began."[2]

Many workers were cautious spenders, seeking some savings to carry the household over during down work times.

"While industrial workers were responsible for the construction of the plethora of new consumer items available during the 1920s, their lack of purchasing power constrained their ability to purchase the fruits of their labors. For a working-class family, there simply was not enough extra income after paying for necessities. Economist Emma Winslow calculated that 95 percent of a working-class family's monthly income went to food, clothing, housing, and utilities. This left a scant 5 percent for education, heath, recreation, and luxury items. Installment buying made some items available, but large purchases such as automobiles, often remained too expensive. Blue-collar Americans had to make do with less costly 'major' purchases such as radios and irons."[3]

Real wages from 1923 to 1929 increased less than 5 percent with mostly the upper tier of workers such as in auto, railroad, construction and printing benefiting the most. The dichotomy of earnings among urban workers may show that in New York City the manual laborer budgeted to spend $40 a week [4]

"Obviously, however, when workers enjoyed only $1 of discretionary income per week, they were unlikely to have the ability to pay the higher rents that almost certainly would accompany private construction of new residential buildings The opportunity to undertake private construction of low-income housing failed to entice many businessmen because of the small likelihood that they could claim quick and sizeable profits. For many Americans, urban life offered great promise, but finding a place to live sometimes was the first difficult trial in a daily struggle to eke out a decent existence."[5] The Average Annual Budget for Working-Class Family of Five in the 1920s looked like this:

The New Consumer Culture

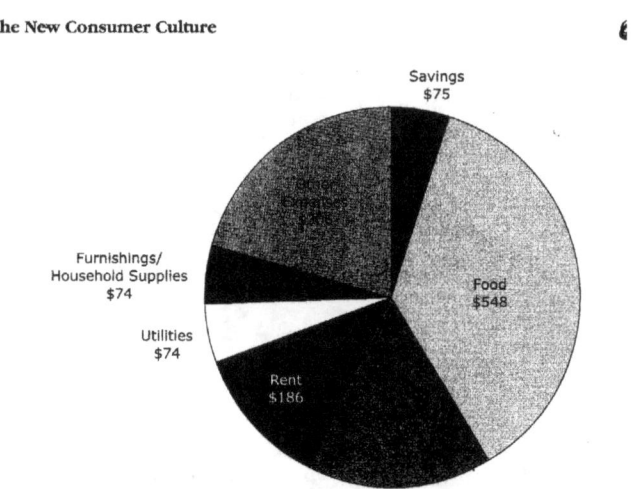

Figure 2.1 *Average Annual Budget for Working-Class Family of Five in the 1920s.*
Source:: *Miller 2003, 282, based on data from Bureau of Labor Statistics.*

What comparisons with today's working class can we make in a relevant manner?

Do we have a class of workers which resembles the workers representing three-fourths of the households of the1920s? Does our comparison require exactly the same percentage of workers to be below middle-class status? Or is the fact that many workers today are being denied the chance to move even into a middle-class status-not alone a professional or business class status make any such analysis valid? It is submitted that any differences between the two working classes are no more than distinctions without a difference insofar as its impacts on the economy.

The following reciting of jobs available in the U.S. economy argue that about 26percent of working Americans have 'nonstandard' jobs:

1. THE FLEXIBLE LABOR FORCE

THE FLEXIBLE LABOR FORCE
By one broad measure, about 26% of working Americans have "nonstandard" jobs

CATEGORY OF WORKER	PERCENTAGE OF WORKFORCE
People who work fewer than 35 hours a week for a particular employer	13.2
Independent contractors (e.g., maids, real estate agents, management consultants)	7.4
Temporary or contract workers	2.1
On-call workers/day laborers	2.0
	0.9
Employees of contractors, such as landscaping or programming services	0.6

Data: Iowa Policy Project and Government Accountability Office, based on 2005 data from Bureau of Labor Statistics

(From "The DISPOSABLE WORKER" by Peter Coy, 7

Consider the following financial and working circumstances of many:

1."About 37% of 18 to 29 year-olds have been underemployed or out of work during the recession, the highest share among the age group in more than three decades, according to a Pew Research Center study released in February."[8]

2. "The generation (above) is the least likely of any to be covered by health insurance. Just 61 percent say they are covered by some form of a health plan, the Pew study said."[9]

3. "Only 58% pay monthly bills on time, a National Foundation for Credit Counseling (NFCC) 2010 survey said." (again, concerning ages 18to 29.)

4. "60% of workers 20 to 29 years old cashed out their 401(k) retirement plans…"

5. "Nearly 70% of GenY members are not building up a cash cushion, and 43% are amassing too much credit card debt, says a November Metlife poll".

6. "On average, Gen Yers each have more than three credit cards, and 20% carry a balance of more than $10,000, according to Fidelity Investments."

7. "Millennials are graduating from college with an average of $23,200 in student debt, according to the most recent data from the Project on Student Debt that is a 24% increase from 2004."[10]

The distressful conditions of employment are not confined to the Gen Yers cited above. Generally, underemployment affects many. People in part-time jobs who want full-time or people in jobs that don't use their education or training has more than doubled to 9.3 million. Ms Dugan who authored the USA Today article above states that if the underemployed are added to the federal count of those involuntarily unemployed, the reach of this affected workforce may be as high as 1 in 5 workers. The consequence of having nonstandard employment may require one to work more than one job as the chart below shows.

Who works extra jobs

About 7.6 million Americans over age 16 work more than one job. The average number of workers, by age group, holding multiple jobs in 2008.

16 to 19 years	230,000
20 to 24 years	750,000
25 to 34 years	1.6 million
35 to 44 years	1.8 million
45 to 54 years	2.0 million
55 to 64 years	1.1 million
65 and older	220,000

Source: Bureau of Labor Statistics

Multiple jobs are necessary due to the low pay of most earnings from one job or the lost of a partner's pay. The above article states that the Bureau of Labor Statistics found that during the first five months of 2009, 5.3 % of all employees worked multiple jobs. This may seem a small percentage, but financial burdens required two-parent earnings and imposed tremendous stress on single-parents.

Those seeking advancement through acquiring a college degree face obstacles contain within the structures of the economy----too many low-skilled, low-paying jobs in service industry and other low-skilled industries--plus the timing of their graduation may impose life-time penalties. Don Peck relates how the specific timing of graduating from college may determine whether the graduate achieves professional opportunities and promotions or lags behind other graduates and be confined to even working low-skilled, low-pay jobs with a life-time curse of never obtaining a professional position. He cites the following consequences:

1. The earnings gap between college graduates benefiting from good economic times at graduation and those not so lucky seems to persist. It persists to the point that "five, ten, fifteen years after graduation, after untold promotions and career changes spanning booms and

busts, the unlucky graduate never closes the gap". [12]

2. The unlucky graduate at mid-career "were significantly less likely to work in professional occupations or other prestigious spheres."[13]

3. The unlucky graduates "clung more tightly to their jobs; average job tenure was unusually long. People who entered the workforce during the recession "didn't switch jobs as much, and particularly for young workers, that's how you increase wages".[14]

4. A 'bad' start in a profession can be a persistent barrier to upward mobility. Peck quoting Lisa Kahn from her study states, "when you're forced to start work in a particular low-level job or unsexy career, it's easy for other employers to dismiss you as having low potential. Moving up, or moving on to something different and better, becomes more difficult."[15]

The similarities between the working conditions and financial insecurity of workers in the 1920s and the past decade of 2000-2010 are fundamental insofar as they suffered from the same employer employment practices. One common source of insecurity was the impact of advanced technology and its accompanying increased productivity. Companies could achieve higher profits through increased output with less workers. The number of factory workers in 1929 was about the same as in 1920.

"In 1922 the country, already enormously productive by comparison with other countries, started a recovery from the postwar depression-a recovery that maintained prosperity, with slight interruptions, until the fall of 1929. The key to the piping prosperity of the decade was the enormous increase in efficiency of production, in part the result of the application of Frederick W. Taylor's theory of scientific management, in part the outgrowth of technological innovations."[16].

Through the implementation of 'Fordism' or the use of an assembly line, plus the substitution of machine power for human labor through the use of electric motors instead of steam engines, employers achieved the following results:

"With more efficient management, greater mechanization, intensive research, and ingenious sales methods, industrial production almost doubled during the decade, soaring from an index figure of 58 in the depression year of 1921 to 110 in 1929.(1933-39 =100) This impressive increase in productivity was achieved without any expansion of the labor force. Manufacturing employed precisely the same number of men in 1929 as it had in 1919."[17]

The strategy common to management in the 1920s and today is to reduce labor to a commodity-a cost that can easily be added or dropped. Consider the Lynds' findings in Middletown:

"For the dominant manufacturing group, the peremptory little figures on the cost sheets require that there shall always be on hand enough workers to take care of any fluctuations in business. The condition of there being more men than available jobs, though dreaded by the working man is commonly called by his bosses 'an easier labor market'. In March, 1924, when the long slump of unemployment was commencing and employers in other cities ran 'want ads' in the Middletown papers offering work, two special delivery letters were laid by the plate of the president of the Middletown Advertising Club at one of its weekly luncheons, asking the Club to use its influence to suppress such advertisements because they tended to draw unemployed machinists from town."[18] In today's workplace, many workers suffer a fate similar to that of being a commodity as they work part-time, as temps, as independent contractors whose contract may not be renewed, and other labor classifications that exempt employers from providing benefits and payroll deductions.

As shown above concerning the typical financial condition of blue collar workers in Chicago, Detroit factory workers fared no better:

"A survey in 1929 found that the average Detroit-area Ford worker earned $1,712. But what was considered 'necessary' by 1929 called for an income of $1,728-$16 short. And Ford workers, as well as any of the semiskilled workers in growing industries such as automobiles, electrical goods, and other mass-production industries, were relatively well paid. Progressives worried that 'dollar-down serfdom' would 'deliver the workman to his employer swathed in the tightly binding bandages of payment due dates', preventing strikes. Consumption on credit was the sure road to lower wages. Only by borrowing from the future could that $16 difference be made up, though, and in the 1920s, Americans choose comfortable serfdom."[19]

Working families in the 1920s may aspire to a middle class status through installment purchases of cars, appliances, and radios. But unlike the blue collar workers of the 1940s, 1950s, and 1960s, the blue collar workers lacked job security and high wages. Workers in the 1920s were faced with layoffs, wage cuts, and other work-related interruptions to financial security. Nevertheless, the urban worker was constantly tempted by advertising to acquire goods beyond his financial means. In mid-twentieth century, a middle class income status could be acquired through decent jobs and only a few sought upward mobility as a route to upper middle class status. Today, a middle class income status for blue collar workers has been undermined by employer practices which minimize the need for skilled workers.

As in the 1920s, productivity increases victimized workers during the past decade. Profits and productivity have been achieved through wage reductions in addition to any technological innovations such as computerized operations. The Wall Street Journal in its article of January 17-18, 2009 entitled "Layoffs and Cuts to Wages Deepen at Big Companies" by Kelly Evans and Don Clark cited the following circumstances and consequences for workers: "But falling prices bring their own troubles as employers make up revenue declines by trimming wages. Employers in recessionary times always feel compelled to squeeze more from less. But with the job market so weak, employees appear more willing to work for less pay than leave behind pensions and health care coverage to brave the worst job market in a generation." They cited several cases of lay-offs throughout some industries. During the 1920s, lay-offs were common for factory workers.

Today, productivity increases have not been necessarily benign. Consider Business Week article of May 25, 2009 entitled "Productivity's Up and That's a Worry" by Michael Mandel. He cites productivity as having provided the impetus for recovery by increasing profits without raising prices which reassured the Fed about there being less danger of inflation. Relieved of inflationary fears, the Fed continued to support low interest rates which were vital for stabilizing the economy. In achieving this productivity, companies have eliminated not only unskilled or semi-skilled workers but also white collar professionals. Mandel cites the following:

"The slide started in earnest after the Lehman debacle. Since August 2008, employment in engineering and architecture occupations is down 10.3 %, computer and mathematical occupations are down 9.3%, and natural and social science occupations are down 2.3%........Together these four occupational groups have lost 1 million jobs since August."

Mandel offers the troubling prospect that companies stuck in slow-growth economy will be slow to rehire professionals who are "the people who do the research, the new product development, the information gathering, the training, and even the marketing which moves the product forward."[20]

Working conditions in many of today's companies parallel those of the 1920s where the fast pace of assembly line work and piecemeal jobs often led to the worker's exhaustion and in some industry men were physically unable to sustain a satisfactory work performance when they reached the age of 40 and beyond. Similarly, while perhaps dismissals of workers due to their physical inability to perform are not as flagrant, companies have other ways of accomplishing the same thing. Downsizing of the number of workers maintained on company payroll has lead to the following consequences as reported in the USA Today, Workers Feel burn of long hours," December 17, 2011:

1. U.S. workers put in an average of 1, 815 hours in 2002 compared to about 1,300 to 1,800 across Europe. Japanese hours of work for the year equaled that of American workers.

2."While extended overtime relieved companies of extra shifts or additional workers, most studies show a negative outcome for companies who insist on sustained performance on those terms. Employees feel the strain. Mounting research shows there's a tangible downside to overwork, from mental health problems to physical ailments and job injuries caused by fatigue and stress. It's also a bottom line issue. A study by the Economic Policy Institute found that mandatory overtime costs industry as much as $300 billion a year in stress and fatigue-related problems."

Another employment policy of today which parallels that in many industries of the 1920, such as the suffering coal and textile industries, was the instituting of pay-cuts. For today's cases see, Wall Street Journal, January 17-18 2009, for its article entitled, "Layoffs and Cuts to Wages Deepen in Big Companies" by Kelly Evans and Don Clark.

An alarming development in the structure of American industry has been noted recently as did President Hoover in the late 1920s--an economy which featured too many low to semi-skilled jobs. In its February 4-5 issue, the Wall Street Journal reported the following results in job-creation:

"Since mid-2011, the U.S. has added 264,000 health care jobs, 167,000 leisure and hospitality jobs-mostly in restaurants---and 94,000 manufacturing jobs. Employers also have hired 109,000 temporary workers, an encouraging sign because companies often hire temps before they add permanent workers."[21] Any optimism contained in this report was greatly restricted by the following caveat:

"The recent employment gains have been concentrated in comparatively low-wage sectors. Hospitals and other heath-care providers have added nursing aides and technicians far faster than higher-paying positions like doctors and nurses. The big gains in business services have come among secretaries and temp workers, not architects or lawyers." "But some economists worry that as the country continues its decades long shift away from manufacturing and toward services, it is becoming increasingly skewed toward low-skill, low wage jobs". Harvard economist Lawrence Katz pondered, "Will it be (an economy) with minimum wage jobs that don't utilize people's potential, or will they be organized in ways that a highly educated work force provides a lot of customized service?"[22] President Hoover's concern derived from what he regarded as excessive use of assembly-line work, but the same outcome concerned him as it did Professor Katz.

It is not surprising that the following headlines reflect the above diminishing opportunities for college grads and trained, skilled workers:

"HOUSEHOLD INCOME SINKS TO '95 LEVEL"

From Wall Street Journal in 2010 in article by Conor Dougherty and Anna Wilds

Mathews.

Or "STUDY; NEARLY HALF ARE OVERQUALIED FOR THEIR JOBS." From USA Today, January 28, 2013 by Mary Beth Marklein.

What social and financial weakening does these headlines spell? Is there any strong possibility of upward mobility even into a high income middle class status? Not according to recent measurements and reporting: Consider Time Magazine's findings in their issue, November 14, 2011 in an article entitled, "WHAT EVER HAPPENED TO UPWARD MOBILITY?" by Rana Foorohar at pages 26-31. Ms Foorohar cites the following conditions which 'haunts' the young:

"Nor are we the world's greatest opportunity society. The Pew Charitable Trusts' Economic Mobility Project has found that if you were born in 1970 in the bottom one-fifth of the socioeconomic spectrum in the U.S., you had only about a 17% chance of making it into the upper two-fifths. That's not good by International standards. A spate of new reports from such groups as Brookings, Pew and the Organization for Economic Co-operation and Development show that it's easier to climb the socioeconomic ladder in many parts of Europe than it is in the U.S."

Although Time concedes that today's workers "live in households with larger incomes, adjusted for inflation, than their parents had at the same age" our examination of even middle income households of today achieve that status only through a two -parent working household. Beyond any such stationary comparisons between the insecure factory worker of the 1920s and any low-skilled, low-pay worker now, another test provided by Time examines the opportunities for all workers-regardless of the family incomes in which they were raised. This test of upward mobility asks, "How we are doing compared with our peers?" "By that standard, we aren't doing very well at all. Having the right parents increases your chances of ending up middle to upper middle class by a factor of three to four."[23] Time provided this chart showing the path to upper mobility:

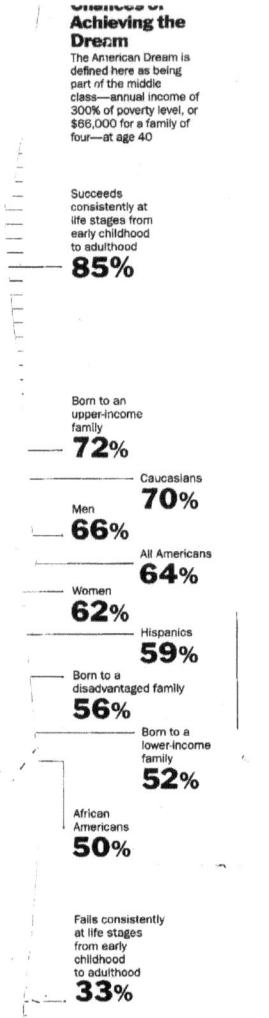

Not all differences in peer chances of upward mobility can be attributed to the favorable conditions of childhood. Remember how graduates of good economic times achieved a permanent advantage over those graduating in poor economic times--particularly if the ones graduating in bad times end up in low-pay, low-skilled jobs for an extended period. They tend to lack professional credibility for jobs for which they originally were educated or trained.

The absence of upward mobility today corresponds generally with the lack of such opportunities in the 1920s. The Lynds in their book, Middletown, cited several cases where the absence of one's getting ahead was voiced by residents of Muncie, Indiana. Their study of six plants showed that "there was a chance for one man in 424 to be promoted." during a year and three-fourths time. Laments about one's spouse's inability to be promoted or to achieve a better job were voiced:

(Husband a machinist, age thirty-eight) "Well, he's been doing the same thing over and over for fifteen years, hoping he'd get ahead, and he's never had a chance; so I don't suppose he ever will."

(Husband a machinist, age twenty-six.) "There's nothing ahead where he's at and there's nothing to do about it".

(Husband a machine-tender, age forty-six) "There won't never be anything for him as long as he stays where he is and I don't know where else he can go."

(Husband a foreman, age thirty-eight) "He's been there nine years and there's no chance of promotion. The work is so hard he's always exhausted. He wants to get back on a farm. He's been lucky so far in not being lay off, but we're never sure."

(Husband a factory laborer, age thirty.) "He'll never get any better job. He'll be lucky if they keep him on this one."[25]

Again the above attitudes showing uncertainty reflect a work environment so unstable as to compel workers to accept pay cuts as they are today.. See Ibid, page 60. To draw a fairer comparison between the 1920s and today insofar as getting ahead is concerned, the Lynds found that the attitude of high school graduates tended to be one of 'just getting a job after graduation- a job which required some vocational training in high school.[24] This attitude of high school graduate of the 1920s correlates very closely with the attitudes of high school graduates in the 1950s when manufacturing jobs were plentiful and marriages often occurring at a young age. In both decades there lacked a culture of self-improvement beyond what the present job might require. Promotion to foreman in the 1950s was probably more frequent than in the late 1920s. Today, upward mobility is lacking despite a perceived need of the young to acquire a college education towards a profession or high-skilled occupation. The need for immediate reward from present jobs in rejecting any schooling which may require deferring enjoyment from spending does remind us of today's generations' preference of instant gratification. The reader is left to his/her own conclusion as to how far the need for instant gratification hampers the young and the quest for better jobs. It seems that a difference exists today from the motivations of the young during the 1920s as noted by the Lynds:

"The dominance of the dollar appears in the apparently growing tendency among younger working class men to swap a problematic future for immediate 'big money'. Foreman complain that Middletown boys entering the shops today are increasingly less interested in being moved from job to job until they have become all-around skilled workers, but want to stay on one machine and run up their production so that they may quickly reach a maximum wage scale."[26]

By requiring college graduates to linger for years in low-pay, low-skill work, we may be creating the same culture and incentives existing above for the youth of the 1920s. As Time Magazine's research showed increased upward mobility for those raised in upper income families, the Lynds' research showed similar advantages for the well-to-do in the 1920s' Middletown. More specifically, their research showed that "the new rush of the children of the business class to college and of the working man's children to high school and college is increasing the vertical mobility of the children by offering all manners of short-cuts to the young man or woman with an education, but once established in a particular job, the limitations fixing possible range of advancement seem to be narrower for an industrial worker."[27] Nevertheless, even with upward mobility for some, particularly those from upper income families, an overriding limitation existed then and today. A limitation that accelerates the growing disparities in earnings:

"With the passing of apprenticeship the line between skilled and unskilled has become blurred as to be in some shops almost non-existent. The superintendent of a leading Middletown machine shop says, 'Seventy-five per cent of our force of 800 men can be taken from farm or high school and trained in a week's time.' In the glass factory………..84 per cent. of the tool-using personnel, exclusive of foremen, require one month or less training, another 4 per cent, not more than six months, 6 per cent, a year, and the remaining 6 per cent, three years."[28]

In the final chapter, we will point to a growing partnership between companies and college in internships in an effort to anticipate and fill future human resource needs--needs that cannot be satisfied by treating labor as a commodity to be manipulated at will by employers. In addition to securing the future of young professionals, this type of response is calculated to strengthen the growth of an upper middle class by offering more middle class income jobs. We will now see that both today and in the 1920s, the middle class was becoming under financial stress,

In the 1920s, a middle class status usually belonged to a professional, a small business owner, a doctor or lawyer, or local business man. Their 'needs' usually consisted of furniture, clothes, doctor's bills, Christmas presents, eyeglasses, schoolbooks, groceries, fuel, rent, lights, phone, Life insurance, auto upkeep, and vacations (for upper middle class) See for example, listings in Borrow,[29] Mass production and sales required consumption by the middle class and the rich. However, to achieve economies of scale in production, the working class, also, would have to purchase considerable amount of goods and services. Great disparities in income prohibited this necessary volume of consumption by the working class. Down payments for autos and other expensive goods prohibited many workers from buying on credit. Continued consumption by the middle class in the 1920s was undermined by two economic adversities: 1. Because banks could no longer gain additional funds from the sale of their bonds, they had no ability to refinance home mortgages as they became due. Home mortgages in the 1920s required only interest payments initially with a balloon principal payment due after a few years. The fatal consequences were portrayed in Josephine Lawrence's "If I Have Four Apples" which represented a reality shared by many in the late 1920s. The book's principle character, a Mr. .Hoe, had benefited from boom times in buying his home which rose in value with the economic times. However, whereas "throughout the 1920s home owners could expect to refinance their balloon mortgages, banks now demanded that they pay off the loan or face foreclosure. Few home owners could pay the principal on their mortgages all at once, having spent the 1920s simply paying the interest every month. Since all the lenders wanted their money at once, properties across the country were foreclosed on, further depressing the real estate market and making investments even more unwise..."³⁰ An additional peril existed for home buyers in the rush to make and buy homes. As related in "If I Had Four Apples"

"Mr. Hoe's fictional problems were all too common real ones. His boom-era house was 'flimsy' and although it could be 'easily improved if he only had a few hundred dollars to spend on it,' all his income went to the mortgage. Because he had paid too much for this shoddily constructed house during the boom of the 1920s, Mr. Hoe could barely meet his mortgage payments as his wages fell. Desperate appeals to the Home Owners' Loan Corporation went unanswered for months and then ultimately denied. Despite his own desire to work and to pay his bills, Mr. Hoe fell prey to forces beyond his control. He had done everything right, yet everything had turned out wrong." As author of Borrow notes, "millions of Americans, following the rules, had had the same experience, and suddenly it was no longer so clear that individuals were completely responsible for their economic lives."³¹ This description of financial disaster clearly is one happening to a middle class family in general as factory workers would not normally be positioned by economic booms to pursue this home-buying strategy based on the ability to refinance. So, as in the recent decade much of the middle class prosperity was fictionally derived--from the assumption that home values would go up without serious interruptions in lowering values. Another false bottom of the middle class path to their status in the 1920s had been pointed out much to the displeasure of lenders and many industries:

"Economists argued, backed by sound reasoning, that by committing their payments to goods already purchased, consumers could no longer buy new goods or services. The expansion of purchasing power in good times through installment credit worked only to prevent spending in bad times, hampering recovery. According to this view, paying back the $3billion of installment debt owed in 1929 required foregoing new purchases, condemning the U.S. economy to years of languishing depression."[32]

In other words, making installment payments now for goods already owned competed with buying new goods. Although Americans repaid most of their installment debt after the Crash of 1929, it resulted in less money available for present consumption. "Durable goods spending fell by half and durable goods manufacturing, on which most installment credit was based, fell to a fifth of it's 1929 level by 1932."[33].

The general condition of the middle class in the 1920s is accurately summarized below:

> "The coupling of increased disposable income and shorter work weeks led middle-class Americans to devote more attention to both leisure and consumption. To facilitate consumerism, businesses began to offer a wealth of expensive products to Americans through the wonder of 'installment buying'. No longer forcibly constrained to be thrifty, Americans gobbled up automobiles (Ride Now, Pay Later," trumpeted the manufacturers), refrigerators, washing machines, and radios with 10 percent down and pledges to make monthly payments. During the decade, more than 85 percent of all furniture sold in the United States would be bought on credit."[34]

The price of achieving a middle-class standard of living through extensive credit was too heavy a load to sustain in the face of economic changes which were often adverse to the middle class as well as to the working class.

"To consume, even at the risk of financial peril, denoted one's success in achieving the American dream, a dream of leisure, comfort, and wealth through keeping up with modern products and technology, middle -class Americans both established their superiority over the drudgery of working class existence and connected themselves with the wealthy. By consuming on the installment plan, middle-class Americans tasted some of the delights of wealth, and by consuming beyond their means they placed themselves in a position that required they continue to work diligently for their employers."[35] (Notably, the next sentence reflects that

"Middle-class Americans, therefore, derived both pleasure and pain from the unequal distribution of wealth", implying that their preoccupation with material well-being contributed to the continued and increased disparities in earnings and wealth. The following paragraph concedes as much.)

The spending spree of the `1920s led to an accumulated personal debt of $3billion.[36]

How does this unsustainable credit-led consumption of the 1920a compare to the ultimate state of today's middle class as a result of their extensive consumption based on credit cards, refinancing, and equity loans?

Remembering that a well-off middle class represents a barrier to extreme disparities in wealth and earnings, we cannot tolerate a great diminished capacity of the middle class's ability to reflect a moderation between great successes of the few and the great disadvantages of the few.

Beginning with definitions of the middle class, the following have been offered by the New York Times:

> » **ECONOMISTS:** The Census Bureau divides household income into quintiles, or groups of 20 percent. Some economists narrowly define the middle class as those in the middle 20 percent of the distribution, earning between $38,000 and $61,000. Others define it more broadly to include the middle 60 percent, between $20,000 and $100,000.
>
> » **SOCIOLOGISTS:** The middle class to them is based on occupation: an "upper middle class" of white-collar specialists (lawyers, engineers, professors, economists and architects) and a "middle class" of lower-level white-collar workers (teachers, nurses, insurance sales and real estate agents). Together, they make up about 45 percent of households.
>
> » **POLLS:** Americans often view "middle class" as something more than specific income levels, which can be affected by family size, expenses and local costs of living. At least two-thirds of adults say being middle class means owning a home, being able to save for the future and afford things such as vacation travel, the occasional new car and various other little luxuries, according to an ABC News poll in 2010.
>
> — *Associated Press*

DEFINITIONS OF 'MIDDLE CLASS'

The "middle class" is an amorphous concept, and the presidential candidates are giving it their own definitions to fit their political purposes. Here are some ways to define it, political, economic and otherwise:

» **POLITICS:** In pushing for tax benefits for "middle-class" Americans, President Barack Obama defines them as families making less than $250,000 — which is 98 percent of U.S. households. Republican challenger Mitt Romney has defined the group as families making less than $200,000.

» **WHITE HOUSE COUNCIL OF ECONOMIC ADVISERS:** In a January speech noting the middle class has shrunk to 42 percent of households, Alan Krueger, who chairs the council, defined the group as those having annual earnings within 50 percent of the U.S. median income. The current median income is $49,445, putting middle-class earnings in a range from about $25,000 to $75,000.

According to the White House Council of Economic Advisors, those in the middle class have an annual earnings within 50 percent of the U.S. median income. The current median income is $49,445, putting middle-class earnings in a range from about 25,000 to $75,000"

Economists in the Census Bureau divides household income into quintiles or, groups of 20 percent. Some economists narrowly define the middle class as those in the middle 20 percent of the distribution, earning between $38,000 and $61,000. Others define it more broadly to include the middle 60 percent between $20,000 and $100,00."

Sociologists give this definition: "The middle class to them is based on occupation; an 'upper middle class' of white collar specialists (lawyers, engineers, professors, economists, and architects) and a 'middle class' of lower level white-collar workers (teachers, nurses, insurance sales, and real estate agents). Together, they make up about 43 percent of households."

According to Public Opinion Polls, middle class levels of income vary and depend upon family size, expenses, and local cost of living. "At least two-thirds of adults say being middle class means owning a house, being able to save for the future and afford things such as a vacation, travel, the occasional new car and various other little luxuries, according to an ABC News poll in 2010.[38]

It is significant that the definition of middle class most subscribed to is that based on income status, not occupation-just as in the 1920s[39] How is the middle class doing today? Growing and prospering or suffering decline under the weight of declining incomes, growing consumer debt, and the decline of upward mobility even into the middle class station of life? The following are offered as the dominant profile of the conditions of our middle class.

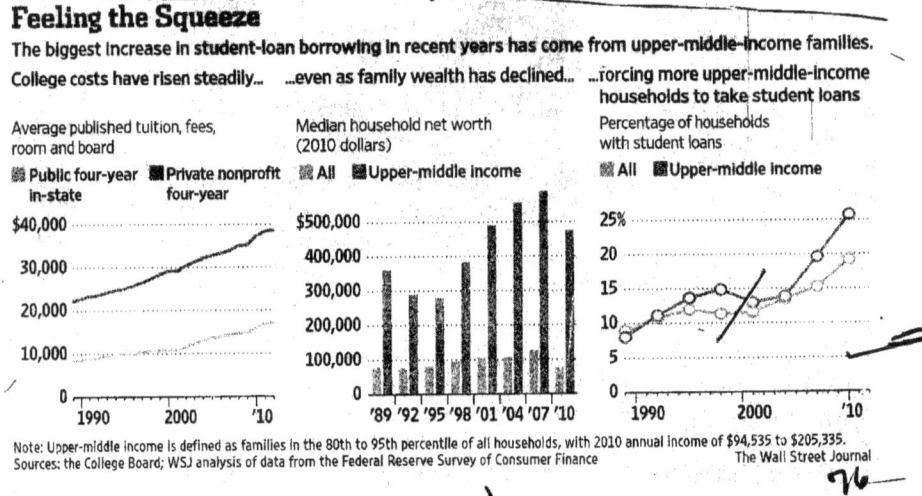

In addition to the decline of upward mobility opportunities, the following provides greater understanding of how difficult it is becoming to be a middle class household:

1. Consider how burdensome mortgage payments can be as a percentage of disposable income. The following graph shows the distribution of mortgage payments as a percentage of income among different income groups.

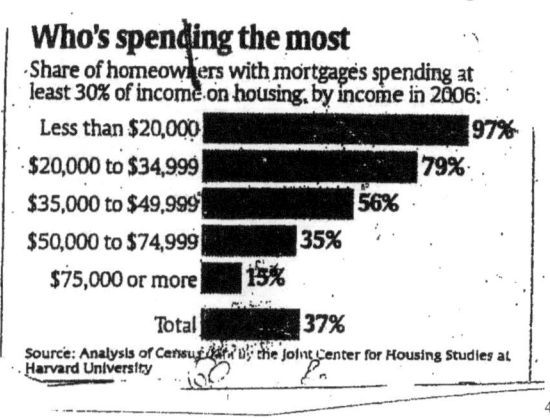

2. Child care expenses reduce disposable incomes. The following chart tracks the incidence of child care cost of state, by single parent experience, and by the two-parent experience.

State-to-state costs vary

Ranking of cost of child care for a 4-year-old;
1 = highest; 50 = lowest.

State	Average annual cost of preschool care	Pct. of median single parent family income spent on pre-school care	Pct. of median two-parent family income spent on pre-school care	Ranking of preschool care as a percentage of income
Alabama	$3,016	18.3%	4.8%	50
Alaska	$6,684	23.0%	8.4%	22 (tie)
Arizona	$5,876	26.2%	9.4%	17 (tie)
Arkansas	$3,884	22.3%	6.1%	48
California	$7,576	31.1%	10.9%	3
Colorado	$7,020	27.7%	9.2%	15 (tie)
Connecticut	$8,459	29.0%	9.0%	19
Delaware	$5,515	23.8%	7.0%	40 (tie)
Florida	$4,948	21.6%	7.8%	32
Georgia	$4,025	20.3%	6.2%	45 (tie)
Hawaii	$5,620	22.8%	7.3%	36
Idaho	$4,803	28.2%	8.4%	22 (tie)
Illinois	$6,806	31.6%	9.2%	15 (tie)
Indiana	$5,408	25.8%	8.4%	22 (tie)
Iowa	$5,375	25.7%	8.4%	22 (tie)
Kansas	$4,446	18.3%	6.9%	43
Kentucky	$4,710	32.4%	8.1%	28
Louisiana	$4,760	30.3%	7.7%	33 (tie)
Maine	$6,344	34.8%	9.4%	12 (tie)
Maryland	$6,535	29.2%	7.2%	37 (tie)
Massachusetts	$9,628	40.7%	10.6%	4
Michigan	$6,216	29.1%	8.7%	20
Minnesota	$8,832	31.1%	11.4%	2
Mississippi	$3,904	26.7%	6.8%	44
Missouri	$3,967	18.7%	6.1%	47
Montana	$4,486	26.2%	8.8%	29 (tie)
Nebraska	$5,190	26.2%	7.0%	31
Nevada	$3,200	14.3%	5.3%	49
New Hampshire	$7,014	24.9%	8.5%	21
New Jersey	$8,985	32.8%	9.6%	8 (tie)
New Mexico	$5,054	35.1%	9.1%	17 (tie)
New York	$8,530	40.4%	11.3%	1
North Carolina	$5,876	31.8%	9.4%	12 (tie)
North Dakota	$4,784	26.3%	7.8%	35
Ohio	$6,159	31.1%	9.1%	17 (tie)
Oklahoma	$4,073	23.5%	7.0%	40 (tie)
Oregon	$5,160	26.0%	8.2%	27
Pennsylvania	$6,800	31.4%	9.6%	8 (tie)
Rhode Island	$7,800	45.3%	10.3%	5 (tie)
South Carolina	$4,180	22.8%	6.2%	45 (tie)
South Dakota	$4,804	24.9%	7.7%	33 (tie)
Tennessee	$4,188	22.3%	7.0%	40 (tie)
Texas	$4,427	21.7%	7.2%	37 (tie)
Utah	$4,764	21.5%	8.0%	29 (tie)
Vermont	$6,537	27.7%	9.5%	10 (tie)
Virginia	$7,852	34.6%	10.3%	5 (tie)
Washington	$6,891	32.7%	9.5%	10 (tie)
West Virginia	$3,886	26.7%	7.1%	39
Wisconsin	$6,968	31.0%	9.8%	7
Wyoming	$5,438	29.8%	8.4%	22 (tie)

Note: Costs of child care are based on the price of care in a licensed child care center. The in-

" Stephanie Amour cites the following facts:

1. "Average child care fee for one infant ranges from $3,083 to $13,480 a year according to the National Association of Child Care."

2. "to afford average-priced infant care in a center, a two-parent family would

need to spend 6 to 10 percent of household income each year."

        3. "Single parents would have to pay nearly $3 out of every $10 they earn."

Moreover, any income advantage gained by a second income earned by a spouse is what eliminated by working expenses such as travel, clothing, meals, in addition to the child care expenses. Both two-parent and single-parent families suffer from the changed workplace. Amour cites changed working conditions as follows: "Current trends add to financial woes. Workdays have been stretched longer due to technology and the 24/7 demands of today's competitive business environment. It used to be that many children didn't begin formal schooling until kindergarten. But preschool is now in vogue--and the costs can be high, with some private preschools running $20,000 a year."[43] Adding to the disruption of family life and to its deteriorating quality is the fact that many two parent workers have different shifts. Census data between 1979 and 2008 shows that 45 % of the children had both parents working full time. This increases the adversity in achieving a middle class income station in life as the following brings to full understanding:

"Working couples have crazy schedules. The majority of families headed by dual-earner parents have experienced non-standard job schedules (defined as other than 9 a.m. to 5 p.m., Monday through Friday), research co-written by Brines suggests. In the late 1980s, 69% of couples had a least one spouse regularly working a night, week-end, rotating, or evening shift. By 2002 that had climbed to 86%"[44]

What about accumulated consumer debt from this attempt at middle class income status? Has it imposed a burden similar to that accumulated by the 1920s' middle class in an effort to 'enjoy the good life'? The following USA Today research shows the condition of consumer debt as of the year 2007:

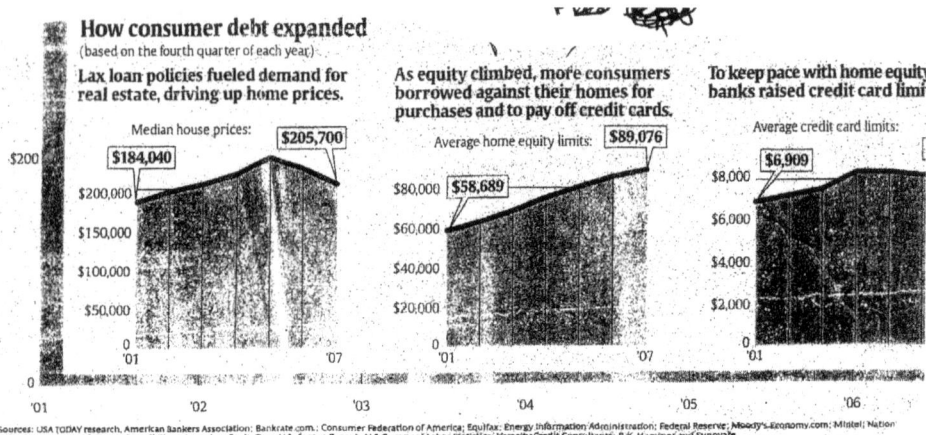

45

The prior chart showing how student debt has impacted even the upper middle class also shows that while consumer debt may have slacken in the years following 2007, household net worth declined through the year 2010. Time magazine has provided, perhaps, the best summarized profile of the declining financial well-being of the middle class-a decline attributable to the lack of upward mobility of younger family household earners.

> "Families headed by people under 35 are almost 70 percent poorer today, adjusting for inflation, than they were in 1984."[46]

The test of a vibrant free society is one that offers security and well-being to the vast majority of its people. Of first priority is the ability to achieve a strong and extensive middle class. This is only a very, but essential, beginning for nation-building and maintaining. Business Week in a recent column noted that "Many nations can move from low-income to middle-income status, but as labor costs rise only countries that boost productivity, improve education, and master innovation fully develop."[47] One hazard of achieving economic growth of significant proportions is the historic great disparities in wealth and earnings which almost invariably occurs. Great disparities in earnings and wealth undermine the first principle of nation-building--the embracing of the economy of the vast majority of families. This has not been the recent experience of Americans according to their earnings. Only excessive consumer debt has permitted the illusion of a vast, well-off middle class.

Chapter Three Notes

1. David Kennedy, Freedom From Fear (New York: Oxford Press 1999) page 24
2. Linda S. Watts and Alice George op. cit. page 342
3. Ibid, page 349
4. Ibid 135
5. Ibid, page 136
6. Ibid page 61
7. Peter Coy, Michelle Conlen, and Moira Herbst, Business Week," The Disposable Worker", January 18, 2010
8. USA Today April 23, 2010
9. Ibid, page 2A
10. All cites are from the above USA Today article
11. Paul Davidson, "Moonlighting becomes a way of life for many" USA Today June 24, 2009
12. Don Peck, Pinched (New York; Crown 2011) page 64.
13. Ibid, page 64.
14. Ibid, page 64
15. Ibid, page 65
16. William E. Leuchtenburg, Perils of Prosperity 1914-1932 (Chicago: University of Chicago 1958) page 193
17. Ibid, page 193
18. Robert S. Lynd and Helen Lynd, Middletown: A Study on Modern American Culture, (New York: Harcourt, Brace, & Co 1929) page 58
19. Louis Hyman, Borrow, (New York: Vintage 2012) pages 56-57.
20. Michael Mandel, "Productivity Up" Business Week May 25, 2009
21. Ben Cassleman, "Recovery Reclaims Labor….." Wall Street Journal February 4-5, 2009
22. Ibid, page 5
23. Time, November 14, 2011.
24. Robert and Helen Lynd, op. cit. page 47
25. Ibid, page 67
26. Ibid, page 81
27. Ibid, page 68
28. Ibid, page 74

29. Louis Hyman, op. cit. page 82
30. Ibid, page 76
31. Ibid, page 81
32. Ibid, pages 84-85
33. Ibid, page85
34. Linda Watts and Alice George op. cit. page 344
35. Ibid, page348
36. Ibid, page 344
37. From The New York Times classification of the middle class
38. Ibid
39. Ibid
40. Ibid.
41. "Feeling The Squeeze", Wall Street Journal, October 26, 2012
42. Forty two
43. Stephanie Amour, "High Cost of Child Care can lead to Lifelong ……" USA Today April 15, 2010
44. Ibid
45. Ibid
46. "How consumer debt expanded", USA Today
47. Time, op. cit. November 14, 2011
48. "The Middle Income Trap", Business Week June 18, 2013

CHAPTER FOUR

PARALLEL CONDITION NO. 2: EASY CREDIT LENDING AND ABANDONMENT OF COMMERCIAL BANKING.

The financing of commerce, investment, and infrastructure: How both the 1920s and 2000-2009 departed from traditional banking and sought quick and fluid profits. In the process, shadow banking and investment banking was beyond the effective reach of Fed monetary policies. In addition, there was excessive reliance upon consumer credit for sustained sales in the effort to repeal the need for increasing disposable income across a broad sector of American workers. Much of the excesses of 1920s economic and financial activities could be ignored until at least three converging influences met: (1) manipulation of stock values invited speculation and the increased use by corporations to obtain needed funds through stock offerings rather than through bank loans. The diminished use of lending to corporations by banks caused the banks to seek profits in non-commercial lending, mainly real estate mortgage lending and call loans to brokers. Also, the absence of profit-making in commercial lending led many large banks to invest in foreign bonds such as Bavarian, Brazilian, and Chili. (2) This hell-bent quest for quick returns through profits made in financial markets deprived the economy of investments in other needed sectors such as steel, coal, textiles, and agribusiness which all suffered decline during the 1920s. (3) sustained consumption through installment lending reached its limits by 1928 as consumer credit doubled in the 1920s. Deprived of purchases by debt-ridden workers, manufacturers were over-producing with the natural response of the companies laying-off workers and reducing output. Excessive bank lending in the real estate mortgage market caused great financial exposure to many banks by the end of the 1920s as foreclosures mounted. Added to this collapsing scenario is the crippling effect of our adherence to the gold standard. (This last factor will be considered separately as another parallel condition between the foreign financial entanglement of our banking and monetary systems in both the 1920s and today)

Perhaps the one driving factor mentioned above which allowed all major economic participants to become complacent and even euphoric was the ability to sustained sales through consumer credit-lending. The credit-lending foundation for mass production in the 1920s has been noted above. The paralleling dependency of recent history leading into its greatest excesses in the 2000-2006 period was anticipated by John K. Galbraith in his <u>The Affluent Society</u>. In it he foretells of the coming of consumer lending as a necessary ingredient of mass production:

"One danger in the way wants are now created lies in the related process of debt creation. Consumer demand thus comes to depend more and more on the ability and willingness of consumers to incur debt.

An increase in consumer debt is all but implicit in the process by which wants are now synthesized. Advertising and emulation, the two dependent sources of desire, work across society. They operate on those who can afford and those who cannot. With those who lack the current means, it is a brief and obvious step from stimulating their desire by advertising to making it effective in the market with a loan. The relation of emulation to indebtedness is even more direct. Every community contains individuals with wide differences in their ability to pay. The example of those who can pay bears immediately on those who cannot. They must incur debt if they are to keep abreast. The great increase in consumer indebtedness in our time has been widely viewed as reflecting some original or unique change in popular attitudes or behavior. People have changed their view of debt. Thus, there has been an inexplicable but very real retreat from the Puritan canon that required an individual to save first and enjoy later. In fact, as always, the pieces of economic life are parts of a whole. It would be surprising indeed if a society that is prepared to spend thousands of millions to persuade people of their wants were to fail to take the further step of financing these wants, and were it not then to go on to persuade people of the ease and desirability of incurring debt to make these wants effective……." [1]

How far consumer credit-led consumption can be extended depends upon the particular circumstances of the times. Circumstances such as increased pension and mutual fund holdings values and rising prices of homes which increased equity-lending led to consumption into the 2000-2008 peroid. This source of perceived creditworthiness did not exist for many in the 1920s thereby curtailing that period much sooner than from the time of Galbraith's book of the 1950s into the first decade of the 21st century. Nevertheless, sooner or later the 'emptiness' of the financial source of debt--that is the lack of adequate disposable income- to support this level of consumption (70% of GDP) must be reckoned with as Galbraith noted:

"As we expand debt in the process of want creation, we come necessarily to depend on this expansion. An interruption in the increase in debt means an actual reduction in the demand for goods. Debt, in turn, can be expanded by measures which, in the nature of the case, cannot be indefinitely continued. Periods for payment can be lengthened, although eventually there comes a point when they exceed the life of the asset, which serves as collateral. Down payments can be reduced, but eventually there comes a point when the borrower's equity is so small that he finds it more convenient to allow repossession than to pay a burdensome debt. Poorer and poorer credit risks can be accumulated, but at last it becomes necessary to exclude the borrower who, as a matter of principle, does not choose to pay."[2]

Could any recounting of the past six to eight years be more accurate than Galbraith's above? Sub-prime lending resulting in zero equities and foreclosures and equity loans which have exhausted homeowners' equity. Bankruptcies in huge numbers. Refinancing of mortgages to lower monthly payments and thereby provide more purchasing power for homeowners---these features of 2000-20008 consumer economy could have easily been inserted in Galbraith's account as examples. The primary distinction between accumulating consumer debt in the 1920s and during 2000-2008 is the methods available in the 21st century of extending credit which were not present in the 1920s such as equity loans for ordinary workers, refinancing for ordinary people, reverse mortgages which permitted people with otherwise limited spending ability to improve their financial situation. (Although some sources of consumer credit were available in the 1920s which can be ignored in assessing the effectiveness of the Fed. Manufacturers often sold on credit their products to their workers and the private finance companies were the 10th largest industry in the U.S.)

The commonality between the 1920s and the first decade of the 21st century can been seen in its aftermath. Most workers in the 1920s had no retirement plans or health plans. They worked until they died or became disabled. Today, many retirement plans have been decimated by stock losses which are not insured by ERISA. This has forced boomers back into the employment lines. Workers dispossessed by outsourcing or relocation of plants such as RCA workers, textile workers, and other manufacturing employees are almost indistinguishable from those laid-off in the late 1920s or from those forced to work part time in the early 1930s or take wage cuts in the early 1930s. The similarities between the down and out of 1930-33 and of today are somewhat concealed by the present economy's niche markets which tend to resist recessionary times. Like the 1930s, today's economy tends to favor women over men in terms of employment opportunities at the entry or unskilled level. The hollowing out of jobs in some sectors as in manufacturing, textiles, electronics in today's economy bears a likeness to the declining employment in mining, textiles, even manufacturing, and agribusiness of the 1920s. Parallel happenings, those not identical, may point to similar causes. David Kennedy in his Freedom From Fear may have identified the most compelling reason for the plight of the 1930s and today's dilemma: "Without broadly distributed purchasing power, the engine of mass production would have no outlet and would eventually fall idle."[3] Seeking Fundamentals of Sustained Consumption: Disposable Income, Installment Payments, Personal Wealth.

Faced with such forbidding market deficiencies in which to sell durable goods, what principles obstructed the path of economic recovery in 1930-31 by way of lower interest rates?

Principle No. 1. Consumption excessively depended upon credit regardless of the status of disposable income of the credit-buying consumers. Note from the graph below, that personal spending has historically depended upon annual disposable income.

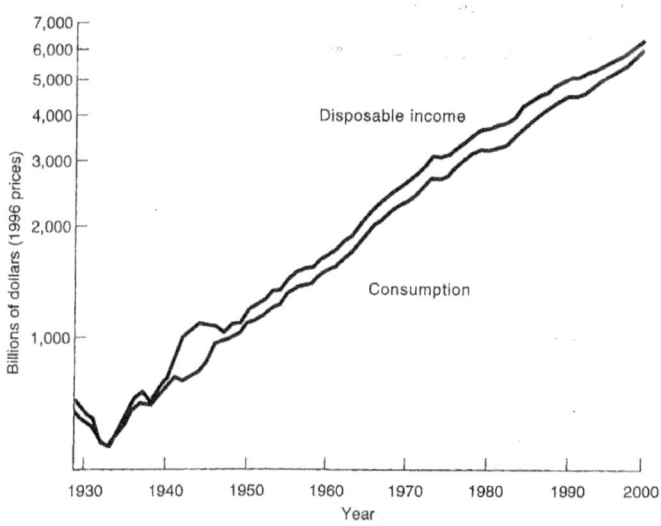

FIGURE 22-6. Consumption and Disposable Income, 1929–1999
U.S. consumption spending has closely tracked the level of personal disposable income over the last seven decades. Macroeconomists can forecast consumption accurately based on the historical consumption function. (Source: U.S. Department of Commerce. Real disposable income is calculated using the deflator for personal consumption expenditures.)

What constraint did disposable income impose on spending up to 1929?

"The stock market crash of 1929 burst the bubble of uncontrolled speculation and business expansion. There were more causes for this economic precariousness, among them the loose regulation of the U.S. banking system. Another factor often cited is the dramatic upturn in consumer credit spending. Prior to World War I most goods had been purchased with cash, even homes were financed with modest mortgages. But beginning around 1923 the concept 'buy now, pay later' became popular as the advertising industry whetted appetites for products of every description. Easy credit convinced the middle class that there was no reason to defer the good life, or at least occasional instant gratification: by 1927 more than 85 percent of the furniture, 80 percent of the phonographs, 75 percent of the washing machines,, 70 percent of the new and used cars, and more than half of the radios, pianos, sewing machines, vacuum cleaners, and refrigerators sold to America were purchased through payment plans.

Consumers made up for the difference between their wages and the costs of what they wanted to buy by borrowing against future earnings. As long as prosperity continued most of the installment debt could be met--but a wavering economy could bring it all crashing down. Yet times had been so good for so long that people had begun to get used to spending on credit; after all, from 1921 to 1928 the economy had enjoyed a generally upward spiral of increased production that created more jobs, which meant more wages that could be spent on more purchases, sending the spiral upward again. Once the direction reversed, factories' output would be reduced meaning fewer jobs and thus fewer consumers able to make purchases which would send the spiral spinning down to more cutbacks in production and employment. In addition, the prosperity of the 1920s had overlooked a large part of the country. More than half of all American families at the end of the decade were living on the edge of the subsistence level and could not afford the consumer goods factories were churning out. Their absence from the consumer credit revolution created a major imbalance between supply and demand that took another toll on the economy." [5]

Principle # 2 Great Disparities in Income as a barrier to recovery.

Any recovery through an increase in Aggregate Demand (total purchases by individuals, businesses, and government) faced economic inertia from the great disparities in incomes earned by the various workers, some of whom we have examined. This dilemma will cause Roosevelt to seek to increase the ability of the "one-third of a nation ill-clad, ill-fed, and ill-housed' to buy the mass output which American industry had the present capacity to produce. The excessive reliance upon credit purchases in defiance of the reality of a weak disposable income foundation for such expansive buying produced a harder fall the longer this manner of buying was pursued as revealed below:

"In 1930, the federal Department of Labor completed an extensive study of Ford's Detroit area labor force. The average earnings for those who met the study's criteria---heads of families who had been employed at least 225 days-were $1, 694. The average annual expenditure was $1,719, the small difference being taken up by gifts from relatives or low levels of debt. Sixty-one percent lived in one-family houses. 32 percent were in two-family houses, and 7 percent occupied apartments. Thirty-six percent owned radios, a fairly smart luxury, while 5 percent had telephones, and 47 percent had cars. The study enumerated every buying decision made by the average Ford family, down to the outlay for asparagus, mackinaws, and books. However, the most telling point in the study was the fact that 59 percent of the families made purchases on the installment plan.

The installment plan makes prosperous times even more enjoyable, but it makes hard times much more wretched, as a whole generation of Ford workers was to find out. In that respect, they were not unlike employees in a hundred other industries, except that there was an extra sense of betrayal and confusion among the workers at Ford."[6]

Principle #3. Many major firms were in oligopolistic industries where lowering prices to increase sales was not (and still is not) an option. This lesson was well-gained from the experience of the giant corporations during the 1890s. Even though some firms, even Ford, attempted recovery through lower prices, the most successful firms such as G.M. and Chrysler sought to increase profits through targeting the well-to-do with sales of luxury models. This had the advantage of compensating lower output of production with selling luxury cars at high prices and not requiring as big a labor force since the luxury market was more niche than mass and also has minimize price competition, historically as noted by the late Professor Walter Adams in his <u>The Structure of American Industry</u> where he states:

> "Parallelism and uniformity in pricing among the Big Three is strikingly and at times, astonishingly close. Although automobiles are highly differentiated products, and although a certain amount of price flexibility occurs at the retail level, there is nonetheless, substantial price uniformity for comparable models offered by different manufacturers. This, in turn, limits price differentials up and down the chain of manufacturing and distribution.
>
> In the small segment of the industry, which is populated by a larger number of competing producers, pricing behavior is distinctively different. There, foreign competitors occupy nearly 40 percent of the field; there is no recognized price leader; there is no rigid pattern of leadership followership, and pricing exhibit's the variability and unpredictability characteristic of a more competitive market." [7]

(Note on a more recent effort by first G.M. then others to recapture market share shattered by globalization through offering zero interest in the purchase of their cars. This had temporary success until G.M was matched by Ford and others. The effort to cease this zero interest plan was resisted strongly by the car companies' customers. Still, the above description has application to the auto industry between 1930-31 when domestic firms went unchallenged by foreign car companies.) Consequently, the disparities in income could not be contended with by lower prices of cars in an effort to bring their price within the range of those in the 30 to 40 percent income group which was excluded from buying on credit during the 1920s.

Principle#4---Selling on credit in an expanding economy invites on the part of wage-paying companies and wage-earning workers in an effort to repeal the natural relationship between annual disposable income and annual consumer debt. This inordinate disregard for a natural range of separation between disposable income and credit buying must be regarded as the Great Temptation of the modern economy, but it had its initiation during the "Roaring Twenties." What does are our recent two-decade old departure from adhering to an attentive respect for the limitations of credit-buying instruct us? Let's review some fundamental considerations, first. As provided in <u>The Secrets of Economic Indicators</u> by Bernard Baumohl, the historical reliance on some indicators such as disposable income changes have alerted policy-makers as to the expected direction of the economy;

"By studying the growth in personal income, you can get some insight into future trends in consumer spending. But one has to be careful about generalizing here. The relationship between income and spending is not as simple as it once was. Since the mid-1990s consumer outlays have been greatly influenced by one's perception of personal wealth. Spending can accelerate if households see the value of their financial and real estate investments growing, a phenomenon known as the wealth effect. For example, economists estimate that for every dollar increase in the value of one's stock portfolio, consumers spend an additional 3 to 6 cents. A one-dollar rise in the value of other types of wealth (such as real estate) raises spending by 2 to 4 cents."[8] "A better portent of future consumer demand can be found in real personal disposable income...:" (Ibid at page 68). Baumohl cautions, "On occasion, households spend more than what they bring home in income, forcing families to dig into savings or borrow money to make up the difference. However, this is not sustainable in the long run, because at some point consumers will deplete their savings or acquire too much debt, or both. Any of these actions can lead to a sharp retrenchment in spending and throw a wrench in the economic expansion."[9] (On page 69, he discusses possible measurements of determining when interest payments are too burdensome and curtail spending by the debt holders) Baumohl cites a troubling abandonment of adhering to a safe relationship between one's annual disposable income and one's annual consumer debt: "Back in 1980, wages and salaries paid for nearly 80 % of all spending, with the rest (20%) being financed by debt and from withdrawing from past savings. By the summer of 2006, wages and salaries financed barely 65% of all expenditures, which meant consumers had borrowed more than ever before as well as tap some savings to fill the gap between income and spending."[10] Is this a path to continued economic growth or to ruin? Could enough consumers in the late 1920s into 1930-31 have followed this path of credit buying assisted by the lower interest rates urged by Freidman and Schwartz? By examining the following from Kevin's Phillips Wealth and Democracy , we will determine the advisability of premising borrowing based on increasing value of mutual funds and other stock holdings (1990s) and then pursuing credit buying through refinancing, equity loans, and other financial devices made possible by historically low interest rates combined high historically high home prices/values. Is our recent two-decade experience based on stock market values and home values a model which lower interest rates would have permitted in 1930-31?

First, review the following graphs provided in Phillips' work which show the continuing departure of consumers from relying mostly on disposable income as a guide for spending:

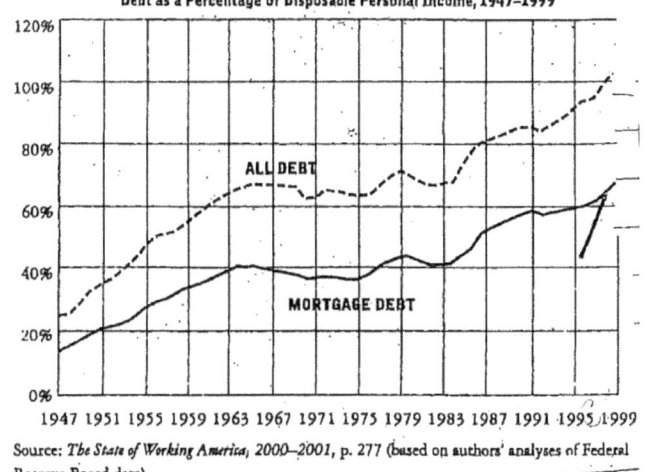

Source: *The State of Working America, 2000–2001*, p. 277 (based on authors' analyses of Federal Reserve Board data).

What accounted for this increasingly reliance upon credit or debt for spending: In the 1990s, it was the relying upon the reported values of mutual funds, stocks and bonds as a wealth-base for consumption-even though no real earnings had been received. When the stock market took a severe hit in 2000, many wondered why they were now saddled with the prospect of bankruptcy or/and delayed retirement. An article in the Indianapolis Star of October13, 2008 page A3 describes the telling blow to consumers:

"Trillions in stock market value-gone. Trillions in retirement savings-gone. A huge chunk of the money you paid for your house, the money you're saving for college, the money your boss needs to make a payroll-gone, gone, gone. Whether you're a stock broker or Joe Six-pack, if you have a 401(k), a mutual fund, or a college savings plan, tumbling stock markets and sagging home prices mean you've lost a whole lot of the money that was right there on your account statements a few months ago."[12]

As the author, Eric Carvin, states, "you might be disappointed to learn that it (the money) was never really money in the first place." Carvin provides a partial quote from Nobel Prize economist, Robert Shiller, who reminds us of this fact in a succinct way: Shiller notes that the 'price of a stock has never been the same thing as money--is simply the 'best guess' of what the stock is worth'. It's in peoples' minds' Shiller explains. 'We're just recording a measure of what people think the stock market is worth. What the people who are willing to trade today-who are very, very few people -are actually trading at. So we've just extrapolating that and thinking, well, maybe that's what everyone thinks its worth."[13]

Shiller gives the following example of how 'lost money' really was not lost money. An appraiser values your house at $350,000 a week after it was appraised at a value of $400,000. Shiller explains, ' In a sense, $50,000 just disappeared when he said that. But it's all in the mind.'[14] (He makes an example of home prices which become the second basis, after the stock market of the 90s, for assuming a financial justification for credit-buying.) This 'magical disappearance of wealth' through descending prices of stocks, bonds, and homes occurred through unrealistic expectations as to what these individual markets could accomplish in a sustained way. Kevin Phillips offers the following observations on how we became addicted to Wall Street quotations of values.

"By way of context, the unprecedented billions pouring into stocks and bonds and mutual funds besides dwarfing any previous totals, marked a historical shift--the overtaking by the hitherto speculative securities sectors of more sedate and long-dominant banking institutions in total assets managed. In reaching $2.6 trillion in November…mutual fund assets for the first time exceeded deposits in the U.S. commercial banking system…"individual financial wealth, a narrow category, went from being 20 percent in stocks to 50 percent. More than ever before, wealth itself was being securitized--traded on exchanges rather than lived in, minted, worn as jewelry, or ridden in leagues and miles."[15]

"Money poured into the capital markets, with the mutual fund assets surging from $1trillion in 1990 to $6.9trillion in 2000 and the number of households owning mutual funds doubling to 52 million.."(page 29 "The Supply-side Economy.)

The second pillar of wealth which seemingly justified credit-driven spending was the soaring prices of houses which along with very low-interest rate loans triggered the spending spree. Both rising home prices and low-interest rates provided a basis for refinancing of mortgages and for equity loans, both of which provided additional spending power but without an corresponding increase in earnings.

(a) Refinancing permit's a home buyer to substitute a new mortgage with less monthly payments for the old mortgage.(Principle of the mortgage is the same). With less monthly mortgage payments, a home owner has more disposable purchasing power. Refinancing became possible through lower interest rate loans made possible by Fed open market buying of government securities which of course provided more reserves to the banks. Advice such as the following from Smart Money magazine in its February 2002 issue, page 76 help ignite this refinancing drive:

> **THEY'RE THE KINDS OF SCENARIOS THAT KEEP YOU UP AT NIGHT: NO SOONER HAVE YOU** broken ground (or linoleum) on a new Sub-Zero kitchen than your company announces it'll be laying off a third of its staff. Your daughter gets her early-acceptance letter from Harvard... just as you finish paying off her older sister's wedding. You have your condo in Boca all picked out when your 401(k) holdings tank (and you're not even at Enron). ✚ These days the late-night what-ifs are all too real. And just when you find yourself in need of some serious cash, all those sources you had available to tap only a year ago have dried up. Your salary is frozen, and your stock portfolio should be so lucky—it lost 20 percent last year. As for that annual bonus? This year it was a fruit basket. ✚ But there is one place you can still turn when you're in a pinch, one investment that *has* done well: your home. While the stock market has slumped the past two years, the average home has appreciated 18 percent, and the typical homeowner now has $50,000 in equity. That makes your house the one lockbox you can still afford to raid. ✚ You wouldn't be alone. As refinancing surged on the heels of record-low 30-year mortgage rates last fall, the hot ticket was a so-called cash-out refi. That's when you replace your existing mortgage with a larger one and pocket the difference. Say you took out a $200,000 mortgage on your $250,000 home two years ago. Because of today's low interest rates and the equity you've already built through appreciation and payments, you could take out a good chunk of cash—somewhere in the neighborhood of $30,000—without lifting your monthly payments. No wonder 63 percent of all homeowners who refinanced in the third quarter did cash-outs, according to mortgage purchasing company Freddie Mac.

The USA Today in an article by Thomas A. Fogarty of August 9th 2001 cites the following impact that refinancing had from 2000 to August 2001: "It pumped an estimated $49 billion in cash into the economy through June, 2001."

Other reports by USA Today cite the following: Refinancing pumped an estimated $250 billion in the economy for the year 2003-2004. The path of both refinancing and equity loans is graphically provided below which depict a descending spiral of financial ruin for many who unwisely pursue home values as a basis for credit-spending: [17]

What caused such a great temptation to rely upon continuing soaring home prices? Especially after many were burned by the stock market crash of 2000. It was the seductive power of soaring home prices which deceived many. Consider this statistic:

"In the value of the total stock of US housing stood at 108 per cent of GDP. In the next year, the one which the stock market rushed to its dizzying climax and then fell back and started its swift earthward plummet, the ratio moved to 113 percent about as high as it had ever been."[18]

After the Fed cut interest rates drastically, "the housing market's total worth took a staccato series of swift steps into entirely new territory. In……it went to 121 per cent of GDP; the year after it was 128 per cent, the next year it struck 133 per cent; and by the third quarter of it stood at 140 per cent.[19] Some foresaw no real problem ahead for increased consumption being based primarily on refinancing of mortgages and on equity loans. For example, Chairman Greenspan reassured us that "because of low interest rates, consumers can more easily handle their debt so the level is not significant cause for concern." Sung Won Suhn of Wells Fargo & Co reassured us that for 'now Americans are OK and should continue to be the driving force in the nation's economic growth' However, The National Association of Realtors offered a caution concerning the housing industry--it has a business cycle like all industries. It recognized that sales growth in homes has a 2 year life cycle followed by a decline rate of increased sales. Also a reported in USA Today, December 12-14, 2008, "As painful as the decline (in prices) has been, history suggests home values still may have a long way to drop and may take decades to return to the height of 2 and one-half years ago." This article also cited an even more troubling comparison of the historical relationship between annual income of homeowners and the value of their homes. The following tables reveals which income groups are the most vulnerable to either declining incomes or declining home prices/values

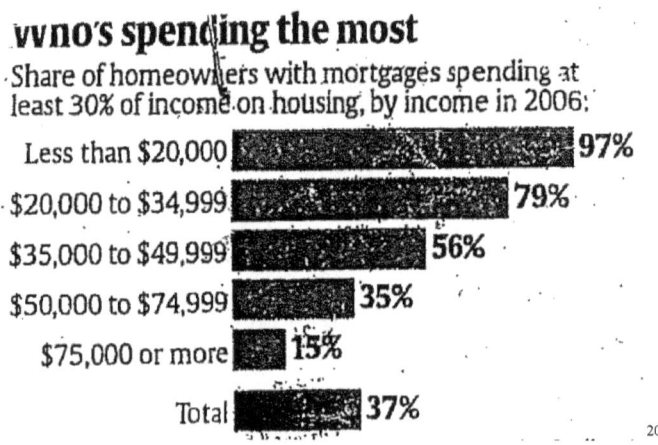

From USA Today findings in its article of November 3, 2009, pp 1B-2B   Estimated number of homeowners with mortgage balances greater than property value:

Q1 2009 14 million   Q1 2011 25 million

The economic squeeze of lost jobs, declining income, excessive spending has resulted in some using their credit cards to make mortgage payments. The credit card debt and its delinquencies in payments summarize the outcome when annual debt becomes so disproportionate to annual disposable income as reflect below as reported by the Chicago Tribune article of May 25, 2008 Section 5, page 3:

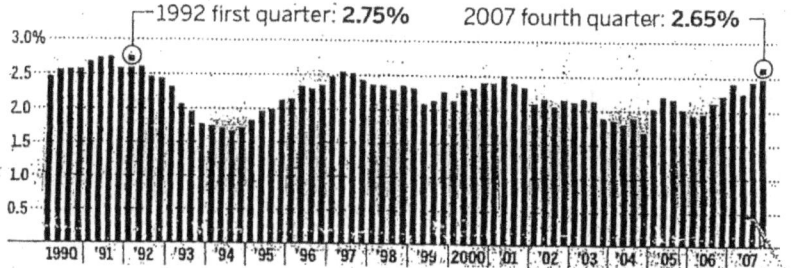

A column by Jeff Madrick in the New York Times of September 4th 2003 (page C2) perhaps anticipated the inability of consumers to continuing ignore the growing distance between their consumer debt and disposable income. The column cites the growing difficulties of lower and middle class Americans to make ends meet. This difficulty stems from the significant increase in the cost of necessities such as health care, education, and a misleading assessment by owners and economists as to the costs of housing. Madrick cites the claim of authors W. Michael Cox and Richard Alm in their book, "Myths of Rich and Poor" that our standard of living is higher than data would suggest because many consumer products such as food, clothing, and electronics cost less than before. However, Madrick is more persuaded by authors Elizabeth Warren and Amelia Warren Tyagi that despite these less costly consumer items, middle class Americans have less discretionary income today (early 2000s) than they did in (1970s). This is due to the fact that " families spend a lot more on.... a house in a safe neighborhood with a good school-____about 70 percent more a year, discounted for inflation, for a typical family of four."

Madrick continued his assessment in agreement with authors Warren and Tyagi by stating that these families are even buying much smaller homes than in the 1970s and that the necessity of having two earners in the family drives up child care costs and costs of eating, clothing, and of course automobile-related expenses. Compounding the burden of these expenses are the increased costs of health care, both treatment, drugs, and insurance. Most middle class Americans' experience would validate these conclusions that in reality middle class has less discretionary income in the 2000s than in the 1970s and it is due more to the increase in the costs of necessities. Given this restricted position in spending, how can refinancing or equity loans hope to continue to lift an economy towards sustained growth. As in the 1920s, exhausted credit by many and the unavailable credit to at least one-third of Americans would eventually impose its natural mandate on Americans in the 2000s--that credit-buying must have a solid foundation in annual disposable income. Despite the limitations imposed by housing and the necessity for a two-income family, most economists place singular importance upon the housing industry for continued economic growth. Consider the following assessments:

"Looking for a single infallible indicator that can foresee the future direction of the economy? Forget it, you won't find any. However, one comes surprisingly close------housing! Excluding one brief instance, there has never been a recession in the U.S. at a time when the housing sector stood strong. Only once since World War II did the economy contract despite a robust housing market, and that was in 2001. Even then, the recession was short-lived and not very deep. This impressive track record is why many experts view homebuilding as one of the most reliable indicators of economic activity. Residential real estate is among the first sectors to shut down when the economy nears recession and it is the first to bloom when the economy starts to turn up."[22]

This influence of housing starts upon economic growth is due to "mainly its sensitivity to interest rates. An overheated economy drives interest rates higher. As mortgage rates climb, this depresses demand for homes and discourages future construction. Builders are also less likely to seek construction loans when rates are high. Conversely, when mortgage rates tumble and home prices decline--events that typically happen during periods of economic weakness---interest in home buying is rekindled now that it is more affordable. Builders, in turn, rush back to banks before the cost of borrowing rises again. "[23] The second impact on the economy felt when housing construction picks up is due to the 'multiplier' effect which construction has on the demand for construction materials. Subcontractors and their employees, and for appliances and home furnishings. "By one estimate, for every 1,000 single-family homes under construction, some 2,500 full-time jobs and nearly $100 million in wages are generated."[24] We will leave aside an examination into the micro-economics of the housing industry and its particular influence on economic growth till we examine the path to recovery from today's Great Recession. Suffice it so ask, "Can recovery be based simply on interest rates or monetary policy independent of across the board increased earnings for most Americans. In other words, are we back to the initial question: What dictates economic sustained growth----lower interest rates or substantial earnings by the workers and the families? The current government effort at stabilizing the economy is through the demand side of financial markets by offering government assistance on mortgages and through resumption of equity loans or refinancing. The supply side of government efforts at rescuing the banks involved extraordinary measures by the Fed not even contemplated during 1930-32. Ultimately, both are part of a problem of a serious credit crunch which, of course, was present in 1930-32. The credit crunch is the result of deceptive and unwise banking practices by commercial banks, investment banks, brokerage houses, equity funds, and other financial institutions of which many were beyond the Fed's legal regulatory authority. The following attempts to show the parallels between banking practices of mid-1920s and of the recent period. Although their methods of financing differed in terms of financial instruments promoted, their same extra-legal content and risk are present in both. The difference exists in the Fed's effort of rescuing the banks from their dubious activities.

Chapter Four Notes

1. John K. Galbraith The Affluent Society (Boston: Houghton 1976) pp. 147-148
2. Ibid. page 151
3. David Kennedy, op. cit. page 22
4. Paul Samuelson and William Nordhaus Economics (New York: McGraw Hill,2001)page 299
5. Douglas Brinkley op. cit., pages 400-401
6. Douglas Brinkley Wheels of the World, Henry Ford, His Company, and a Century of Progress (Adams, The Structure of American Industry, page 111
7. Walter Adams, The Structure of American Industry 7ed. (New York: Macmillan, 1986) pp. 133-136
8. Bernard Baumohl The Secrets of Economic Indicators (New York: Pearson Ed. 2007) page 66
9. Ibid, page 68
10. Ibid, page 65
11. Kevin Phillips, Wealth and Democracy (   ) page 134
12. Indianapolis Star October 13, 2005 citing Eric Carvin
13. Ibid, page A3
14. Ibid, page A3
15. Kevin Phillips, op. cit. 141
16. Smart Money, February 2002, page 76
17. USA Today August 9th, 2001 article by Thomas Fogarty
18. 18 Peter Hatcher, Bubble Man: Alan Greenspan & the Missing 7 Trillion Dollars (New York: Norton 2006) page 24
19. Ibid, page 24
20. US A Today, December 12-14 2008
21. Wall Street Journal January 2010
22. Bernard Baumohe op. cit. page 178
23. Ibid, page 178
24. Ibid, page 179

CHAPTER FIVE

PARALLEL NO. 3: FINANCING BEYOND BORDERS AND REGULATORS: UNSOUND OR UNETHICAL BANKING PRACTICES AND THE 'SHADOW' BANKING SYSTEM.

Can unsound and unethical banking practices impose economic harm to the extent experienced under the Great Depression and the recent Great Recession? Or is any damage caused by the banking and financial sector merely collateral and therefore can be dismissed as an extraneous consideration in determining the causes of these economic crisis? If the banking practices of the 1920s and during the first decade of the 21st century cannot be a primary culprit, then how can monetary policies be the solution? Giving undue attention to Fed responses to these crisis may be misplaced and we should consult other avenues of policy corrections. However, the financial institutions are vital to the performance of an economy and their contribution to any economic great disequilibrium must be taken into account. Any banking and investment practices which deflected the economic attention away from the real world of goods and services must bear some responsibility for the demise. Accordingly, a comparison of banking and investment practices of both the 1920s and during the first decade of the 21st century reveals improprieties which had far ranging adverse consequences and cannot easily be dismissed as inconsequential. Insofar as investment banks and other 'shadow' banks assisted or perpetrated these practices, the economic damage will be even more wide-spread as the latter financial entities are unregulated or beyond the jurisdiction of the Fed.

The following similarities of banking and investment practices existed in the 1920 and 2000-2007.

1. In both periods less commercial lending was done by commercial banks.

Due to corporate use of stock offerings to finance their needs, commercial banks did less lending for business purposes of buying equipment, building facilities, or buying inventory. Denied these commercial lending opportunities, banks sought profits in call-loans to brokers, in foreign bonds, in commercial real estate and residential mortgage lending. Associate institutions of commercial banks, investment banks hawked or promoted bonds or foreign entities, or corporate stock without doing due diligence- they did not bother to investigate the soundness of the securities they were promoting. Stock values seemed a better investment choice due to the high prices which pooling and selling on margin promoted. Stock such as RCA rose to great highest due to stock pooling, a device in which many prominent men would agree to buy a designated stock together at the same time. This had the effect of creating stock prices far exceeding any market value. Having achieved this high price, the members collectively sold the stock at the high price but causing the price to plummet afterwards due to this collective dumping of stock.

What about 2000-20007? Paul Krugman answers any question about a corresponding abandonment of commercial lending during this period with the following observation:

"In early 2007, asset-backed commercial paper conduits in structured investment vehicles, in auction-rate preferred securities, tender option bonds, and variable rate demand notes had a combined asset size of roughly $2.2 trillion. Assets financed overnight in tri-party repo grew to $2.5 trillion. Assets held in hedge funds grew to roughly $1.8 trillion".[1]

These financial instruments only connection to the real economy of goods and service was the originating real estate mortgages (many subprime) which were then securitized into packaged levels of different risk-bearing mortgages, auto loans, credit card debts, etc. Mark Zandi, in his

Financial Shock, states the growing invasion of shadow banks this way:

> "Banks were happy to originate loans-- processing borrowers and accepting originating fees-- but less interested in actually funding the loans, which required them to hold more capital in reserve Funding for loans thus came increasingly from nonblank institutions. These institutions were a mixed bag: they included investment banks, hedge funds, money market funds, and finance companies as well newly invented entities called 'asset-backed conduits' and 'structured investment vehicles. Together they formed a shadow banking system, which was subject to little regulatory oversight and also not required to publicly disclose much, if anything, about itself. By the second quarter of 2007, just prior to the financial shock, the shadow banking system provided an astounding $6trillion in credit and was rapidly closing in on that provided by traditional funds."[2]

Commercial banks who had initiated the residential mortgages often had associated member investment banks, just as in the 1920s. Any assets held by the member investment banks were off the balance sheet of the parent commercial bank.

Can Milton Friedman and his 'followers' be correct that despite the improprieties of financial marketing described previously concerning the investment banking practices and the noncommercial lending by commercial banks, the banks were capable of being almost immediately restored as lenders to risky ventures or even the companies of the commanding heights of the 1920s economy? Does not the actual economic and financial debris which lay in the path of destruction after 1929 discredit the notion that the banks were less culpable than others for the economic crisis of 1930 and therefore, all that was needed was for the Fed to refill the coffers of the banks so that they could resume lending (one must wonder to whom, commercially, given their practices of the late 1920s). Does the recent experience following 2007 when the Fed resorted to what may be regarded as "extra-legal' intervention to save not only commercial banks, but the leading actors of the financial melee -the investment banks, themselves. Does the rescue of the following institutions or the failure to intervene for some shed enlightenment on whether the Fed could have saved the economy in the 1930 with 'looser' money supply? Does the fact that the enormous unorthodox responses of the Fed during the recent years has basically failed to recharge the economy support Friedman's theory or does it tend to refute the notion that monetary policy can rescue an economy on the brink of disaster by simply lower interest rates or in Friedman's terminology simply expand the quantity of money. The primary distinction of circumstances may be that in our current crisis, the shadow banking system created vulnerability not in existence in the 1920s-that of electronic transactions and the speed with which currencies and financial instruments can be traded. Does modern financial trading technology create a distinction from the crisis of 1929 to an extent that the Fed was still capable of rescuing the commercial banking system due to the absence of a deeply penetrating nexus of buyers and sellers in the 1920s.(In 2000-2007, holdings of financial instruments may be thrice removed from its originator.) Maybe, if the deteriorating conditions of banks were the only flaw of the economy in 1929. Can we ignore the other conditions militating against a mass consuming economy such as for example insufficient number of consumers due to great disparities of income? Any damage caused by the banking and investment practices cannot be confined to just winners and losers in the investment game. There were other casualties --more specially opportunity costs. The opportunity costs were not simply those potential losses contained within the investment community below in which many were rescued from their plight by the Fed and the Congress. These institutions listed below exposed more than their own solvency to risk, their activities deflected true investment away from the real economy of goods and services as they did in the 1920s.

1. American International Group. (AIG)
2. Bear Stearns
3. Country Wide Financial
4. Wachovia
5. Washington Mutual
6. Citigroup
7. Bank of America
8. Goldman Sachs

In that there was little separation of financial markets from its consequences for the real economy, the financial debris of both 1929 and of total could not be contained within the parameters of the financial participants.

Chapter Five Footnotes

1. Paul Krugman, Return to Depression Economics and the Crisis of 2008 (   ) page161

2. Mark Zandi, Financial Shock (Upper Saddle River: Pearson Ed. 2009) page 122

CHAPTER SIX

PARALLEL NO. 4 OPPORTUNITY COSTS OF YESTERDAY AND TODAY

Whether the banking and investment practices must bear a major responsibility for the economic crisis of 1929 and today and that the financialization (to borrow Kevin Philips expression) of an economy imposes such deep caverns in the conduct of the real economy as to make monetary policy responses akin to first aid, the following view of Lawrence E. Mitchell in his Business Week column of July 30, 2007 may provide the insight necessary to pursue this inquiry with reasonable conclusions.

His column, "The Tyranny of the Market" regards the on-going crisis as being caused by "The real culprit is the growing preeminence of finance over operations. It causes stock market considerations to trump those that improve the actual workings of a business. And the quicker the stock payoff can be engineered, the better. Until that changes, don't expect CEOs to stop gaming the system."[1] He relates how "this reward bias toward finance has been with us since the creation of the giant public corporation in the late 19th century. Almost overnight, U.S. business was transformed from making money by controlling costs and increasing productive efficiency, the way John D. Rockefeller and Andrew Carnegie did, to reaping instant riches from stock sales--such as the $1.5 billion stock fee (in 2006 dollars) that the J.P. Morgan syndicate earned in 1901 putting together the factories that created U.S. Steel."[2]

Mitchell continues, "Today you see the consequences of this financial dominance. Ask the 400 CFOs who in a 2005 survey revealed a consensus opinion that they would mutilate their own companies to keep stock prices high. Ask the derivatives traders and hedge fund managers who control the direction of the market by trading in instruments that have nothing to do with financing the production of goods and services and everything to do with stock price movements..."[3] Perhaps his key insight can be reduced to the following: "An economy grounded in short-term, rapid-fire finance is an economy likely to self-destruct over the long haul. To avoid that fate, we must construct incentives to redirect both management behavior and executive compensation toward the long term." [4] The effect of stock market expectations has consistently given disincentives for company R and D or any efforts at long term capital investments. See Wall Street Journal in 2003 entitled "Profits No Match for Rising Bar" by E.S. Browning.

   The opportunity costs-what opportunities a person, company, or nation loses by making other choices in investments- are present in the 1920s and today.

In the 1920s, the diverting of money and spending to stocks and bonds, both domestic and foreign, from the excessive profits being earned by corporate giants denied potential investments in industries which were in decline such as agriculture, clothing, heat, shoes, and agricultural products. The unrealistic prices of stock such as RCA augmented by pooling and margin buying became too tempting for potential investors in other industries. Stock prices also hindered the need for commercial lending by banks for the real economy of providing goods and services. Without the overpriced stock market, banks may have attracted more business customers. Many customers disappeared as a result of corporate mergers in the 1920s. (Perhaps as many as 2000 companies disappeared a year as a result of mergers or acquisitions.) Mergers went hand in hand with stock transactions then and today. In fact, enhanced stock values may provide the primary motivation for some mergers. Robert Schaeffer makes these observation concerning the impact of mergers.

> Mergers make many workers in combined firms redundant, as occurs when banks with branches across the street from each other merge into a single firm. When corporations move overseas, they eliminate workers and assign their jobs to others, often to temporary workers who receive wages that are typically 60 percent of full-time workers ' and who receive few if any of the benefits associated with full-time employment. And new technologies make it possible to do the same amount of work, even more, with fewer employees. The net result is massive job loss.
>
> The New York Times reported in 1996 that 'more than 43 million jobs have been erased in the United States since 1979'. Reporters noted that 'in one third of all households, a family member has lost a job' and that 'one in 10 adults—or about 19 million people, a number matching the adult population of New York and New Jersey combined---acknowledged that a lost job had precipitated a major crisis in their lives.' And over time, they said, the pace of layoffs had accelerated, from 1.42 million in 1980 to 3.26 million in 1995.' Most laid –off workers find new jobs elsewhere, but 'only 33 percent of them earned as much as or more than they had before.' [5]

He notes other occupational distortions caused by mergers:

> Corporate managers pursued mergers with enthusiasm. Because stock prices typically increase when mergers are announced, managers can claim that they have increased the value of the firm. And because their compensation is often tied, in part, to stock price performance, they have financial incentives to reap the benefits associated with a rise in the price of the firm's stock. Under these conditions, it is not surprising that corporate managers have sought to acquire other firms or that CEO salaries have soared. In 1995, 'CEOs at the largest 500 companies earned $4.06 million on average, or 197 times as much as the average worker, a 15 percent increase from the previous year.' This represented a substantial increase from CEO salaries twenty years ago. When 'the typical chief executive officer of a large American company earned about 40 times as much as a typical worker did.'

This emphasis upon the financial side of corporate performance skewed the focus on product development within the company and allowed financial results to dictate how the company was ran. Dr. Schaeffer provided this scenario which became common at Ford Motor Company during the 1950s after Ford went public;

> Corporate managers no longer direct a company's nuts-and-bolts production of a particular good or service. They manage stock prices, stock-equity ratios, mergers, divestitures, and dividends in an inflationary stock market environment. This new role explains in part why the disparity between CEO compensation and factory-floor wages has grown. It has grown because executive compensation is linked to the stock market, which is willing and able to provide huge rewards to managers for their efforts to increase payouts and stock prices. [6]

Also, mergers reinforce the drive for wealth from stock ownership, not manufacturing. Dr. Schaeffer states the following stabilizing effect of mergers on the stock market.

> Corporate managers, investment bankers, and stock market investors supported mergers because they believed that the newly consolidated firm would be more efficient and more profitable. Larger assets and higher profits would increase the value of the firm, making possible higher dividend payouts to shareholders and/or a higher price for the company's stock. [7]

Moreover, indirectly, stock market investors' demand for continued extra-profit performances lead to management policies which were detrimental to their workforce. Corporate pursuit of technological improvements took the path of process engineering-not product engineering. Professor Schaeffer notes the adverse impact of financial markets dictating the direction of managerial decision-making.

> "Of course, corporate managers must also seek to improve their company's performance. They have done this by introducing new technology and by restructuring the business to increase productivity. New technology is expensive. For industrial firms, the introduction of new technology often requires the construction of whole new factories. For many years, large industrial firms were reluctant to make substantial new investments of this kind. But as they came under increasing pressure from the stock market, from companies that might try to buy them, and from foreign firms that had grown strong in the postwar period, industrial firms began investing in new technology in the 1980s, building factories, and reorganizing their businesses. Between 1979 and 1995, for example, Caterpillar, a heavy equipment manufacturer, closed nine plants and spent $1.8 billion to modernize its remaining factories. As new technology was

introduced, the firm cut its workforce from ninety thousand to fifty-four thousand and increased production..........

Similar practices continued into the 21st Century as cost-saving devices were purchased as labor-saving, leading to a 'jobless' recovery in 20006-2010.[8]

If these business had remained solitary companies, the chances of seeking business loans would have been enhanced. Also, an economy which is unbalanced toward the marketing and selling of financial instruments also affects the professional and occupational opportunities which the economy offers. While marketing of products did open up as a career opportunity and other business positions became necessary and wanted, the composition of the 1920s economy offered no rescue for sharecroppers, cotton field hands, miners, textile workers, and others who composed one-third or more of those hovering near poverty. Moreover, even manufacturing had about the same number of factory workers in 1929 as it did in 1921. The absence of a growing line of business borrowers caused banks to over-invest in commercial real estate and in subdivision housing. Although housing was not the cure-all for homeowner financial security or for any need to gain immediate profits as 'securitization' became in the 21st century, it did represent an industry which had overinvestment in part because of the lack of customers for commercial purposes. The latter was cause in great part because of the stock market investing which diverted capital from real business purposes.

Misdirected capital investment in today's economy has been cited by Michael Mandel in his column of Business Week June 6, 2005 cites the following as costs resulting from housing speculation and its allied industries. "But whether prices level out, crash, or even keep going up, the housing boom is already having pernicious economic effects. The real problem: the incredible amount of resources-workers, materials, and money-being sucked into home construction and renovation. Michael Mandel cited that residential investment has become a black hole absorbing a staggering 5.8 % of gross domestic product."[9] He offered a distinction between the housing boom of the 2000s and that of the late 1940s. "This time, Americans are building second homes and enlarging current ones at a record pace." He could have added a growing trend of buying homes as an investment to 'flip' and sell without having resided in it. Perhaps as much as 17% of the sales during the housing boom were of this kind. In particular the opportunity costs which an unbalanced economy has imposed despite the immediate positive results are noted by Mandel:

"But what is certain is that housing-driven growth, while creating jobs and lifting wealth, is also distorting the economy, benefiting low-tech commodity sectors rather than the high tech industries at the heart of America's competitive strength. New homes are built mainly out of materials such as wood for frame and floors, plasterboard for the walls and fabricated metal parts for plumbing fixtures. High-tech equipment plays a very small role. Even when new homes include cable for the broadband so-called structured wiring--the high-tech compound accounts for at most 1% or 2% of the entire cost of the home"[10]

"So, what" one may ask? A former Secretary of Defense said 'chips are chips' whether 'potato chips or computer chips'. Mandel provides the why:

1. Only 1.6 cents of every construction dollar was used for info-related products and services such as "computer gear, data-processing services, and technical services.

2. Other industries such as "retailing, manufacturing, education, and health care are much heavier users of 'info-tech."[11]

3. Mandel provided a chart which shows the high-tech input of various industries:[12]

Mandel continued his assault against the direction taken by our economy is an article in Business Week, on September 25, 2006 "If current trends continue, 30% to 40% of all new jobs created over the next 25 years will be in health care. That sort of lopsided job creation is not the blueprint for a well-functioning economy."[13] And the consequences for people seeking jobs in industries other than health or services is clear:

"…using health-care spending to create the vast majority of new jobs, while beneficial in the short run, is not desirable over the long run. A well-balanced economy needs to provide a wide variety of jobs, not just positions for doctors, nurses, ad medical technicians."[14]

Mandel's complaint is a rather tardy one. Kevin Phillips noted in his Wealth and Democracy how much of GDP consisted of insurance, finance, and real estate industries. This disproportionate growth has gone unabated as shown by the chart provided in Anthony Downs' Real Estate and The Financial Crisis: [15]

The importance of this unbalanced economy lies in the types of jobs which each industry offers. Do the jobs offer decent -middle-class earnings on a traditional work schedule or do the jobs consist of a number of high paying jobs with a large number of low paying jobs with few in between of moderate to high pay. This is important economically, socially, and politically for without a vast number of secure middle class paying jobs, the domestic and foreign security of a nation will be at risk. Kevin Phillips has provided a narrative account of nations' abandoning the real economy of goods and services for the fast-paced, mobile, easily entered and exited, economy deeply committed to a financial market-driven economy. He lists Spain during the times of South America exploration, the Dutch during times of the 'tulip' boom and bust in which the Dutch squandered their led in world commerce, and finally Great Britain's great temptation at being the 'world's banker' in which international finance crowded out the goods and services industries of Britain as the dominant industry, Phillips speculated that the U.S. trajectory favoring finance, insurance, and real estate may have a result as unfavorable as those of Spain, Holland, and Great Britain. This end result has been energized by the securitization of mortgages which allies real estate with finance. When one falls, so does the others. Neither would be protected by any 'wall of separation'. If we add other facts to the picture which has been described concerning the abandonment of the real economy by banks, investors, and the business themselves, one conclusion may be unavoidable---we must take Mr. Lawrence Mitchell's advice and began to put in place incentives to restructure the economy by redirecting capital investment to high tech and other desirable and needed industries. Also, we need to remove the Wall Street imperative of expected quarterly returns from the natural business imperatives of our companies. Is this the necessary path to take? Aren't any short term remedies available and sufficient? If one examines the following in conjunction with historical habits of spending and investing and the opportunities of professional careers lost due to the industrial emphasis given, what other conclusion is available?

Consider Kevin Phillips and his findings during the 1990s:

> "By way of context, the unprecedented billions pouring into stocks and mutual funds, besides dwarfing any previous totals, marked a historic shift-- the overtaking by the hitherto speculative securities sector of more sedate and long-dominant banking institutions in total assets managed. In reaching $2.6 trillion in November 1995, mutual fund assets for the first time exceeded deposits in the U.S. commercial banking system. By 2000, their margin had widened to several hundred billion dollars, in retrospect, a leading indicator of vulnerability. At the same time, sweeping deregulation was further blurring the lines between the banking and investment sectors. To flesh out the transformation, the percentage of U.S. individual wealth committed to stocks jumped during the 1990s from 12 percent to 26 percent. Individual financial wealth, a narrower category, went from being 20 percent in stocks to 50 percent. More than

ever before, wealth itself was being securitized--traded on exchanges rather than lived in, minted, worn as jewelry, or ridden in leagues and miles."[16]

Note Phillips use of the word securitization. When the stock market fell in 2000, money flowed in from home and abroad to invest in real estate. The temptation for securitization never abated as banks and their investment banks rushed to create another method of securitization. Other shadow banks sought their own methods of quick and mobile returns. From securitization of stocks to securitization of mortgages, credit card loans, car loans, and other "innovations", the indictment issued by William Greider in his <u>One World Ready or Not</u> against finance capitalism rings too true for effective denial:

> "In the history of capitalism's long expansionary cycles, it is finance capital that usually rules in the final stage, displacing the inventors and industrialists who launched the era, eclipsing the power of government to manage the course of economic events. As capital owners and financial markets accumulate greater girth and a dominating influence, their search for higher returns becomes increasingly purified in purpose---detached from social concerns and abstracted from the practical realities of commerce. In this atmosphere, investors develop rising expectations of what their invested savings out to earn; and the rising prices in financial markets gradually diverge from the underlying economic realities. Since returns on capital are rising faster than the productive output that must pay them, the process imposes greater and greater burdens on commerce and societies--debt obligations that cannot possibly be fulfilled by the future and, sooner or later, must be liquidated, written off or forgiven."[17]

Is Greiger's description of the unfolding of an economy mislead by its financial sector close enough to that of the Crash of 1929 and to today's crisis as to not permitted nay-saying? Hopefully as this is developed here in the next chapter and others, the answer will become clearer. How does an economy dominated by finance, real estate, insurance, and service industries reflect an imbalance within the development of an economy? The imbalance reveals itself in the scarcity of high-paying, middle-class jobs which generally involve product-making.

Process-engineering is generally pursued by firms in retreat, seeking cost-reduction in order to maintain satisfactory bottom-lines for the financial markets. An incentive associated with the emphasis upon finance is the preference for MBA to seek finance positions rather than in product development. We have noted how Ford Motor Company shifted from product development to bottom-line protection of its stock value once Ford stock was offered to the public. David Halberstam took note of this in his book, <u>The Reckoning</u>. The rising priority of finance over product development was revealed in the arrogance often shown by Ford finance officers:

> "They were the right men for the era. Starting in the late fifties and then more rapidly in the sixties and the seventies, Ford and companies like it promoted men who would conserve what existed, rather than men who would risk what they had for an increasingly expensive shot at gaining even more. The growing power of the finance people made the creative people more vulnerable than ever. For the creative people always, no matter how good they were, made mistakes. No product man was perfect; for every model that was a success, there were others best forgotten. By contrast, the finance men were careful. They never identified with a particular product. They never created anything. In meetings they attacked but never had to defend, while the product people defended and could never attack. Once Iacocca told Lundy, "Ed, the great thing about being in finance is, you don't have to worry about ten-day reports, you don't have to worry about sales, you don't have to worry about design, you don't have to worry about manufacturing breakdowns--just what is it you guys do for a living?"[18] (Halberstam noted that such comments by Iacocca were always made when no one else was around.)

Halberstam cites the changed attitude of Wall Street investors who found that "the traditional blue-chip companies were no longer very interesting, because they had completed their principle growth; they were already big and rich. The trick now was to find a company that was just about to make it and catch it before everyone else got in on it, to ride it while it was hot and then get off just before it reached its plateau."[19] Citing the 'go-go market', Halberstam states a driving force which prevails today, "Profit was no longer enough now; super profit was of the essence. This trend placed an exceptional burden on traditional companies, companies whose profits, no matter how considerable, had leveled out."[20] The consequence was that "it was no longer enough simply to make good product and a solid profit; now more and more the object was to drive the stock up."[21]

The resulting changes in management policies must be regarded as imposing 'opportunity costs'--the lost opportunities for electrical, mechanical, and industrial engineers whose talents lie in making things. Other 'lost opportunities were implicit in the fact that "preoccupation with the stock forced old-line companies to make short-range moves designed to make the present look good as the expense of the future. Research and development were chopped back because they were expensive and cut into profits and hurt the way the company looked on its books."[22] Halberstam cited the developing scarcity of professionals and skilled workers caused by the drain of these positions by college graduates now seeking instant wealth in finance. The following influences caused this distortion of the labor market:

1. The old stock market turned over at 10 or 12 percent while the new 'hot' stocks brought 40 to 50 percent.

2. Given the prestige of finance, who, by the early sixties, "wanted to go from Harvard Business School to U.S. Steel, or Ford or some small-parts manufacturer in Ohio when Xerox or Donaldson, Lufkin & Jenrette or other comparably exciting company beckoned. Why go to an already carved-up and probably diminishing world when there were brand-new worlds opening up right in front of you? And of those whom older companies were able to woo from the great business schools, who wanted to go out and work in the assembly plants?"[23] In any event, "the fast track, with quicker advancement and bigger pay and bonuses, was in management, which now meant the financial end, and the slow track, for the second-class citizens, was in the factories."[24]

3. The loss of skills willingly and able to make things or to assist in their

production must be regarded as a great loss and undoubtedly contributed to our decline in global market of manufacturing. A growing disdain for traditional 'roll -your-sleeves-up' work came somewhat natural to business school graduates who were guided into finance and its allied courses as majors. The attitude associated with the growing preference for finance and its allied fields reflect an impatience with getting ahead and with learning new engineering and scientific fields. Consider the temptation for new graduates in the late 1950s, the 1960s, and 1970s: "One could make far more money by playing the market on Wall Street--where cleverness was rewarded immediately--than by joining a company and getting in line to do something as mundane as producing something. The effect of this drain of ability away from the companies themselves was incalculable."[25] How can such a great distortion of the labor market not come back to haunt a country saddled with the loss of its manufacturing advantage in the 1970s and beyond. How can such a distortion of professional opportunities not ultimately penalize a country built on product innovation and its improvement? The following limited participation by engineers in automobile-making undoubtedly contributed to the decline of the industry--in particular the inattention to quality control urged upon the industry by W. Edwards Deming in the 1970s.

"In the late 1950s and beyond, engineers in the automobile industry "were still showing up in Detroit…..but their hands were clean now. Rare was the new engineer who had ever actually built something. The nation's technical knowledge was becoming more and more abstract. The brightest young men went to law school and business school; the best engineers wanted to work in the space program or in defense."[26]

Today's emphasis upon computerized financial and currency transactions and upon 'virtual reality' approaches to communication derived somewhat from this past experience of the 1950s and 1960s and beyond. Emerging technological innovations tended to strengthened finance over product-engineering as noted by Halberstam:

"So there were more people than ever from the business schools, and where they had once had only slide rules for their calculations, now they had computers, which greatly increased their capacity to quantify any concept and to put those numbers to use. Computers were a powerful new weapon for the finance people. Every year now they had greater access to financial detail and greater skill in using that detail within the company, With the coming of computers, the financial people were like prophets armed."[27]

(As pointed out above, even computerization in manufacturing tends to favor process-engineering rather than product engineering, given the emphasis on cost-reduction.)

Any opportunities to pursue product-engineering, especially in the traditional industries, and reverse the unnatural preference for finance has been obstructed by the emerging and sustained Wall Street mania fueled by institutional holdings of stocks and bonds and by financial wealth-seeking through immediate gratification via computerized trading. Thus, not only was an imbalance created within American industry but also within many firms compelled to ignore their main business ad instead seek 'artificial' methods of profit-enhancement. Under the duress of investors' expectations, firms and industries were distorted:

Between 1982 and 1996, stock prices soared. "The Dow Jones Industrial Average climbed from 777 to over 6,000, the longest bull market in U.S. history, but this was also a period of corporate downsizing, which resulted in massive job losses and stagnant wages for American workers. As we will see, these two developments-rising stock prices and widespread job losses--were closely related."[28]

During the 1980s, new government policies directly or indirectly encouraged investment in the stock market. As new investment flooded into the market, stock prices rose, bid up by growing demand. But while this stock price inflation was good for investors, it put companies under enormous pressure to boost their profits, payouts, and stock prices to meet investors' rising expectations. So corporate managers merged with other firms, sold off parts of their business, introduced new technology, and laid off workers to raise productivity, cut costs, and increase profits. Higher profits could then be used to increase shareholder dividends and boost stock prices. The problem is that as stock prices climbed, job losses have mounted, wages have stagnated, and the gap between rich and poor has widened [29]

The consequences of financial market dominance over corporate America are easily detected if one can visualize what the economy of today would look like and how it would differ from the present landscape of finance, real estate, insurance and retail service industries with only the health and education industries provided limited relief for job-seeking Americans.

1. This consequence translates throughout each firm's preference for workers, size of work force, amount of pay, and security of employee employment. "Corporate managers no longer direct a company's nuts-and-bolts production of a particular good or service. They manage stock prices, stock-equity ratios, mergers, divestitures, and dividends in an inflationary stock market environment. This new role explains in part why the disparity between CEO compensation and factory-floor wages has grown. It has grown because executive compensation is linked to the stock market, which is willing and able to provide huge rewards to managers for their efforts to increase profits and stock prices."[30]

2. The following outcomes must be regarded as opportunities loss by workers so impacted by the emphasis upon financial wealth.

　　A. "Between 1979 and 1995, for example, Caterpillar, a heavy equipment manufacturer, closed nine plants and spent $1.8 billion to modernize its remaining factories.--as new technology was introduced, the firm cut its workforce from ninety thousand to fifty-four thousand and increased production. 'We almost doubled our productivity since the mid-1980,' Caterpillar executive James Owens said."[31]

B. Wall Street investor's pressure resulted in outsourcing. "In 1987 for example, auto makers spent $28 billion on parts manufactured overseas, up from $8blllion ten years before. The Big Three went from importing 500,000 engines in 1983 to 1.92 million in 1987."[32]

C."From 1979 to 1992, thanks to automation, manufacturing output rose 13.1 percent, while the workforce declined by 15 percent."[33]

D. The use of technology in reducing costs was transferred to the service industry. While quality and accuracy and accountability improved through the use of bar codes, scanners, and computers, the industry' usage 'has contributed to the loss of 400,000 jobs in retailing since 1990."[34] "In the banking industry, experts predicted in 1995 that 'half of the nation's 59,000 branch banks will close and 450, 200 of the 2.8 million jobs in the banking industry will disappear' a product both of mergers and of new technology like automated tellers (ATMs)"[35]

Should we be concerned that certain professions and skilled occupations are not in high demand-at least not in demand for tenure or full-time employment? Is an economy serious out of kilt when it is heavy-laden with health care jobs, service jobs, and finance? Consider how the failure of capital to be invested heavily in product-making, in scientific pursuits, in research and development has translated into the following outcomes: Robert Schaeffer reported the financial dilemma of many families in the early 1990s. This description bears an unchanged condition for many today who seek to maintain a middle-class life style.

"Overall, real wages fell 9.6 percent between 1979 and 1993. Households were able to maintain their collective income during this period only because an increasing number of women took jobs: 56.6 percent of women work in paid positions. But while this has helped support family income, it meant that parents had less time for their children. 'Parents are spending 40 percent less time with their children than they did 30 years ago More than two million children under the age of 13 have no adult supervision either before or after school.' wrote MIT economist Lester Thurow"[36] What is perhaps even more critical is that the inequalities in earnings will become even greater: "The economic gains made by mergers, restructuring, and new technology have been distributed upward, claimed by corporate managers and stockholders, not by workers."[37]

As in the 1920s, excessive spending or 'investing' in stocks and bonds and the direct or indirect impact of ignoring other capital investments, many of them needed in industries such as mining, textiles, agricultural goods, clothing. These industries lagged in the 1920s. It seems peculiar that necessities such as clothing, shoes, boots, and food products would suffer from consumer demand. But with one-third of a nation in poverty, it is no surprise. Unlike economic shortcomings, the social and emotional effects of unemployment, persistent low-pay employment, and a life-long denial of callings which college education and vocational training are calculated to instill---all of these cannot be corrected within a few years. In fact the emotional and skill entropy will require years of rehabilitation -which the present society is ill-inclined to wait for.

The final outcome from a imbalanced economy may resembled that described as caused by a lingering Great Depression where when there finally was a need or demand for skilled workers--none where qualified to apply because the economy of the 1930s misused these talents and caused them to languish.

"The economic waste was easy enough to see, and it was, of course, astronomical in terms of the value of goods and services the unemployed could have produced. Less calculable but more tragic was the waste of human skills. People took any kind of job they could get, regardless of training or aptitude. When the Government needed skilled war workers, a test survey in Kokomo, Indiana disclosed that, as a result of Depression emergency, almost half the workers in town were in the wrong jobs: a sheet-metal worker was a shipping clerk; a die maker was running a sewage plant; a drill-press operator was a janitor, a molder was a policeman, and a barrel reamer was digging ditches." We cannot repeat even a semblance of this tragic misdirected economic development--even more so since we presumably have some capacity greater than those during the Great Depression to change the direction of our capital investments in industries which justified young adults going in to debt in the multi-thousands of dollars for training or an education.

Chapter Six Footnotes

1. Lawrence E. Mitchell, "The Tyranny of the Market" Wall Street Journal July 30, 2007
2. Ibid, page 90.
3. Ibid, page 90
4. Ibid page 90
5. Robert Schaeffer, Understanding Globalization (Lanham: Rowan & Littlefield, 2009) p131
6. Ibid, page 129
7. Ibid, page 125
8. Ibid, page 129
9. Michael Mandel, "The Cost of All Those Mansions". Business Week, June 6, 2005 page
10. Ibid, page
11. Ibid, page
12. Ibid, page
13. Michael Mandel, "What's Really Propping Up The Economy?" Business Week, September 25, 2006 page58
14. Ibid, page 60
15. Anthony Downs, Real Estate and The Financial Crisis, (Washington D.C.: Urban Institute, 2009) page
16. Kevin Phillips, op. cit. page 141
17. William Greider One World Ready Or Not, (New York: Simon & Shuster, 1998) page
18. David Halberstam, The Reckoning (New York: Morrow, 1986) page 258, 269
19. Ibid, page 247
20. Ibid, page 247
21. Ibid, page 247
22. Ibid, page 247
23. Ibid, pages 233-234
24. Ibid, page 233
25. Ibid, page 233
26. Ibid, page 246
27. Ibid, page 246
28. Robert Schaeffer, op. cit. page 121
29. Ibid, page 121
30. Ibid, page 129
31. Ibid, page 129
32. Ibid, page 130
33. Ibid, page 130
34. Ibid, page 130
35. Ibid, page 130
36. Ibid, pages 132-133
37. Ibid, page 133

CHAPTER SEVEN

PARALLEL NO. 5 SEEKING DOMESTIC ECONOMIC STABILITY UNDER THE COERCION OF FOREIGN FINANCIAL DEALINGS AND MOVEMENTS

International trade is premised on the notion of comparative advantage which states that some nations have a resource advantage in some product-making over other nations. This is not an absolute advantage in that Brazil has a more soybean production capacity than the U.S. in that it can out produce the U.S. in soybeans, but that Brazil sacrifices less resources than the U.S. in producing even the same output. Several things interfere with the satisfactory application of comparative advantage. Countries using very low wages and ignoring health and safety requirements in the workplace can achieve lower production unit costs than companies operating in countries which require a minimum wage and a safe and healthy workplace. Other 'unfair' trade advantages may be present in these developing countries. However, for our purposes we need to focus on the financial aspects with accompany the conduct of international trade. We need to see if any parallel dilemmas exist between the Fed's attempt to reconcile domestic needs with any international imperatives in the late 1920s and the last decade-2000-20010. While trade disputes may occur regarding unfair labor costs or importing goods with prices below cost (dumping), these differences can be identified, corrected, and resolved by legal and judicial determinations. Currency trading and the international selling and buying of securities have been able to avoid similar restrictions available in trade resolution. Speculation and currency devaluation have imposed artificial results on international trade and development. The gold standard which governed during the 1920s was designed to prevent currency distortions which would impair business and national global transactions. In order to establish and promote global trade and investment, nations adopted the gold standard as a means of disciplining countries' monetary policies. The gold standard sought to ensure that traders and investors would be paid in stable currency values and not be blindsided by dramatic changes in foreign currency values caused by currency devaluations or by great inflation. Benjamin Frieden summarizes the requirements imposed on nations seeking to adhere to the gold standard:

> The gold standard symbolized financial rectitude because it required governments to fit their economic policies to global economic pressures. Adherence to gold forced national economies to adjust when they spent beyond their means. If a nation ran a trade deficit, importing more than it exported, it spent more money-that is gold- to pay for imports than it earned for its foreign sales. As gold left the country, the domestic supply of money declined, and the nation's purchasing power also declined. This reduced demand and made it hard for national producers to sell their goods. Producers had to cut prices and force wages down. So by the inherent working of the gold standard, a country spending more than it earned was compelled to reduce wages and prices, spend less and produce more cheaply. If the process ran smoothly, the economy would soon rebound. As local wages and prices dropped, foreigners would buy more of the country's goods and nationals would buy fewer imports. Thus imports would drop and exports would rise, returning the country to balance. [1]

Restating the gold standard requirements as they applied specially to domestic economic policies, Frieden poses the dilemma for governments seeking to resolve only domestic consequences of market directions:

> Governments searching for alternatives to deflationary paralysis and financial ruin ran into an apparently immovable international object-gold. Attempts to half deflation and raise prices were blocked by government commitments to the gold values of their currencies. As two economic historians put it, the gold standard's 'rhetoric was deflation, its mentality was one of inaction'. Countries on gold had to let prices take their course, for national prices were simply a local expression of world prices. Attempts to print money would lead investors to sell off the (debased) currency for gold. The gold standard ruled out monetary stimulation. [2]

The restriction on monetary stimulation meant that a nation could not lower interest rates to increase lending and spending just because of any domestic economic recession or even depression. It could lower interest rates only if under the gold standard requirements, a bank's country held too much gold (from a favorable trade balance) and was obligated to restore a global trade balance among nations by lowering its interest rates so that investors would take their money/gold out of the nation which is lowering rates and invest in a nation which offered relative higher interest rates. The obligation to adhere to gold standard requirements as dictated by trade balances impaired a nation's policy leaders to address economic crisis whose cause lie in domestic disequilibrium. As Friedman explained, "Gold retarded a government's response to the crisis and it also sped the international transmission of financial shocks. The slightest hint that interest rates in, say, Belgium, might go down led investors to pull money out of Belgium and put it somewhere safer. As capital fled Belgium, the fears became self-fulfilling: Money became scarcer, debtors defaulted, and banks failed." [3]

Thus, if Belgium lowers interest rates in order to stimulate spending and thereby revive her economy, she would invite her undoing as investors abandoned hr banks, covert her currency to gold, and then convert the gold into a currency of a nation offering higher interest rates. Friedman recounts the consequences for the United States from the 'international transmission of financial shocks' caused by the British abandoning the gold standard in 1931.

"The American authorities were besieged after the British devalued against gold in October 1931. Investors cashed in their dollars for safer gold, while American bank depositors pulled money out of the banks in anticipation of a financial crisis. The Fed responded in classic gold standard fashion, raising interest rates from 1.5 to 3.5 percent in a week to keep money in the country and in the banks. The logic was clear but perverse. Without the commitment to gold, "the Fed could have lowered interest rates, stimulating the economy by making borrowing, spending, and investment easier. Instead, shackled to gold standard requirements, the world's most important central bank imposed even more austere and restrictive policies (during a increasing gaining economic depression.)" [4] (It remains for us to determine whether lower interest rates would have improved economic conditions during 1930-1932. The arguments presented so far would indicate "NO", since there were very few creditworthy people or companies and the companies that remained were ones that had not sought capital loans during the 1920s and would now be seeking to be "rescued" or "bailed out" by loans. To restate the main proposition in this effort, experience persuades us that lower interest rates can at most only stabilize an economy and is not capable through a increase in the quantity of money of creating economic growth of significant and sustainable proportions. Even in stabilizing an economy, experience suggests that this is possible only when improvements are possible on the margin-- not requiring great departures of corporate or government operations or policies. This would be pursued later in more specific details which place responses by companies and government with the corresponding economic conditions of 1930-32 and today.)

The crisis of 1929-32 played out initially with the Fed having concern over the speculation on Wall Street. However, it was not that clear as to whether the Fed should intervene simply to address Wall Street investment practices. Perhaps the most admired Federal Reserve Board member, Chairman Strong, had reservations about the Fed targeting its policies primary at Wall Street investing.

But as an experienced Wall Street hand, he was quite aware of how difficult it was to identify a market bubble--to distinguish between an advance in stock prices warranted by higher profits and a rise driven purely by market psychology."

Strong recognized his own highly fallible judgment about stocks was a very thin reed on which to conduct the country's monetary policy."[5] Strong relinquished to his uncertainty regarding judging stock market conditions and stated that he believed that as stated by him; "He feared that if he added yet another goal--preventing stock market bubbles- to the list he would overload the system."[6] Strong put this way, "Must we accept parenthood for every economic development in the country? That is a hard thing for us to do. We have a large family of children. Every time one of them misbehaved, we might have to spank them all"[7]

But it was not easy to ignore the collateral damage which speculation on Wall Street was causing. The following facts cited in <u>Lords of Finance</u> seemed to compel Fed actions against Wall Street speculation:

> 1. New York was 'sucking' in capital from abroad as a result of the speculative mania.
> 2. This was draining capital from Europe that was very dependent upon American money.
> 3. Germany and Central European countries were the most vulnerable to the consequences of this drain.

. Bank of England was losing gold, going from reserves of $830 million to below $700million and still declining. In the past Strong would have been asked by the Bank to lower interest rates in the U.S. which would then provide incentives for foreign investors to take their money out of U.S. banks and deposit in England where rates were higher.

The following scenario illustrates that gold balances achieved through changing the trade balances may have represented the 'pure' theory of the gold standard, but when faced with extraneous influences on currency exchange differences such as caused by the flight of capital to the U.S. to speculate on Wall Street, other approaches to secure gold other than as a result of restoring trade balances were pursued.

He arrived in New York on January 27 armed with his new proposal. Meeting with Harrison at the New York Fed, Norman now surprised everyone by arguing for a sharp rise in U.S. rates, possibly by 1 percent, even by 2 percent, taking the discount rate to 7 percent. The Fed should try to break "the spirit of speculation", "prostrating "the market by a forceful tightening of credit. Once a change in psychology had been achieved, interest rates could be then brought down again and capital flows to Europe would resume. For some reason Norman thought the Fed could pierce the bubble with a surgical incision that would bring it back to earth, without harming the economy. It was a completely absurd idea. Monetary policy does not work like a scalpel but more like a sledgehammer. Norman could neither be sure how high rates would have to go to check the market boom nor predict with any certainty what this would do to the U.S. economy.[8]

This approach by the Bank director of England, Norman, exposes a vulnerability of the Fed and its monetary policies---can they serve both domestic and international needs simultaneously or must it choose a priority based on circumstances and alternative policies other than monetary? Reviewing the series of Fed actions supports the notion that its adherence to gold requirements disabled it from responding effectively to the aftermath of the Crash of 1929 and may have contributed to the Crash. Consider the priority given by the Fed to gold standard disequilibrium.

1. In 1927, the Fed made large number of open-market purchases and a discount rate reduction which lower interest rates.[9] "By mid-1927, stock exchange speculation began to take a more prominent place in policy discussions. Common stock returned 37.5 percent in 1927 Returns in 1928 were larger still, 43.6 percent, so the compound total return for these two years was 98 percent. Between July and November 1927, loans to brokers and dealers in New York increased more than $300 million."[10]

The Board was confronted with the question: "Should they respond to large increases in asset prices or confine their attention to prices, output, money, or foreign exchange."[11] The idea of raising interest rates and increasing security sales to fight speculation was opposed by Governor Strong. He stated his objection as follows:

"I have not felt that such a policy was justified by the facts, that any effort through higher rates directed especially at stock speculation would have an unfavorable effect upon business generally, and that this would be particularly unfortunate at a time when we are producing a surplus of exportable farm products which cannot be marketed abroad unless the country remains a free loaning market for the rest of the world. (Strong to Young. Board of Governors File, box1436, October 19, 1927." [12]

Lower interest rates were established instead to help restore the gold reserves of Great Britain who was losing gold to the U.S. due to the high returns offered by Wall Street speculation. This policy was taken without any serious regard for any domestic consequences in the U.S. This is the view taken by scholars such as Elmus R. Wicker as noted in Monetary Policy 1923-1933, page 145 below:

'Two historians of the period, Lester V. handler and Elmus R. Wicker, note that Governor Strong initiated the policy after a visit from Montagu Norman, the governor of the Bank of England Hjalmar Schacht, president of the German Reichsbank, and Charles Rist, deputy governor of the Bank of France, in early July. They had urged that rates be lowered in New York as a means of stabilizing the European monetary situation in line with the plan for the resumption of gold payments. However, while Chandler argues that Strong had good reason to favor lower rates in view of the domestic situation, Wicker discounts domestic considerations. He argues that the recessionary tendencies apparent in the summer of 1927 were not sufficiently severe to warrant the actions taken, noting that production had taken 'a much sharper dip between September and December 1926' and that, by July, when easing began, the wholesale price index was rising for the first time in almost two years.' Wicker suggests that the easy-money policies of 1924 and 1927 were undertaken to establish the international gold standard and that in both cases the action merely 'coincided with the goal of domestic stability'" Wicker's position is basically supported by the recent study, Lords of Finance, which provides a narrative account of the relationship between Norman and Strong in their efforts to support the gold standard.

David Kennedy in his Freedom From Fear offers support for Wicker's argument that lower interest rates were established in 1927 so that the interest rates in Britain and elsewhere would be higher than in the U.S. This would encourage deposits in those banks and thereby bring gold reserves into these banks.

> "This easy-money was due largely to the influence of Benjamin Strong, the stern and influential governor of the New York Federal Reserve Bank. Strong's policy was meant to support the imprudent decision Chancellor of the Exchequer Winston Churchill had made in 1925 to return Britain to the prewar gold standard at the old exchange rate of $4.86 to the pound. That unrealistically high rate crimped British exports, boomed imports, and threatened to drain the Bank of England of its gold reserves. Strong reasoned, not incorrectly, that lower interest rates and cheaper money in America would stanch the hemorrhage of gold from London to New York, thus stabilizing an international financial system that was still precariously recovering from the strains of the World War. The same policies, of course, facilitated vast speculative borrowing in the United States. It was that disastrous consequence that prompted Herbert Hoover's contemptuous description of Strong as "a mental annex to Europe."[13]

Caught in a conundrum of balancing consideration for stabilizing the gold standard system and discouraging Wall Street speculation, the Fed, "recognizing that the easing of credit policy in the middle of 1927 had been a mistake, "raised rates from 3.5 percent in February 1928 to 5 percent in July 1928. But as the stock market began its second leg upward in the middle of 1928, the Fed fell silent and disappeared from view, divided about how to react."[14]

But the dilemma would not simply and silently go away. Speculation continued and any raising of interest rates to discourage call lending may penalize legitimate lending for businesses. Also, raising interest rates would undo the restoration of gold reserves which may have been accomplished through the lower interest rates established in 1927. "Moreover, capital had once again begun flowing in from abroad, attracted by the returns on Wall Street. Were the Fed to raise interest rates now, it might well pull in even more gold, possibly even forcing sterling off the gold standard."[15] Before his death, Strong began urging the others not to tighten money any further "but step aside in the hope that the frenzy would burn itself out."[16]

Some governors of the Fed felt reassured in April 1928 as reported in New Procedures, New Problems 1923 to 1929:

"Chase was optimistic when the Governor's Conference met at the end of April (1928). With call money rates at 5 percent and discount rates at 4.5 percent at several banks, the credit situation seemed well in hand. (Such a spread of .5 percent difference between what the bank paid at the discount window and what it could earn with call loans seemed too small to justify banks to pursue call loans in great numbers.) The French elections had been won by Raymond Poincare, so French stabilization and continued United States gold outflow seemed likely."[17]

France's position in the gold standard system brings to light both a concern over the flow of gold and over the exchange value of the franc. Concern over the exchange value of the franc which was declining, "[t]he authorities still had one weapon in reserve to break the downward spiral---the more than $1billion in gold holdings of the Banque de France, some $700 million parked in its vaults on the Rue de la Vrilliere, and a further $300 million held abroad with the Bank of England."[18] Noting that the French held gold as a national treasury and were even unwilling to use it for the war effort, Liaquat Ahamed states "In early 1926, the government, its finances now restored but its currency still inexorably and inexplicably falling, tried to persuade the Banque that now was the time to redeem its pledge by supporting the franc with foreign currencies borrowed against the security of the gold. The Banque refused. "[19] Efforts by the French government to persuade Benjamin Strong to lend $100 million from the New York Fed was rejected as Strong felt that the Banque should offer the gold as collateral to any loan from the Fed. Strong stated succinctly that the dilemma was 'when they would be unable to pay, the Americans would have to physically take the pledged gold reserves from the vaults of the Banque, for which they would be 'excoriated from one end of France to the other."[20] The French sought loans from private banks and were rejected. (They wanted loans in order to buy francs on the open market. This would tend to raise the value of the franc.) Eventually the franc would increase in its exchange value and pose a different controversy-- should its rise be capped (not allowed to increase any further)? Should the franc be corrected in its exchange value by the natural consequences of trade surpluses and deficits? Some argued that it should be lowered by intervention in the market--that is selling francs for other currencies which would create a bigger demand for the purchased currencies while disposing a number of francs tends to lower its currency exchange value.) What to do?

"The truth is that at that time, very few bankers could claim to understand fully the situation of France in 1926, particularly the complicated dynamics between the inflow of money and its effects on the exchange rate and domestic prices and, in turn, their impact on the overall economy."[21]

The fatal flaw in focusing excessively upon trade balances and currency exchange rates was to ignore the economic consequences for a nation's people. Those who favored placing a cap of the franc's exchange value won the battle.

"By the middle of 1927, it was clear that Moreau had won. Waves of French capital that had fled to London or New York had washed back home, allowing the Banque to accumulate a foreign exchange chest of $500 million dollars, most of it in pounds At 25 francs to the dollar, French goods were among the most competitive in the world, exports were booming, while prices were stable. It seemed as if, thanks to Moreau, France, of all the European countries, had finally hit upon the right recipe for dealing with the financial legacy of the war, avoiding the two extremes of German-style inflation and British-style deflation."[22]

Moreau's mistake was to assume that the value of the currency of a major economic power such as France, the fourth largest industrial economy, was a matter for that country alone. Exchange rates, by their very nature, involve more than one side and are therefore a reflection of a multilateral system."[23]

This optimism proved to be misplaced. As instability in Europe forced European central banks to raise their rates even higher. "Many Reserve officials felt that pushing member banks' indebtedness to this level (loss of gold due to European high interest rates) had been beneficial in that there had been a definite decline in the rate of expansion of bank credit extended for brokers' loans. They had not yet realized that the decline had been more than offset by a tremendous increase in loan funds supplied by nonbank lenders-an increase of $750 million in the first six months of 1928." (Again the appearance of a shadow banking system feeding the stock market speculation.)[24]

This lending by nonbanks continue into 1929 as reported in Kennedy's Freedom From Fear:

"When the demand for call loans overwhelmed even the abundantly liquid resources of the banking system, corporations stepped in. They accounted for roughly half the call-loan monies in 1929."

> Much blame has been leveled at a feckless Federal Reserve System for failing to tighten credit as the speculative fires spread, but while it is arguable that the easy-money policies of 1927 helped to kindle the blaze, the fact is that by late 1928 it had probably burned beyond controlling by orthodox financial measures. The Federal Reserve Board justifiably hesitated to raise its rediscount rate for fear of penalizing non-speculative business borrowers. When it did impose a 6 percent rediscount rate in the late summer of 1929, call loans were commanding interest of close to 20 percent-a spread that the Fed could not have bridged without catastrophic damage to legitimate borrowers. Similarly, the board had early exhausted its already meager ability to soak up funds through open-market sales of government securities. By the end of 1928 the system's inventory of such securities barely exceeded $200 million--a pittance compared to the nearly $8 billion in call loans then outstanding"[25] (With only $200 million of government securities in its inventory, The Fed could hardly compete with the $8 billion available for call loans. The Fed could remove only $200milllion from the money supply of banks by selling them government securities which would become assets of the banks and not reserves to be loaned.)

4. After the Crash, the Fed devoted immediate and almost exclusive attention to the domestic crisis. It purchased over $150 million government securities during the panic week of October 29-30, 1929 and had purchased over $1billlion of government securities in an economy that at the time had a nominal GDP of $50 billion during 1931.[26] This undivided effort at the domestic crisis came to a sudden interruption in 1931 due to Great Britain's taking the sterling off the gold standard. Both borrowed reserves and interest rates shot up the fourth week of September 1931 and remained high until early 1932. The Fed raised the discount rate during

this period but made no open-market purchases in response to the British abandonment of the gold standard which triggered the Fed policy above. (Interest rates may have gone up through demand and supply effects, alone, because of less cash reserves to lend due to the drain of gold from the U.S. and cash withdrawals from banks by customers. The gold stock of the U.S. declined by $727 million by October 28, 1931 and cash withdrawals from banks increased by $544 million between mid-September and the end of December in 1931.[27]) The Fed had increased the discount rate from 1.5 percent to 3.5 percent to ward off the drain of gold from the U.S. Donald Wells explains the crisis imposed by Great Britain's going off the gold standard:

> "When Britain declared it would no longer redeem its pound sterling in gold, there was a large increase in demand by Europeans for gold. Since the dollar was still redeemable in gold, there was a run on the dollar. Foreign banks exchanged their dollar deposits at the New York Fed for gold. In six weeks, over $700 million of gold left the U.S. for Europe. Governor Meyer did believe that the gold standard should be maintained; therefore, he agreed with the New York Fed that it should raise its discount rate and stop open-market purchases of securities. The belief in the gold standard was very strong among financial leaders in not only this country but also in most European countries. But with central banks exercising discretion, the rules of the gold standard were often ignored, especially by the nation losing gold. This external pressure on banks from the loss of gold was matched by an internal drain by the public for more currency because people realized that many banks were failing. In 1931, a total of 2,293 banks failed. Banks losing reserves from the gold drain increased their borrowing from the Fed even though the discount rate was increased. Banks also dumped their commercial paper and government securities on the market to get needed reserves, but this caused the prices of these assets to fall and their yields to rise. By this dumping on the market, banks were only pulling reserves from one another."[28]

From the above narrative of converging demands upon the Fed from Wall Street speculation, concern over maintaining the gold standard (in particular the vulnerability of Great Britain) and the obligation under the law to maintain price stability and support economic growth, what should be the priority of the Fed? Should the Fed give main emphasis to the domestic concerns of speculation and price stability, or focus upon attempting a 'soft landing' of the Wall Street bubble by raising interest rates, or give priority to saving the gold standard? Authors cited above give sound reasons as to why attacking speculation would have been futile (given the shadow banking system which had superior funds for such lending) and these authors also cite the stranglehold which the gold standard imposed upon a strictly domestic monetary response to domestic crisis in disobeying the gold standard mandates. We will return to this dilemma later when a conclusion is drawn on lessons to be gained from the Fed's responses of the 1920s and early 1930s and today. Presently, we now focus upon a condition today which in its international dimensions parallels that of the 1920s. Suffice it to say that if the gold standard required a nation to raise interest rates due to its trade deficits causing an unacceptable imbalance of gold reserves, that nation would raise interest rates despite, say, 14% unemployment rate domestically. This is untenable in a representative democracy. This will be further developed from Dr. Jeffrey Frieden's observations in his Global Capitalism, pp. 13, 182, 184,

Chapter Seven Footnotes:

1. Jeffrey Frieden, Global Capitalism: Its Fall and Rise In The Twentieth Century, (New York: WW Norton, 2006) page 18
2. Ibid, page 182
3. Ibid, page 184
4. Ibid, page 184
5. Liaquat Ahamd, Lords of Finance: The Bankers Who Broke The World, (New York; Penguin Press, 2009) page 276
6. Ibid, page 277
7. Ibid, as quoted on page 177
8. Ibid, page 370
9. Benjamin Anderson, op. cit. page 139
10. 10 Liaquat Ahamd, op. cit. page 224
11. Ibid, page 224
12. Ibid, quote at page 225
13. David Kennedy, op. cit. page 36
14. liaquat Ahamd, op. cit. page 318
15. Ibid, page 318
16. Ibid, page 318
17. Ibid, page 229
18. Ibid, page 253
19. Ibid. page 253
20. Ibid, page 253
21. Ibid, page 263
22. Ibid, page 268
23. Ibid, page 268
24. Elmo Wicker, op. cit. page 151
25. David Kennedy, op. cit. pages 36-37
26. See article by James Butkiewiz at page 186 in Economics of the Great Depression E. Wheeler.
27. David Wheelock, "Monetary Policy in the Great Depression and Beyond: The Source of the Fed's Inflation Bias", Economics of the Great Depression Wheeler ed. Page 158
28. David Wells, The Federal Reserve System: A History (Jefferson ,N.C.: McFarland & Co. 2004) . page 52

CHAPTER EIGHT

PARALLEL NO. 6 CONFRONTING INTERNATIONAL CURRENCY TRADING AND THE FED'S EFFORTS AT POLICY CORRECTIONS.

Before addressing immediately the current global financial crisis and the policy responses of the Fed and Congress, it would be useful to gain an overall understanding of the Post-World War II international efforts at correcting global and domestic trade and investment practices which contributed to the world-wide great depression of the 1930s. This overall view of post-war efforts to reconcile foreign and domestic needs will be instructive in drawing this parallel between the 1920s and today.

In both periods, what is the Fed's primary responsibility and what comparisons can be made as to its response during both? Should the Fed's standard guide line be; What are the consequences domestically if we choose to give international financial market stability the highest priority? What are the consequences for the global economy if we choose to give domestic price and economic stability the highest priority? Who should bear primary responsibility--the U.S., foreign governments, or international organizations? Does it in turn rest upon which economic or financial force is the main cause of the distress? Does origin determine responsibility for correction and if so which correction, foreign or domestic, is appropriate? One should ask him/herself as he/she examines the currency and trading regimes established after World War II, is the new international trading and investing order meant to be self-executing and self-correcting in a manner reminiscent of that design of the gold standard. In other words, less government intervention is to be accepted in the interplay of demand and supply of goods, services, capital investment as established and even altered by autonomous actions of businesses, foreign and domestic. And in facilitating this exchange system under demand and supply, national currencies should adjust accordingly as dictated by the established exchange ratios under Breton Woods. Again as the reader examines the following narrative of the evolution of the international trade rules as governed by GAAT and the late 20th century modifications of GAAT, ask yourself is not the same deference to international trade and investment governing principles being asked of sovereign nations as the gold standard required. Can or should the Fed bow to the imperatives of national trade rules even if the neglect of its domestic responsibilities is at risk. We saw how the Fed during the late 1920s attempted to serve two 'masters', the gold standard and its mandates under the Federal Reserve Act. Keeping in mind the Fed's working toward mutually hostile targets, maintaining the gold standard and Great Britain's adherence to it and attempting to establish an easy money supply and credit to fight the beginnings of the Great Depression, observe any contradictory policy-actions during the crisis of 2006-2010.

1. The international financial and trade environment: 1945----2010.

The Frustration of Competitive Advantage by Currency Trading.

Decades after World War II, all foreign currencies had a fixed relationship to the dollar. Thus, a pound was always worth the same specific amount of dollars. Similarly, the mark, yen, and franc maintained a fixed value pegged to the dollar. Most nations initially desired this fixed relativity to the dollar for several reasons: primarily, the experience of the 1930s involved a free floating relationship whereby a pound may be worth two dollars and then become worth three or four dollars as a result of nation's devaluation--simply unilaterally changing the value of its currencies. These changes were not due primarily to changing economic factors of relative costs in say Britain as opposed to cost of similar goods in the U.S. Nor were these currency exchange values caused by the natural play of demand and supply of the currency over an extended period of trading by nations. Any attempt at devaluation of a nation's currency in order to export surplus goods which domestic consumers were unable to buy would be resisted and met with similar devaluations by nations who were targeted for imports. This war of currency devaluations proved to be destructive and provided the incentive to avoid these currency efforts after the War. Secondly, this fixed exchange value system was acceptable because of the ability of the dollar to secure the workings of such a system. The dollar was the soundest currency after the War and the United States provided the hegemony necessary to lead, stabilize, and secure the new trading order visualized by world leaders. America possessed enough financial and economic resources sufficient to provide management and discipline to this global trading and investment order under GAAT.

However, as nations emerged from the ruins of World War II and initiated their own version of economic growth and development, the fixed currency rates fell into disfavor. Capitalism is an on-going economic system which introduces changes and thus instability concerning prices, employment, and quality of life. Secure jobs are replaced by new jobs created by an innovating business environment. National crisis of inflation, unemployment, and inadequate capital investment have their impact locally in towns, cities, farming communities across a nation. A recession may require lower interest rates be established by the central bank in order to make more money and loans available to consumers and businesses. Also, increased government spending to stimulate the economy may be required in order to restore employment. However, what if in lowering interest rates and in increasing spending, the government must ignore the Bretton Woods mandate of fixed exchange values which the country's currency must maintain with other currencies? Or America might institute a soft money policy to stimulate consumption through lower interest rates. But, the French, Germans, Japanese and English possessing dollars in American banks will exchange dollars for their currencies of francs, marks, yen, and pounds in order to transfer their currencies to other foreign banks now offering higher interest rates than the U.S. banks. This transference of dollars by foreign depositors to foreign banks reduces banking reserves and thereby reduces the amount of reserves a bank has to lend. By reducing the reserves of U.S. banks, the removal of dollars by foreign depositors impairs our government's effort to stimulate the economy through lower interest rates. Our government must accept the demanded foreign currency in order to accommodate those foreign depositors seeking to relocate their accounts to higher paying foreign banks. Yet, our government must in turn accept dollars in order to maintain the fixed exchange value imposed by Breton Woods. "The basic problem, of course, is that a governmental proclamation that a dollar will be worth so many pounds does not mandate stability with respect to the demand for and supply of pounds. As demand and supply shift over time, governments must intervene directly or indirectly in the foreign exchange market if the exchange rate is to be stabilized."[1]

If in the example above, the Fed's easing of money through lower interest rates altered the fixed currency relationship between the dollar and other nations' currencies, then there was a requirement to buy or sell currencies, ours or others, in order to reestablish the fixed value of the dollar to other currencies as mandated by Breton Woods. This reestablishing of currency equilibrium often conflicted with the needed fiscal and monetary policies of a nation. For example, to avoid intolerable balance of trade deficits, a nation might have to employ restricted fiscal and monetary policies under the fixed rate regime regardless of the condition of its domestic economy, (This conflicting circumstance could exist due to the ability of multinational companies to manipulate prices and costs through their intra-firm transfers.) The benefit of a fixed rate of exchange is the minimization of financial extraneous influences on prices, costs, and demand. Currency has a de minimus role in trade as relative prices driven by relative costs of products in respective nations become the determinate factor in exporting and importing transactions.

Faced with the dilemma of neglecting domestic economic needs in order to conform to the mandated fixed exchange values, nations began to adopt a floating exchange rate system during the 1970s. This was due primarily because America was no longer able to support the dollar in a manner which enabled other countries to rely upon American trade deficits. The eclipse of American hegemony required each nation, including America, to fall back upon its own devices. Nations desired an ability to manage their own economic destiny independently of natural market influences which international demand and supply concerning currencies may impose. They desired emancipation from the discipline of free trade as governed by comparative advantage and its pursuit by industries. Thus, a floating exchange rate emerged allowing nations to have discretion in seeking domestic economic goals. Ideally, floating exchange rates could operate in a self-adjusting manner similar to even the gold standard by allowing a nation's exports to increase appropriately (as its currency value lowered) and then correct an excess trade balance caused by a currency low exchange value when demand for the nation's exports caused its currency to increase in its exchange value and begin to make the nation's exports more costly due to the increase exchange value of its currency. Professor Campbell McConnell explains in his textbook:

1. Exchange rate can be determined by the unimpeded play of demand and supply (with freely floating exchange rates) for example, if pounds become less expensive because the value of the dollar rises this causes Americans to demand larger quantities of British goods since now a dollar has become worth more pounds then before and will buy more British goods then before. However, if American demand for British goods continues to be strong, the pound will eventually rise in its exchange value with the dollar due to Americans asking for more pounds in exchange for their dollars at the foreign exchange banks in order to buy the British goods.

2. If the dollar price of pounds rises (meaning that a pound is worth more dollars then before), the British find that American goods are cheaper. This results in the British buying more American exported goods to Great Britain and in buying American exports (imports in Britain), the British must exchange pounds for dollars. If British continued for a sustained period to buy American imported goods to Great Britain, more and more pounds are substituted for dollars and this substitution of pounds for dollars represents an increased demand for dollars, making the dollar to have an increased exchange value with the pound. This increased exchange value of the dollar with the pound (due to the increased need for British consumer to have dollars) causes the dollar to begin to increase the price of American goods imported into Great Britain. In this manner, currency exchange values tend to self-correct--but only if the trade patterns between the two nations are well developed so that there tends to be an approximate trade balance over time between America and Great Britain. (This last view is the author's only. For example, American dependency upon Arab oil created a trade imbalance as our imports far exceeded any exports to the Middle East. Under these trade patterns, there is insufficient trade going back and forth between the U.S. and the Middle East to allow self-correction. The same may be true with our trading with China today. No self-correction is possible through shifting demands by Chinese for American exports and demands by Americans for Chinese imports since one far outweighs the other.)

By the way, currency exchange values of the Yuan and the dollar could be self-correcting if more Chinese began to buy American goods imported into China in great quantities or the exchange values could be restored by increased Chinese capital investment in the U.S. However, for any small currency exchange value between the yuan and the dollar similar to the pound and the dollar to presist, both national economies must assume approximately the same dimensions in GDP and other significant economic indicators. Our extensive trade relations with Japan has not produce an exchange value of yen to dollars which maintains the same smaller dimensions as pounds to dollars do. This would seem to have some significance in the ability of currency exchange values to self-correction (return to their normal exchange value).

3. The interplay of pounds and dollars as explained and illustrated above affects the trade balances of Great Britain and the U.S. Exchange values can affect the final prices of goods offered to consumers in Great Britain and in the U.S. Also, along with differences in exchange value of the dollar and the pound, the demand for a nation's products are determined by price, tastes, and national distribution of income.[2]

Exchange rates may be altered by changes in tastes, inflation, or interest rates of nations. They may also change because of micro and macroeconomic influences. Here are three economic factors which may change a nation's rate of exchange for its currency.

1. The rapid increase in national income will result in more imports, causing an increased demand for foreign currency.

2. A rapid rise of domestic prices relative to other nations' will result in an increase domestic demand for imports.

3. Higher interest rates will increase the demand for a nation's currency, causing the currency to increase in the exchange rate.[4]

The floating exchange rates are theoretically self-correcting in that when demand for exports becomes too large, imports are encouraged since the dollar in our case will increase in its exchange value (due to our nations' demanding more dollars to buy our exports). The increased exchange value of the dollar will allow Americans to buy cheaper imported goods (cheaper, in this case, due to the lower exchange value of the foreign currency of the importing nation). However, many nations, including America, have a persistent imbalance of trade, importing more than they export or vice versa: thus floating exchange rates perform in a less than perfect or satisfactory manner as they are theoretically constructed. Much imperfection is due to national devaluation of currencies by thee nations, trade barriers interfering with a natural mutual exchange of goods and services by nations, and oligopolistic dominance in international commerce. In addition, speculation in currency distorts and aborts natural processes which would correct imbalances of trade which is allowed to work themselves out completely. For example, if British goods are in demand by Americans, the demand for pounds will eventually become so strong as to change the currency ratio from one pound to, say, two dollars to, say, one pound to three dollars. At this point American goods achieve an advantage in that they become cheaper for the British to buy since now one pound can buy three dollars worth of American goods, rather than two dollars of American goods under the initial circumstances above. Consequently, British subject begin to buy more American imports which tends to correct any unnatural exchange value between the pound and the dollar (which historically seems to have been an acceptable rate which promoted not only trade between America and Great Britain but throughout the globe.)

    However, any natural correction of currency exchange value resulting from the ebb and flow of international trade can be impaired, even prohibited, by speculation of banks, hedge funds, currency funds, and by the intra firm transfers of multinational companies who assign costs to their transfer semi-finished goods (really imported goods to be assembled in another country) not only incurred costs of labor, materials, and overhead but on the perceived need to reduced prices of their goods in the imported domestic market. If the cost of goods manufactured should be $1000 per unit, but is listed as $1500 because intra firm transferred semi-finished goods were coasted at $800 instead of actual costs of $300, the discipline provided by international trade under comparative advantage is subverted. If, for example, the pound is reaching a new exchange rate of 3 to 1 dollars from an initial rate of 2 to 1 dollars due to great demand for British products by American consumers, speculation in currencies can abort any self-correction provided by the pound reaching an exchange value of 3 dollars and becoming too expensive for American purchasers. Speculators do not hold currencies for long-term purposes; their game is to use the short-term to achieve immediate profits from economic results which speculators anticipate would occur, even without their intervention. Thus, through sustained mutual trade between Great Britain and American, the pound may become worth 3 dollars, making it become too expensive for Americans to buy the British imported goods since now it takes 3 dollars instead of 2 to buy the same imported goods. If this pattern of exchange value alterations has a repeated history, that is all speculators need to intervene with assurance that they can make instant profits through buying pounds making the pound achieve a higher exchange value than the dollar (which the speculators may use to buy the pounds). Suddenly, within a short period of say days, the pound is now worth 3 dollars or more due to the buying of great quantities of pounds by the currency funds (other currencies besides dollars would likely also be used to buy the pounds.) Demand for pounds has been artificially increased significantly while the supply of pounds has remained unchanged within this short time frame. Thus, one pound may now equal 3 dollars within days, rather than as a result of months, maybe years, of international selling and buying of goods. (That is why the increased value of the pound is called 'artificially' increased since it was not increased in association with any economic purpose-the making and selling of goods.) As a result Great Britain sells less goods to Americans since the dollar rises to the artificially induced value of 1 pound to 3 dollars before the quantity of goods sold by the British would have produced that exchange value. Is this distortion caused by speculation and other non-economic transactions (such as manipulating infra firm transfer costs) a huge peril to the natural exchange of goods and services as dictated by relative prices, costs, and even the resulting currency exchange value alterations? An overwhelming "YES" must be asserted in view of the following findings:

1. It was estimated that in 1986 only 16% of foreign exchange financed trade or consumer accounts with speculation accounting for the other 84% and 90% of currency exchange being in the hands of primarily banks, then.[5]

2. A recent publication cites an even more distorting influence of currency and financial trading on the sale of goods and services across the globe:

"Money now moves around the world at a speed that defies and baffles government regulators. Policies to 'liberalize' (lift barriers to) investment, combined with advancements in information technology, have facilitated the explosion of private financial flows described earlier and allow about $1.5 trillion a day of travel across borders as foreign-exchange transactions. Only one to two percent of these transactions are related to trade or foreign direct investment. The remainder is for speculation or short-term investments that are subject to rapid flight when investors' perceptions change."[6]

3. One cannot dismiss the impact of multinational corporations' policies upon the natural flow of international trade of goods and services under the principles of comparative advantage or any emerging attempts to modernize these principles. Consider the following findings of those who have researched and analyzed the effects of multinational companies.

A. It has been estimated that 40 percent of U.S. exports and nearly 50 percent of its imports are goods traveling through intra-firm trade of multinationals and that globally 40 percent of global trade occurs through intra-firm trade within multinationals.[7] Moreover, Lawrence B. Krouse concluded that only about 15 percent of global trade occurred in free-market circumstances-.i.e. between unrelated buyers and sellers under no compulsion to trade with each other.[8]

Any Fed policy on the dollar's value would be neutralized to some extent by the fact that much trade is accomplished through bartering, perhaps as much as 30% of trade.[9]

    4. Other distorting influences could be cited such as below poverty wages in developing countries given their exports an "unnatural" advantage over manufactured products in developed countries where fair labor standards and workplace safety and health conditions are sought. However, for the purpose of drawing parallel circumstances between the foreign crisis confronted by the Fed in late 1929 and the Fed's dilemma today with the foreign entanglement of securitized mortgages, auto loans, credit card loans, etc., it is sufficient to draw the comparison which confronted the Fed today with that posed by the gold standard to the Fed's responses during 1928-1932.

    (B) Lets pursue how the currency exchange rate relates to government fiscal and monetary policies and how the Fed attempts to seek a resolution of the international financial crisis which had its origin and cause in U.S. financial market transactions. Let's continue to develop the reason for nations' abandoning the fixed currency exchange rate adopted after World War II by examining more deeply the dilemma which being compelled to adhere to the fixed currency exchange rate comprised and even prevented nations to respond effectively and politically responsibly to domestic economic crisis. After reviewing the recent three decade history of domestic policies attempting to accommodate both or either domestic economic needs and international banking views on America's dollar exchange value vis-à-vis the value of other nations' currencies and the burden which the dollar may pose we will be positioned to critique the circumstances of the Fed during the recent decade in attempting to prevent another "Great Depression".

Even the freedom of discretion provided by floating rates for currency exchange to tax, spending, raise or lower interest rates can be impeded by the mobility of capital. (If the abandonment by Britain of the gold standard in 1931 had not been followed by the instant capability of countries and investors to immediate withdraw their dollar deposits in the U.S. and demand gold instead, would the Fed had more time and flexibility in responding to the Crash and its aftermath?) "By the mid-1970s, due to new technologies and the deregulation of national financial institutions, the volume of the international flow of capital assets exceeded the volume of world trade many times over. According to one estimate, in 1979 total exports were $1.5 trillion compared to foreign exchange trading of $17.5 trillion, by 1984 whereas exports had increased only to $1.8 trillion, foreign exchange trading had ballooned to$35 trillion."[10]

The implications for domestic macroeconomic policies are severe in the face of financial transactions which are autonomous from both government regulation and even from the immobility that committed capital involves in physical investments of plant and equipment or even research and development. To make the counter-influence which currency trading has upon government policies and their intended results, consider the following description of currency traders' practices with the examples of government polices afterwards:

Chairman Volker relates the type of strategies employed by traders "who care little about basic economic trends" or their domestic consequences if not corrected or promoted.

"What interest them is the current fashion in the market, or what they think is motivating their counterpart in other banks and their customers to buy or sell currencies. Suppose they think interest rates are important (as indeed they often should.) As the traders follow the business news on their screens, they may catch predictions by economists working for the large banks and brokerage houses that, say, payroll employment is expected to fall by 100,000, a figure that will be published by the government first thing in the morning. If the number of jobs actually declines by 150,000, the market figures that the Fed is more likely to cut interest rates and that some customers and other traders will sell dollars. So some will rush to be the first, initially depressing the value of the dollar. If it looks like a trend, then others will follow, and the shift in exchange rates may end up far out of proportion to the significance of any particular item of economic news.

Changes in exchange rates influence the prices of imports and exports, and changes in prices of course eventually affect their volume. In general, a decline in the value of a currency will therefore reduce a trade deficit by making imports more expensive; a rise produces the reverse effect. But the actual flow of funds in the market these days is not dominated by transactions in trade but in huge movements of capital chasing higher investment income, and the exchange rate therefore reacts more sharply to those capital flows. And those flows may be influenced by something as straightforward as a higher rate of interest or as unpredictable as a change in a country's politics."[11]

Now, consider how speculation and related financial trading can impose such uncertainty or irregularity on the global economy as to divert attention from domestic solutions to saving or restoring the value of the dollar, of the yen, of the mark, or other currencies which are so grossly misaligned in their currency exchange rates from this speculative and related trading. William Greider recited his findings from the perspective of the mid-1990s.

"The dollar, the deutschmark and the yen, in descending order of importance, were the three main reserve currencies that served as anchors for global trade, but each was subject to its own continuing uncertainty and dramatic volatility. The monthly swings in exchange value between the dollar and the deutschmark, for instance, typically ran around 5 percent a month and frequently greater than 10 percent. In 1995, the dollar lost 20 percent of its value against the yen in three months. Then, as the three leading governments intervened to staunch the decline, the dollar lurched back upward and three months later, was 20 percent stronger. How could the market be right about money-values when it was always changing its mind?

Across several years the market shifts in currency values were so extreme and contradictory they might be described as irrational. The dollar, for example, was said to be worth 260 yen in 1985, then marked down to 130 yen by 1987, then up to 160 yen in 1990, down again to 80 yen in early 1995, then up to 100 yen a few months later. Nothing in the economic reality corresponded to those violent swings in financial numbers. The United States did not suddenly become half as strong, then suddenly much more productive nor did Japan's underlying value as a national economy abruptly weaken, then surge. As Rob Johnson said, everyone runs to portside, then to starboard, but the boiling process of reallocations never achieve equilibrium."[12]

The volatility of the dollar-yen exchange rate could not have resulted from changing trade balances between the two nations. The U.S. has continued in an uninterrupted fashion to have a trade deficit with Japan. The clear separation of currency exchange values from economic purpose (selling of goods and services) is illustrated by the outcome of efforts of the U.S. and Japan in 2000 to keep the dollar from declining. Despite significant intervention efforts in buying dollars by both the U.S. and Japan, the actual result in the exchange value of the dollar remained unchanged due to the enormous selling of dollars by currency funds to the point that their speculative strategy involving many more reserves of currencies nullified the joint effort of the U.S. and Japan.

Given the above showing of the volatility of currency exchange rates, one can easily see the difficulty of a nation exercising established fiscal and monetary policies addressed to the domestic conditions of a nation. Consider the following attempts at national economic domestic policies:

For example, " if a country restricts its money supply in order to fight inflation, the consequent rise in the domestic interest rates causes an inflow of capital that then defeats the original policy objective and raises the exchange rate."[13] (The fight against inflation is defeated by the increase in the money supply and therefore bank reserves which inflows of deposits in

U.S. banks cause. This makes more spending domestically possible and there would re-ignite inflation. The higher interest rate offered initially at American banks increases the demand for dollars to be deposited here. This increased demand will tend to increase the exchange value of the dollar which is collateral to the government's initial purpose.) Thus although the floating exchange rate is desired by nations because it frees them to ignore any mandatory fixed value of its currency to other foreign currency and allows them to address monetarily and fiscally domestic economic needs, there remains the distortions caused by speculation, multinational intra-firm transfers, and temporary capital transfers as responses to domestic policies but have no real connection to domestic goals--that is these capital flows are only opportunistic and not committed investment. Arthur Burns in testifying before Congress in 1973 offered these objections to the floating exchange rate system:

> "First, in my judgment, the floating exchange rate systems that has figured so heavily in academic discussions is a dream that will continue to elude us. Even for a country with as low a ratio of international trade to gross national product as that of the United States, the repercussions of exchange rate changes on the domestic economy can be substantial. Under a floating exchange rate system, governments are always apt to be subject to political pressure by business, agricultural, and labor interests for   protection against large movements of exchange rates--which may mean new controls or central bank intervention or both.
>
> Second, a system of floating exchange rates may lead to political friction and competitive national economic policies. From time to time suspicions will be generated that this or that country has been manipulating its exchange rate at the expense of the interest of its trading partners. In such an atmosphere, whether for defensive or retaliatory reasons, governments may impose controls on capital flows or on current transactions. It is true, of course, that suspicion and political friction may be present under any type of exchange rate regime.
>
> Third, the uncertainty associated with floating exchange rates may lead in time to some erosion of international trade, particularly in the case of

equipment purchases that require long-term financing and when profits margins are slim. These uncertainties may also weaken private foreign investment--especially in long-term bond issue.

Fourth, exchange rate fluctuations under a floating regime may add further to the difficulties that some governments already have in carrying out suitable fiscal and monetary policies. There is a danger, for example, that a temporary exchange rate depreciation will get translated into permanent price level increases through upward revisions of nominal (money) wages. Moreover, floating exchange rates may themselves become a tool of business cycle policy, and thereby lead at times to neglect of appropriate domestic policies."[14]

Before one is eager to be persuaded by Burns and the subsequent global experience with floating exchange rates, we should be reminded why the fixed rate exchange system proved too burdensome for national domestic policies. Let's use an example to remind us: Suppose France is required under the fixed exchange rate system to maintain a ratio of 8 Francs to a Dollar. Then suppose that France begins to experience annual inflation of 15% due to her scarcity of productive capabilities after World War II making domestic goods hard to find and therefore expensive. To lower inflation, France raises interest rates at her banks to 9 percent, about 3 percent above that offered in the U.S. Due to France's higher interest rates, investors/depositors in U.S. transfer their dollars to France in exchange for francs which are then deposited or invested to take advantage of France's higher interest rates. Because of an increased demand for francs and a decreased demand for dollars, the franc assumes an exchange value rate of 5 francs to a dollar. Under Bretton Woods, France is obligated to restore the exchange rate of 8 francs to a dollar. How would this be accomplished--by increasing the demand for dollars and reduced the demand for francs. France could buy enough dollars to increase the demand for dollars by selling francs. This assumes sufficient French reserves of francs and other currencies to use to buy the dollars. In attempting this method, France has to battle speculators who have many more currency reserves and any global trade and investment disturbances which this effort to correct a currency imbalance may trigger. The primary immediate tool for France is to lower her interest rates and thereby lower the international demand for francs. This move would contradict the initial effort at fighting inflation with a smaller money supply which high interest rates could establish. So what is the solution for all purposes, both domestic and international, commercial markets and financial markets? And how absorbed should the Fed become in wrestling with the value of the dollar, with trade deficits, with speculation? Has the global significance of the dollar empowered the Fed with greater ability to exercise its monetary powers effectively or has the Fed been somewhat disabled by the fact that the prominence of the dollar in international economic transactions created the "Tiffin dilemma" which holds that the more the dollar is used throughout the world as the means of exchange the weaker the controls become of the United States in maintaining the strength of the dollar vis-à-vis other currencies. This is due to "the fact that the world economy needed the United States to pump dollars into the monetary system to maintain liquidity' lead to "to the fact that doing so undermined the value of the dollar and its role as a global monetary standard" (Robert Schaeffer op. cit page 39). Moreover, the extensive acceptance of the dollar as a stable currency for oil transactions, in particular, created an independent pool of dollars beyond the immediate regulation of the Fed or the U.S. Treasury. This leveling influence began with our military presence in Europe and in Japan where dollars were used extensively for military purchases and payroll. From this beginning the path of our financial exposure to world-wide economic transactions became even more intricate and beyond our government's control. One such independent source of dollars was the "Euromarket" which evolved mostly from the dollars provided by the earnings of the oil-producing countries.

"By the 1970s, for every dollar U.S. banks were lending to non-Americans from their domestic bank offices, they were lending six or seven more from offshore facilities that collectively came to be called the Euromarket. This pooling of funds, mostly in dollars, started in Europe to accommodate the financial needs of Communist China, but it soon became a global money pool that could be used by borrowers anywhere. The distinguishing feature of the Euromarket is that the money is denominated in a currency different from the official currency where the deposits are located. All such money is largely beyond the reach of national regulators in the countries of origin. When U.S. companies in need of capital abroad resorted to the Euromarket, they were complying with the U.S. policy to restrict capital outflows from the United States. But the buildup of this huge pool of offshore dollars created a formidable alternative to the U.S. capital market. IBM was the pioneer among U.S.-based companies to make creative use of the Euromarket, but soon many U.S. companies operating outside the United States were financing their overseas operations without resorting to banks in their home country. The Euromarket expanded into bond issues and then began offering a menu of increasingly arcane money products. Soon it was serving as a 'connecting rod' for financial markets around the world that once were entirely separate."[15]

Added to this 'Tiffin effect" of the profusion of dollars throughout the world was the intensified spread and use of 'Eurodollars' deposited by Arab oil-producing countries from their earnings. Enormous holdings of dollars in European banks by Middle East oil producers and others tended to lower the value of the dollar. Countries found it necessary to depart from any fixed value of their currencies to a dollar. The result was a series of U.S. policies which reflected a dollar in decline as the accepted currency for global trade and investment:

(1) In 1971, Nixon closed the 'gold window', declaring that the dollar would no longer be redeemed in the U.S. in gold.

(2) Federal Reserve Chairman, Paul Volker, raised the interest rate to fight inflation. However, since the dollar was a reserve currency for the world, the Fed had unwittingly raised interest rates everywhere. The result was fluctuating interest rates and currency exchange rates throughout the world. This transformed the international trading of goods and services into "buying, selling, and lending of monetary products worldwide."(Ibid

p369 "Most of it had little or nothing to do with investment in either production or commerce" (See Robert Schaeffer, Ibid page 369) With financial markets left unrestrained or weighed by concrete investment in plants, equipment, or R&D, the electronic ease in transmission of trading in financial instruments and currencies became even farther removed from the real world of goods and services.

(3) The U.S. perceived need to increase exports in the late 1970s in order to rescue an economy impacted by 'stagflation'(double-digit inflation and double-digit unemployment) resulted in the U.S. efforts to have European nations to stimulate their economy so that more U.S. exports could be purchased abroad. Either through lower interest rates or increased government spending, the European countries were to create a 'locomotion' effect whereby European economic growth would lead to U.S. economic growth through exports. This reflected a decreasing autonomy by the U.S. to correct economic domestic distress through monetary or fiscal policies of our own.

(4) Ironically, the dollar was considered to be too high in the mid-1980s, leading to the Plaza Accords which initiated an effort by Japan, Germany, the U.S. and others to lower the value of the dollar

(5) By all accounts, the Plaza Accords failed to achieve the desired devaluation of the dollar and this lead to the Lourve efforts at international coordination in finance.

All of the above are indicators of the loss of autonomy, perhaps sovereignty, by governments in the efforts to stimulate their own economy and/or maintain price stability, and protect the value of their currency in the international economy. Barnett and Cavanaugh provided this troubling look in The Confidence Game written during the 1990s:

"Governments are periodically taught chilling lessons about how much control they have lost over the money they print. In September 1992, a frenzy of twenty-four-hour-a-day trading in European currencies forced the central banks of Finland, Italy, Spain, and Britain to devalue their currencies and to spend DM24 billion to prop up the lira and f10 billion to keep the British currency afloat. The British prime minister, who had made a public vow never to do what currency speculators around the world forced him to do, could not defend the pound even after the Bank of England raised interest rates 5 percentage points. The exchange of one currency for another, according to estimates of the Bank of International Settlements, is now about $640 billion a day. Not more than 10 percent of this huge volume of currency trading that causes governments to quake and some to fall has anything to do with normal commercial transactions, in which people or companies actually need to convert one currency to another to purchase foreign goods or services No longer rooted in any community or nation, money was losing any relationship to the concrete world of goods and services. The value of money was now totally afloat and was based solely on how it was viewed by money traders and speculators.'[16]

Chapter Eight Notes

1. 1. Campbell McConnell, Economics, (New York: McGraw-Hill, 1981 8th ed.) page 851
2. Ibid, page 848
3. Ibid, pages 849-850
4. Ibid, page 848
5. See Kelko, Restructuring the World Economy,(New York: Pantheon, 1988) pages 79, 113. And 193
6. 6. Sarah Anderson and John Cavanagh With Thea Lea, Field Guide to the Global Economy, (New York: Free Press,2000) page 33
7. William Greider One World, Ready or Not,(New York: Simon & Shuster Touchstone, 1998)page 137 for global trade in general and pages 22-23 for U.S. trade.
8. Ibid, page 137
9. 9. See Kolko op. cit. pages 26-27 and Gilpin in The Political Economy of International Trade (Princeton: Princeton U. Press 1987) page 195
10. Gilpin op. cit. page 144
11. Paul Volker Changing Fortunes (New York: Times Books, 1992) pages 231-232
12. William Grieder op. cit. 249
13. Gilpin op. cit. page 195
14. As quoted in Campbell McConnell op. cit. page 856
15. Barnett and Cavanaugh "The Casino Economy" page 320
16. Ibid, page 320

CHAPTER NINE

PARELLEL 7 CONFRONTING INTERNATIONAL CURRENCY TRADING; IDENTIFYING CAUSES AND EFFECTS TO DETERMINE APPROPRIATE POLICY RESPONSES:

GLOBALIZATION GONE TOO FAR

Scholars have taken a recent view that the nation-state will be or is undergoing a fundamental transformation whereby the forces of globalization will compel nations to abandon their modern duties of 'establishing justice, ensure domestic tranquility, provide for the common defense, promote the general welfare, and secure the blessings of liberty' as set forth in the U.S. Constitution. These obligations of representative government will be replaced by the dictates of a rather suffocating global economy. Philip Bobbitt set forth in his <u>Shield of Achilles</u> that the following path of modern governments will be altered:

> Very simply, the victorious Western nation-states of the Long War, plus West Germany and Japan, by relying on the market to allocate resources efficiently within their domestic economies effectively extrapolated this approach to all the states of their alliance. What had been true within a single state proved true among states. The attempt to control currencies and investment in the socialist states turned out to be a crippling mistake, draining away investment that might have been indifferent to the human rights shortcomings of such regimes and walling those states off from international trade that require convertible currency. The nation-state which had established its reputation as a provider of welfare to the nation by guaranteeing a unified nation market and providing protection against foreign competition and access to foreign markets, was super-charged when the liberal democracies applied the same principles to their interstate trade and finance. The effect of the reduction on direct controls and taxes on capital movements, the liberalization of long-standing regulatory constraints on financial services, the expansion of relationships with offshore financial harbors, and the disintermediation that accompanied these steps made states much wealthier. At a price.* (Shield of Achilles, page 220)

The nation-state will be obligated to abandon the above conditions of legitimacy and morph into the market state in the following manner:

What are the characteristics of the market-state? Such a state depends on the international capital markets and, to a lesser degree, on the modern multinational business network to create stability in the world economy, in preference to management by national or transnational bodies. Its political institutions are less representative (though in some ways more democratic) than those of nation-state. The Open Market Committee of Federal Reserve and the electronic referendum (to take two extremes) are more characteristic of market-state than the elegant electoral representative institutions envisioned by Hamilton and Madison or the mass election campaigns of Roosevelt and Johnson. Like the nation state, the market state assesses its economic success or failure by its society's ability to secure more and better goods and services, but in contrast to the nation-state it does not see the State as more than a minimal provider or redistributor. Whereas the nation-state justified itself as an instrument to serve the welfare of the people (the nation), the market-state exists to maximize the opportunities enjoyed by all members of society. For the nation-state, a national currency is a medium of exchange; for the market-state it is only one more commodity. Much the same can be said about jobs; for the nation-state, full employment is an important and often paramount goal, whereas the market-state, the actual number of persons employed is but one more variable in the production of economic opportunity and has no overriding intrinsic significance. If it is efficient to have large bodies of persons unemployed, because it would cost more to the society to train them and put them to work at tasks for which the market has little demand, then the society will simply have to accept large unemployment figures. Mark Tushnet has noted this development:

Small-scale programs with modest aims characterize the new constitutional order: any deficiencies in the provision of health care or in income security after retirement are to be dealt with by market-based adjustments rather than ambitious redistributive initiatives. Similarly, poverty is to be alleviated by ensuring that the poor obtain education and training to allow them to participate actively in the labor market, rather than providing generous public assistance payments.

Nothing facilitates this transformation more completely and unaccountably than the financial market's grip on global commerce whereby currency and security trading far exceeds that of goods and services. National central banks attempt to compensate for any economic distortions caused by currency speculation or improper banking practices. This chapter seeks to expose the innate contradictions contained in the Fed attempting to conform internationally and at the same time performing according to its domestic mandate. (A simple review of how international currency exchange rates are supposed to work would assist the reader.)

Is a currency misalignment (a dramatic historical departure from exchange rates) due to

(A.) a national extraordinary economic surge in growth expressed in exception trade surplus such as in China, today? Or

(B.) is it due to national manipulation of its currency to accommodate perceived need to increase exports or even to increase demand for its currency through higher interest rates. Or

(C.) is it due to natural swings in currency exchange rates caused by the emergence of newly developed nations or nations nearing economic development. The changed nature of participation by these nations in their trade participation causes a change in demand and supply of their currencies. For example, developing countries which predominately exported commodities and imported finished goods would have a deficiency of dollars, historically. These countries converting their economy to a more balanced one between commodities and finished goods would alter the demand and the supply of their currencies in the global market. Recent articles illustrate this as shown below:

From Wall Street Journal, October 15, 2010, page A15 read the headlines: EMERGING-MARKET CURRENCIES SOAR; Investors Push U.S Dollar lower, Further Fueling Tensions Among Economies Competing on Exports. This graph illustrates this changing currency exchange rates and the conflicts it invites.

Financial Friction: Asian Currencies Rise, U.S. Dollar Falls as Trade Deficit Widens

Low interest rates in developed countries and the prospect of easier Federal Reserve policy are sending a flood of money to emerging markets, pushing up their currencies faster than some governments would like.

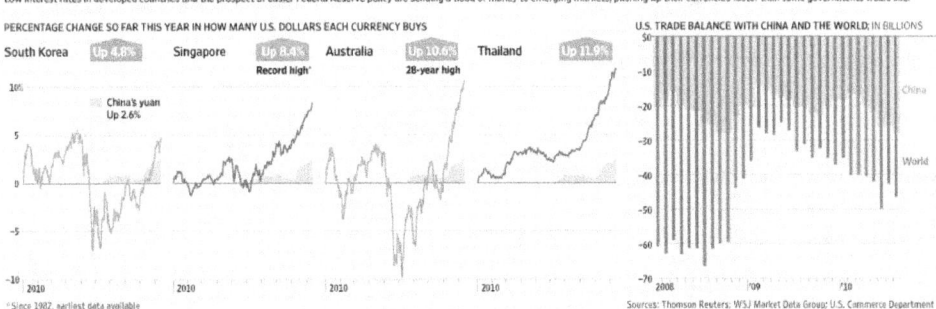

How should economies compete with each other? 1. Through productivity improvements? 2. Through resource advantages? 3. Through the development of resources from their natural or original condition? 4. Through entrepreneurship and marketing--the management of the firm and industry? 5. Or if all of these fall short of national advantage, resort to monetary solutions such as devaluation of the currency or raise/lower interest rates which are artificially (unrelated to the making of goods and services) designed to make one's products cheaper on the international market or alternatively raise the value of one's currency by raising interest rates.(For sole purpose of stabilizing one's currency)

If a nation seeks competitive advantage through currency manipulations, what consequences adhere to this policy for that country and its trading and diplomatic relationships throughout the globe? When does the exchange value of one's currency become the highest priority, both domestically and internationally? Consider the following Business Week article, "What Happens If The Dollar Crashes?" Trade wars could break out, overexposed banks might collapse, and that just for starters.

Coy lists the following possible consequences if the dollar declined another 25% against each major world currency (in addition to the 15% decline since March 2009)

(a) It would take $2 to buy a single euro, leading to more sales globally for U.S. manufacturers and more foreign tourism in the U.S.

(b) But inflation would rise as imported goods would now cost more since it would take $2 to buy one euro price of an imported good from Europe as well as increased number of dollars to buy Chinese imported goods.

(c) With the dollar declining, investors would sell their holdings of dollars (deposited in U.S. banks or throughout the world) for other currencies. This means, for example, less dollars in U.S. banks to lend to U.S. consumers and business.

(d) The lower dollar value hurt those nations such as Japan and China who depend upon exports for economic growth and dollar reserves as a source of investment capital.

(e) This could lead to trade wars conducted through currency devaluations, producing swings in the exchange rates and even more incentives for currency speculation.[2]

Coy notes in the article that federal regulators are sensitive to possibilities similar to those listed above. He quotes an anonymous federal source, "We're not looking quarter to quarter, we're looking hour to hour and minute to minute at what these risks are."[3] Coy cites that (as of October2009) the dollar is down 11% against the Japanese yen, 16% against the euro, 21% against the Canadian dollar, and about 30% against the Brazilian and Australian currencies which are benefiting from a commodity price spike. Against a broad market basket of all U.S. trading partners and adjusted for inflation, the dollar has fallen 15% from the spring high."[4]

Fueling this decline is the 'rock bottom' federal funds rate of zero to 0.25% which allows investors to borrow cheaply (under U.S. interest rates) and then sell the dollars for currencies of countries who offer better returns through stocks and bonds earnings.

The Wall Street Journal article, "New Euro Woe: 'Carry Trade"[5] cites this practice of borrowing cheap in one currency to invest in a nation's currency offering higher returns as using the euro as a favorite funding currency of the 'carry trade' as the practice is called. Concerning the usage of the dollar, Coy cited U.S. trade deficits as driving down the dollar. Foreign central banks have begun to buy less dollars for their foreign currency reserve holdings. Countries which have revealed their new stance in foreign currency reserve holdings "have designated 63% of their new reserves into lures and yen in the second quarter"[6]

While a devalued dollar increases the competitiveness of U.S. exports, any significant movement towards a trade advantage for American business could trigger a sense that as Coy states "that the dollar's decline was starting to snowball out of control. "At that point," Coy continues, "the invisible 'force field' protecting the dollar would fade away, says Martin D. Weiss, chairman of Weiss Group, a financial data and analysis firm from Jupiter, Fla. Says Weiss: "We could become ordinary mortals and more vulnerable to attacks on our currency." [7] As Coy indicated any attempt by the world's central banks to protect the dollar would probably be defeated by currency speculators. (As happened in late 1990s when the yen and the dollar alignment efforts were undermined by speculators.) The possibility that the decline of the dollar could reach crisis proportions has been estimated by Ashraf Laidi, chief foreign exchange strategist at CMC Markets, a London currency and commodity brokerage, at around 30% to 40%. Any great decline could produce the following as described by Coy:

"If the dollar did tumble, import prices might rise faster than most economists now expect. New research by Columbia University economists Emi Nakamura and Jon Steinsson shows that the 'pass-through' from a cheap currency to high import prices was underestimated because poor data. In other words, inflation could emerge more quickly than is commonly believed. It would be disastrous for the economy if the Federal Reserve had to raise interest rates.[8]

Does the following present an ominous peril to the U.S. economy as to justify Fed intervention to support the dollar or is the author of this piece overly concerned as are others. Reviewing the path of the dollar as shown below, should we be concerned enough to give monetary priority to stabilizing the dollar's value?

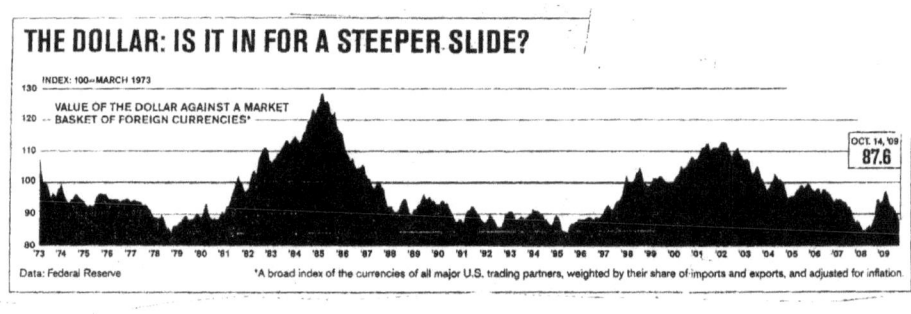

The volatility in the value of the dollar as shown above has resulted in the dollar steadily eroding in value against the euro and other currencies "since 2002 as U.S. budget and trade deficits ballooned, but fears of an American recession and credit crisis have sent the dollar to stunning lows amid predictions that the slump will continue for a long time."[10] The Indianapolis Star reported the following decline of the dollar's exchange value:

"The euro traded for a record $1.5625 before declining to $1.5586 Thursday, while the dollar dropped below 100 Japanese yen for the first time since November 1995. It traded as low as 99.75 yen before recovering some ground to 101.68 yen. The dollar also recently hit a 10-year low against the Chilean peso and fell to its lowest level against Brazil's real since the nation floated its currency in 1999."

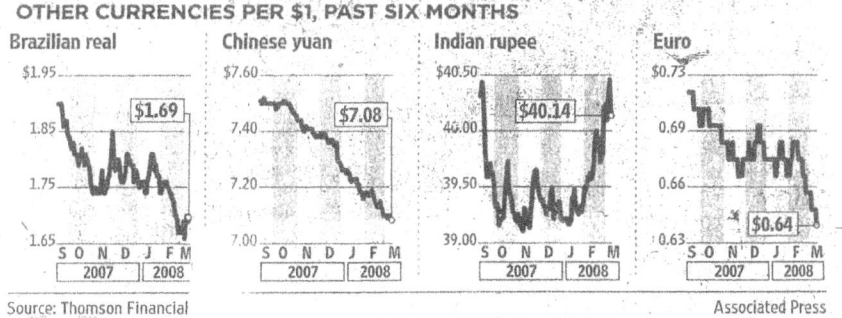

DOWN ON THE DOLLAR
Volatility in the value of the dollar has encouraged people of other countries to use the euro and their own currencies.

OTHER CURRENCIES PER $1, PAST SIX MONTHS

Source: Thomson Financial — Associated Press

The difference between any crisis described above and previous ones could be critical in the way the Indianapolis Star cited:

> "While low dollar cycles have come and gone for decades, experts caution that it's now much more difficult to predict when this one will end because the euro didn't exist as competition for the dollar before.
>
> During previous U.S. economic downturns big foreign funds typically snapped up U.S. treasuries, helping to shore up the dollar to a certain degree. But the euro and currencies from other nations are now seen as legitimate options, and interest rates are higher outside the United States.--meaning the funds can get better returns on investments elsewhere."[11]

Any disturbing misalignment of the dollar exchange value cannot expect to be moderated or corrected through the international trading of goods and services. We have seen how financial trading far exceeds the dollar value of goods and services trading globally. Adding to this disproportionate number of financial transaction world-wide is the manner in which they are conducted. The hazards which electronically transmitted financial transactions are accomplished pose to responsible and effective fiscal and monetary policies of nations has been revealed in the past few decades of the 20th century and the first decade of the 21st century. Consider whether the following characteristics of electronically transmitted financial/currency transactions promote economic vitality in growth with acceptable price levels:

(a) "The number of electronic transfers amounts to only 2 percent of the total transfers yet these transactions involve 5 out of every six dollars that move in the world economy"[12]

(b) "Well over $2trillion a day travels across the street or across the world at unimaginable speed as bits of electronic information."[13]

This removal from the real economic world of goods and services exchanges is reflected in the description below:

"As Felix Rohatyn of Lazard Freres puts it: 'People buy and sell blips on an electronic screen. They deal with people they never see, they talk to people on the phone in rooms that have no windows. They sit and look at screens. It's almost like modern warfare, where people sit in bunkers and look at screens and push buttons and things happen.' (Sampson 1989)[14]

(c) Shifted investment in labor (clerks, tellers, messengers, etc.) to capital investing of $15billion for information technology of automatic systems by commercial banks.[15]

(d) Adding to the volatility is the recent adoption by China of electronic trading in its currency, the Yuan. As reported by the Wall Street Journal article of October 8, 2010 "it is a small start, and trading is limited to the relative small pool of Yuan circulating in Hong Kong. Still, the advent of electronic trading of the Yuan and its likely expansion to traders beyond

Hong Kong mark an important step toward building the infrastructure to support a global market for the currency." The article noted that, "China's government has made a series of moves in the past year to encourage the Yuan's use outside of China, an effort to become less dependent on the dollar for trade and investment. The moves are allowing pools of Yuan to accumulate in bank accounts outside of China, particularly Hong Kong."[16] Electronic trading of the Yuan has already lead to offshore trading by German banks where in offshore trading the "Yuan has traded as much as 1.6% stronger against the dollar than it did onshore, according to data from Deutsche Bank."[17] Despite the emerging growth in the use of the Yuan, China has made an effort to keep the yuan from rising too fast in its exchange value. This effort at suppressing the exchange value of the yuan has led to conflicts between China and Japan, China and the United States, and with others. Are the following reported currency conflicts to be regarded with deep concern or will they be reconciled through the play of demand and supply for currencies imposed by economic development throughout the world as we have noted the growing attractiveness of the currencies of Brazil, Australia, and others experiences growth.

What role should Fed monetary policies of interest rates assume in the following currency debates/challenges? An examination of the proper role of monetary policy will be postponed until the completion of the development of this parallel between the 1920s struggle with the gold standard and dealing with the aftermath of the Crash of 1929 and today's dilemma for the Fed which the international financial crisis and the on-going conflict presented by currency policies of various nations has done. Also, perhaps the final parallel between 1929-32 and today is the credit crunch which both periods suffered. When this final parallel is developed, we will pursue the proper role of the Fed.

What responses, fiscal, monetary, or legislative should the U.S. take in response to our perceived China exploitation of its currency, the Yuan, in keeping it artificially low in order to promote its exports. The Wall Street Journal in its issue of June 22nd, 2010 reported the following : "Although China's Yuan rose against the dollar on June 21, 2010 perhaps signaling a Chinese willingness to 'ease the currency peg' against the dollar, Congress still has the following legislation pending to correct the alleged misalignment of the Yuan against the dollar:"

"Senator Charles Schumer (D. NY) a loud antagonist on the issue, intends to move forward with legislation aimed at China that would give the administration power to take action against countries with 'misaligned currencies'. The legislation would authorize a range of actions, including pursuing settlement proceedings through the World Trade Organization." Among legal accusations would be the assertion under this new law that misaligned currencies constitute a subsidy from that country's government. The rise of the yuan is attributed to an increase demand by investors for the currency. This promise of a market correction is cautioned by the authors of the article, Batson and Hitt, with the following observations:

"Trading in the Chinese currency was closely watched Monday as investors and policy makers world-wide tried to gauge the significance of the policy move. How much China lets the currency move will help determine to what extent it can defuse tensions with its trading partners and help shift the balance of its own economy toward consumer spending. In the past, the central bank has generally used the central parity rate to manage daily trading in the yuan. Officially, the rate is based on market forces, but in reality is up to the central bank's discretion, and is taken as a signal of policy intentions. Market participants said it was significant that the central bank allowed the Yuan to strengthen in spot trading, where it often intervenes."[18]

Was this a signal that the Chinese would permit the exchange value of the Yuan to be determined by market forces of supply and demand without intervention by its central bank? This issue may have been somewhat 'mooted' or postponed by the action taken by Japan concerning the yen. In order to lower the exchange value of the yen, the Japanese sold an estimated trillion yen in exchange for $20 billion. Japan was concerned about the rising value of the yen and its harming of Japanese exports. It is being speculated that this action by Japan "could take pressure off the Chinese to allow their own currency to appreciate."[19] The action of the Japanese to prevent the appreciation of its yen typifies policies of other nations who are greatly dependent upon exports for growth. Wall Street Journal in its article of September 29, 2010 pages C1-C2 recites this currency disposition:

> "Tensions are growing in the global currency markets as political rhetoric heats up and countries battle to protect their exporters, raising concerns about potentially damaging trade wars. At least half a dozen countries are actively trying to push down the value of their currencies, the most high-profile of which is Japan, which is attempting to halt the rise of the yen after a 14% rise since May. In the U.S., Congress is considering a law that targets China for keeping its currency artificially low, and in Brazil, the head of the central bank said the country may impose a tax on some short-term fixed income investments, which have contributed to a rise in the real."[20]

Some currency movements are caused by market influences which are opposed by central banks attempting to manage their currency values.

> "Part of the challenge is that the moves in the currency markets that are raising the ire of central banks and politicians are being driven by longer-term investors.
>
> Stronger economies in the emerging markets are attracting capital from the developed world, pumping up demand for local currencies.
>
> Talk of additional quantitative easing in the U.S. signals to investors that interest rates there will remain close to zero for a long time.
>
> Meanwhile, inflation is building in Asia, forcing interest rates higher. Investors see that mismatch and are shuttling money from west to east, attracted to the higher yields."[21]

"Malaysia, on the other hand, has allowed a stronger ringget for the independence a free-floating currency gives to monetary policy makers and the spur it gives to its exporters to become more efficient."[22]

A currency conflict is brewing among China and her Asian trading partners as the lower Yuan has made the Japanese yen and other Asian currencies nuncupative in their exports. Wall Street Journal, September 17, 2010 cited the following:

"Japan launched its battle against a strong yen this week, joining other Asian governments facing a common currency predicament: competing with China.

While attention was focused on the yen's 15-year high against the dollar as Japan began currency intervention Wednesday, the yen also was near its highest point against the Chinese Yuan in a decade.

That puts Japan---an advance country--in the same boat as such export-dependent economies as South Korea, Thailand and Taiwan, which both compete and trade with China and find it necessary to routinely intervene in currency markets to adjust their currencies, taking the yuan into account."[23]

Some adjustments in currencies are needed because of currency trading and speculation which distort any natural changes in currency exchange values from the buying and selling of goods and services. Even the efforts of nation's central bank's intervention can distort any natural changes in exchange values caused by the selling of goods and services across borders.

"In reality, Asia's economies outside of China have seen their currencies rise in anticipation of, rather than in reaction to, China's currency moves. Since China signaled a change in its foreign-exchange policy on June 19, investors have sent money into other Asian currencies, hoping to ride the currency wave higher, even as the Yuan has stayed mostly still.

South Korea, Thailand and Singapore have all seen their currencies rise about 3% against the Yuan since last June announcement, exacerbating worries about export competitiveness. All three, in addition to Taiwan, have been active in currency markets, buying dollars and pushing their reserves to record or near-record levels. Asian countries outside China hold $2.9trilllion in reserves. China has $2.5 trillion.

These countries have decided to intervene, according to analysts, in part because not doing so would cause their currencies to rise and make them less competitive in relation to China. In Japan's case, China and the U.S. are the most important trade partners, with China receiving 18% of its exports, while the U.S. accounts for 16%. While Japan has been staying out of the currency intervention in line with general agreement among Group of Seven countries, some economists see it as one of Tokyo's few options to protect its fragile economic recovery."[24]

However, these currency maneuvers by the Chinese, Japanese, and others may be only 'sparring' before a full-blown crisis erupts as speculated in its October 1, 2010 the Wall Street Journal in an article entitled, "Dollar, Euro, and Yen Engage in 'Ugly Contest'" page C5.

B. WORKING THROUGH THE EXCHANGE AND INTERNATIONAL FINANCIAL MARKETS TO ACHIEVE DOMESTIC PRICE STABILITY AND A SOUND EXCHANGE VALUE FOR THE DOLLAR:

In measuring which priority to give an emphasis, what guidelines has the past provided the Fed in seeking domestic price stability and a sound dollar on the international currency exchange market? Have the Fed's selections of policy emphasis in either deferring to domestic needs or alternatively showing overly concern for the exchange value of the dollar been in harmony with the economic wisdom on these matters? In will be helpful to examine how the currency exchange regimes were designed to work and why some were abandoned for an alternative currency exchange policy. In examining the rise and fall of the exchange value of the dollar during recent decades perhaps we can detect different influences acting upon its value, internationally. Look for two or three commanding factors which can determine the value of the dollar: (a) domestic economic trends, (b) government intervention to protect or alter the value of its currency, (c) or international coordinated effort by the central banks of the major trading nations. Study the following path of the exchange value of the dollar during the 1980s as an example of differing influences coming to bear on the dollar's exchange value.

   1. The dollar rose in value between 1980 and 1985 despite the U.S. running a large and growing trade deficit. Conventional economic thinking would hold that since Americans are buying far more imported goods and exchanging dollars for foreign currencies, the dollar would decline as more dollars were being supplied to importers than foreign consumers were demanding dollars to buy our exports. By any economic model of demand and supply where supply increases without a corresponding demand, the price/value of that item (in this case the dollar) will decline. However, the dollar rose in value during this period because of offsetting U.S. domestic economic influences of high interest rates which provided incentives for foreigners to exchange their holdings of foreign currencies to obtain dollars for depositing in American financial institutions or for other investment purposes which would earn the high interest rates. Also, the U.S. economy began to grow during this period and thereby provided other investment opportunities for foreigners who would trade their foreign currencies for dollars to make investments. Both of these factors increased the demand for dollars to the extent that it offset any decline in the dollar attributed to our growing trade deficit.
Political instability in nations that otherwise would have been attractive investment opportunities also increased the demand for dollars as investors sought a stable, developed nation in which to place their currency holdings.

   This rise in the exchange value of the dollar resulted primarily from autonomous domestic policy dictated by domestic crisis of stagflation. There was no currency intervention by the Fed or any coordinated effort by the central banks of the major trading nations. However, the sustained rise of the dollar became a concern for other nations as the U.S. continued to attract investments due to its high interest rates. This led to the Plaza Accords.

    2. The rising trade deficit of the U.S. reached an historic high of $160 billion as the rising dollar made American exported goods too expensive compared to the price of competing foreign goods. In September 1985, the Group of Five central banks of Great Britain, France, Japan, Germany and the United States met at the Plaza Hotel in New York. They reached an agreement called the Plaza Accord which decided that most major currencies needed to appreciate vis-à-vis the dollar. These central banks pledged to intervene in the foreign exchange market by selling dollars to buy the other currencies. (The dollar had begun to weaken that summer). Buy selling dollars to buy the yen, the mark, the franc, the pound the demand for other currencies increased and the supply of dollars increases (with demand unchanged). With more dollars now circulating internationally, its value becomes lower as an increase in supply with demand unchanged causes that item to have a lower value.

    3. The dollar continued to decline until early 1987 when the Group of Five met in Paris and reached a new agreement called the Louvre Accord. The new agreement stated that exchange rates had been realigned sufficiently and that the task now for central banks was to support this new currency exchange realignment through buying and selling of currencies (intervention-not through the normal demand and supply results which global trade would impose.)

    The necessity for government intervention in the currency exchange market has been intensified by the abandonment of the fixed exchange regime installed by Bretton Woods after World War II. Under that agreed exchange system, each foreign currency would retain a fixed exchange rate with the dollar and if their currency would stray from this fixed exchange rate, that government must buy or sell dollars to reinstate the fixed exchange rate. Similar to the gold standard of the 1920s, domestic needs were to be neglected in order to retain this fixed exchange rate. The exchange rate may wander off from the fixed rate due to the normal business activities across the globe which may affect the demand or supply of a currency. Excessive demand for the pound due to its international trade balance would cause a 'misalignment' with the fixed rate of the pound to the dollar. This is unavoidable. British business would not alter their exports or imports day by day or month by month just to keep the pound in harmony with the fixed exchange rate. In fact, ideally trade balances would be self-correcting insofar as currency values are concerned as the demand for British exports would eventually increase the demand for pounds (to buy the exported British goods) so great as to increase the value of the pound vis-à-vis other currencies as to begin to cause a decline in exports. This is the design which comparative advantage translated through currency exchanges is supposed to provide a self-correcting mechanism. However, domestic crisis of inflation or unemployment often took center stage, politically, and mandated that domestic needs be given first priority over any commitment to the fixed currency exchange rate, consequently nations began to impose different commitments to the currency exchange market. One adaptation was the floating exchange rate. Under the floating exchange rate, nations give themselves a viable option in addressing domestic economic needs while providing some conformity to a currency exchange system. The floating exchange rate system permitted a nation to allow its currency to stray from any fixed rate but only within acceptable ranges. In other words, a currency would not be permitted by the Group of Five to assume an historic misalignment where it exchange rate becomes abnormal. However, with the rise of new economic giants like China, who is to say what an acceptable exchange rate for the Chinese yuan is. China's economic experience today bears no meaningful relationship with the history of trading among nations. Arguably the exchange value of the Chinese yuan should evolve as a result of the maturing trade relationships China develops over an extended time.

Some argue that under floating exchange rates, "market forces have produced a volatile dollar exchange rate. Governments have responded by buying and selling dollars to limit the market's volatility and to correct what they see as overvaluation (in 1985) or potential undervaluation (in 1987) of the dollar. The frequency of government intervention in the foreign exchange markets explains why the currency system is often referred to as a managed-float system or a dirty float system."[25]

They argue that the abandonment of the fixed exchange rate system has led to corruptive influences and distorting practices of currency speculation. Countering this opposition, are those who support a floating exchange rate system because it allows a nation to implement monetary policies according to the perceived economic needs of the nation. The arguments pro and con breakdown to these:

For the Fixed rate system: 1. Provides monetary discipline which prevents governments from easily giving in to political pressures to expand a money supply far too rapidly to stimulate growth. 2. It fights against currency speculation which the floating rate invites. "If foreign exchange dealers see a currency depreciating, they tend to sell the currency in the expectation of future depreciation regardless of the currency's long-term prospects." This speculation tends to destabilize the value of a currency by "accentuating the fluctuations around the exchange rate's long-run value." This has the effect of distorting export and import prices.[26]

3. Floating exchange rates causes uncertainty in the business world as volatile changes in the value of the dollar, for example, in rising 6 percent one month but falling 6 percent in the next month. Such volatility hampers business's long term plans or even the execution of short-term contracts for supplies and semi-finished goods. (Intra firm transfers of multinationals are somewhat immune to this destabilizing effect.[27]

Those who favor a floating exchange rate offer the following: 1. They help adjust trade imbalances. This argument is strenuously resisted by those favoring the fixed exchange rate. They question the "closeness of the link between exchange rate and the trade balance." "They claim that trade deficits are determined by the balance between savings and investment in a country, not by the external value of its currency." Depreciation in a currency leads to inflation caused by the resulting increase in imports prices. (it takes more of the nation's currency to buy the import.) The debate on whether the ability of a currency to wander on its own in determining its exchange value often centered on this comparison; "Those who favor fixed rates point out that the 40 percent drop in the value of the dollar between 1985 and 1988 did not seem to correct the U.S. trade deficit. In reply, advocates of a floating exchange rate regime argue that between 1985 and 1992, the US. Trade deficit fell from more than $160 billion to about $70 billion, and they attribute this in part to the decline in the value of the dollar."[28]

Some nations have adopted a pegged system where the" country will peg the value of its currency to that of a major currency so that, for example, as the US dollar rises in value, its own currency rises too. Pegged exchange rates are popular among many of the world's smaller nations." The virtue of the pegged system is as in the fixed rate system, a nation's currency is bound to the fixed 'pegged' rate of another major currency. The country monetary system is disciplined in this way. Yet, the major currency to which the small nation's currency is pegged may change or 'float' in response to currency exchange market changes caused by the changing demand and supply for the major currency. However, if capital is flowing out of the country using the peg and foreign exchange traders are speculating against the pegged currency, smaller nations may feel compelled to abandon the pegged system. This happened to several Asian countries such as Thailand and Malaysia in 1997. However, this capital crisis and currency crisis could have been avoided perhaps if these nations had addressed the domestic irregularities of excessive private-sector debt and expanding current account trade deficits. However, Hong Kong succeeded using its currency pegged to the dollar at "about $1=HK$7.8 despite several concerted speculative attacks." Hong Kong fought off these attacks through the efforts of its currency board which upheld its committed to back its currency with the promise of conversion into dollars. "A country that introduces a currency board commits itself to converting its domestic currency on demand into another currency at a fixed exchange rate.. To make this commitment credible, the currency board holds reserves of foreign currency equal at the fixed exchange rate to at least 100 percent of the domestic currency issued."[29] Hong Kong's success using a currency board has led to other nations' adopting them. At the conclusion of the 20th century, the use of various exchange rate regimes looked like this below:

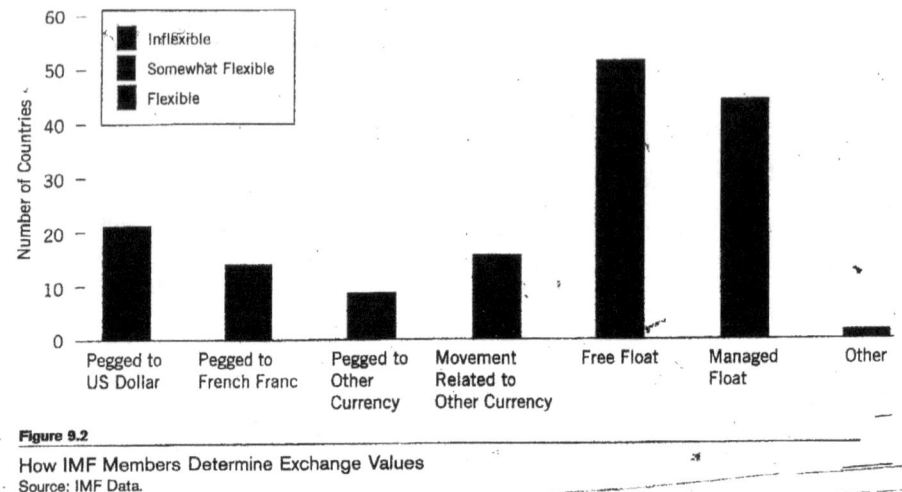

Figure 9.2
How IMF Members Determine Exchange Values
Source: IMF Data.

CHART OF EXCHANGE SYSTEMS[30]

How does today's crisis with China compare to previous confrontations with nations over the value of the dollar, the yen, or the euro?

China seems to subscribe to a managed currency which is unrelated to its Yuan's proper alignment with other currencies as changing economic circumstances in China, Asia, and the developing world would compel. (One does not maintain a trade surplus over an indefinite sustained period when other nations have begun to participate in a more full capacity in the use of natural resources, in the marketing of autos and other durable goods throughout the global economy rather than be content with providing the raw materials.)

What is a proper alignment of major currencies? Such a present stable exchange rate exist today between the Chinese Yuan and the US. Dollar? Or are both nations occupying different stages of economic growth which necessarily cause a significant realignment of the exchange rate of the Yuan and the dollar? Can a nation now committed fully to the international economy retain a stable currency as it currency becomes more available through global markets? On the other hand can nations who have given great emphasis to exports to drive its economy continue to expect countries such as the U.S. to remain content to be the consuming partners of these exporting nations without the latter making any efforts to reverse their trade deficits or their national consuming habits.? Must these nations who depend excessively upon their exports and therefore make every effort to maintain the low exchange value of its trading currency, the yuan in China, come to a realization that a proper economic balance must be achieved through profit-making through exports and through selling to its own citizens/customers. Can such a transition of from an economy of say 70-30 in favor of exporting to one of 50-50 balance between selling abroad and at home be achieved without destabilizing their currency? This may be the agenda for today and for tomorrow. Let's examine the conclusions of most observers on the matter of the role of exchange rates on trade balances. Are these conflicts between China and the U.S. and Japan and others over the alleged artificially low value of the Chinese Yuan unnecessary because currency advantages are marginal and temporary? It is only the immediate advantage gained from devaluation that provides both political and economic gain from it to be irresistible despite the long-term misalignment among currencies it may invite.

Increasing the money supply (expansionary monetary policy) increases national income, lowers the value of the national currency, and increases the price of domestic goods and services. Of these three influences, the income effect tends to predominate in the short and in the long run. By increasing national income, a nation experiences increased purchases of imports with no effect on its exports. (a firm does not increase exports of automobiles or computers as a result of your domestic consumers' increased income. A consumer would go to the local Chrysler dealer to buy a Chrysler, not to Paris Chrysler dealership to buy one.) Expansionary monetary policy decreases domestic interest rates thereby lowering the value of the national currency.(due to reduced demand for the currency for investment in certificates of deposit, bonds, or the currency denominated financial instruments.) Expansionary monetary policy also tends to result in increased domestic prices due to increased consumer demand which easy credit stimulates. However, the exchange effect and the price effect tend to cancel each other in the long run, making the income effect the most predominate trade balance influence[31] (for this effect and for all related effects of exchange, monetary, and fiscal policies referred above and in the following.) Reducing the money supply (contractionary monetary policy) increased the value of the currency, reduces national income, and reduces prices of domestic goods. As in expansionary policy, the income effect predominates as the exchange rate effect and price effect cancel each other. Thus contractionary monetary policy reduces income and a nation's desire for imports.

Expansionary fiscal policy (increased government spending and /or tax reductions) tend to increase national income and thus a nation's purchases of imports without having an effect on its exports. (I.e. increased consumer purchasing power does not increase exports.) Also, expansionary fiscal policy increases demand for domestic products and services with higher prices resulting. These higher prices reduce the competitiveness of the national exports.

A third alternative, other than monetary and fiscal policies, to improve a nation's trade balance is to devaluate its currency. The effect of fiscal policy on exchange rate of a national currency is ambiguous or unclear. Expansionary policy increases a nation's domestic prices and thus increases our trade deficit due to the less competitiveness of our products, both domestically produced and those exported.) Ironically, this non-competitiveness reduces demand for the nation's currency thereby lowering its exchange value. This is an ambiguous effect since domestic inflation cannot be simultaneously a net burden (increased price of exports) and net benefit (reduced exchange rate for the currency.) Thus fiscal policy would normally be conducted without regard to influencing the trade balance through its effect on the exchange rate of the nation's currency. Similarly, contractionary fiscal policy (reduced government spending and/or increased taxes) normally is pursued without regard to any effect on a nation's currency exchange rate. (Since as in expansionary fiscal policy, the effect of contractionary fiscal policy is ambiguous with regard to exchange rates.) However for the United States, international concern for the value of the dollar has resulted in the United States' persistent budget deficits made possible by our high interest rates (during the 1980s) creating investments in our dollar-denominated financial instruments. During the 1980s high interest rates attracted a supply of dollars into the U.S. to be deposited in our banks and other financial institutions and thereby compensated for any 'crowding our' of savings or other sources of capital funds absorbed by government borrowing.

As an instrument of trade policy via its effect on the exchange rate, monetary policy has limited appeal. Its main effect on trade deficits and surpluses is through its effect on national income (contractionary monetary policy of high interest rates reduces national income and therefore decreases imports while expansionary policy of low interest rates increases income and increases imports). While contractionary monetary policy (higher interest rates) will increase foreign investment in the nation's financial institutions, this is normally a short-term effect since these foreign holdings may be immediately transferred to other national accounts in foreign financial institutions. Such 'benefits' derived from high interest rates cannot be regarded as a trade surplus due to their short-term commitment and volatility.

While fiscal and monetary policies have positive/negative effects on our trade balance, they cannot be regarded as essentially trade policy vehicles. They are inherently domestic policy choices in a democracy where the peoples' welfare cannot be subordinated to international goals. Any positive effect of fiscal or monetary policy on a trade balance must be regarded as incidental to the intended domestic economic corrections for which the policies are designed. Where unemployment is high and domestic producer investment low, a nation must address the need for expansionary policies regardless of its immediate effect on trade balances. (However, enormous debt accumulations cannot not be ignored if they are perceived to destabilize the nation's currency and are providing a conduit through which government borrowing is tolerated because foreign deposits in our high interest rate accounts tend to compensate for capital funds which are 'removed' from banks through government sell of its bonds, treasury notes, and other government securities which do not represent liquid lending funds to businesses and consumers.)

Thus, lower exchange rates for a nation' currency must be regarded as an aberration to be sought in circumstances so abnormal as to suggest not only international disequilibrium but also serious disequilibrium in the domestic economy. The correction of one rarely leads to the correction of the other--at least not through the vehicle of financial healing. Under such circumstances of currency/monetary internationally as under the gold standard in the late 1920s and the reoccurring perceived need for Group of Five nations' central banks to reach a coordinated solution on misaligned currencies, it is submitted that the real difficulty lies in the structural inadequacy of domestic economies. For example, the unbalanced economy of the 1920s in which industries such as shoes, clothes, coal mining, textiles, and farming lagged due to lack of investment, infrastructure and business capital. Today, it can be argued that our trade deficit and the volatility of the dollar's exchange value is due to the present unbalanced economy which has 80 percent service industry and an excessive reliance upon imports for durable goods and necessities such as apparel, shoes, coats, etc. This excessive reliance upon imported goods has at least two detrimental effects: (1) this pattern of domestic capital investment deprives our people of jobs which will enhance their skills, security, and well-being. (2) Continued reliance upon 'cheap' imported goods by our low-income families and individuals only secures tunnel vision and provides political, social, and economic resistance to change. Consequently, our exports are impaired by imported goods which may have a modern artificial advantage due to subpar wages and unregulated workplace. Also, the demand for foreign currencies to pay for the imports has an unnatural economic effect on the dollar. This imbedded reliance upon low-priced durable goods (necessary for a middle-class life) and low-priced necessities (necessary for low-income earners to remain above poverty) can only be corrected by structural reform led by capital investment in industries which produce goods desirable and necessary for a modern life style. Part of the dilemma in approaching any solution to this dependency lies in other nations, particularly China, which artificially keep their currency low. These nations are depended upon their exports for growth and typically do not place emphasis on growth through domestic consumption. (Remember the U.S.'s GDP typically has 70 % consumption of its total.) This policy of keeping or placing a nation's currency at a lower exchange rate is known as 'devaluation' of one's currency.

Due to the ambiguous/unclear long term effect that monetary or fiscal policies have on the nation's currency exchange value, some nations which have a great dependency upon their exports will resort to devaluations of their currency. This has been noted above as the reason for the present on-going crisis among China, Japan, the U.S., Asian nations such as South

Korea, and even European concerns. Devaluation is the lowering of the exchange value of a currency through the direct intervention of government policy-not as a result of the interplay of supply and demand in the global exchange of goods and services. If a dollar is reduced from a value of two to every pound to three for every pound, the goods of the United States become cheaper for the British to buy as a pound now will purchase $3 worth of U.S. goods exported compared to the formerly $2 worth of goods a pound would buy. However, if devaluation occurs at full employment, any competitive advantage could be cancelled by domestic inflation which would occur from a reduced supply of goods offered for consumption domestically as goods otherwise available for sale domestically are exported. Exported goods lowered the quantity of goods available for sell on the domestic market. Thus supply of domestic goods is reduced while the demand for those goods remained unchanged or even increased.--this is a recipe for inflation of the prices of exported goods or their substitutes. Devaluation at full employment must be accompanied by increased economic growth or by increased savings. Devaluation remains primarily a device for export-led growth in a depressed economy. However, any economic benefit in terms of jobs, profits, will likely be short-lived as other nations respond with devaluations of their own. Being an artificial advantage not resulting from economic advancement, devaluation has limited success in reversing a nation's trade deficit. Moreover, devaluations by many nations or even a major nation can create financial uncertainty among the trading entities of the global economy. The limited sustained success of currency devaluation, of monetary and fiscal policies, and of trade barriers in international trade and investment lead to regional solutions such as NAFTA and other regional trading blocks consisting of trade agreements between nations concerning tariffs, currency exchange values, labor conditions and environmental control. This feature was not present during the 1920s and will not be developed since this part is concerned only with the parallel concerning the disability that the gold standard imposed on the Fed and what disabilities the Fed faces today for currency conflicts and from the consequences of securitization of financial and security instruments whose destabilizing effects penetrated the banking system of Europe and others. The Fed was compelled to confront the gold dilemma in 1930-31 as it is obligated to rescue banking institutions here and abroad from unsound practices whose consequences joined domestic and international problems and attempted solutions.

Before the fall of Wall Street in 2000-2006: Fed Currency Policies-1987 and Beyond.

On February 18, 1985, Treasury Secretary Baker said he would "not be displeased" if the dollar fell further. Next day, Chairman Volcker countered publicly that the "dollar may have fallen enough."[32] Volcker also rejected a U.S. Treasury communique, recalling, "In a communique proposed by the U.S. Treasury, the significance of which I might have underestimated at the time, there was an effort to include a few words about monetary policy that, to my sensitive ears, at least, suggested that monetary policy should be or would be eased. The wording was rejected by Karl Otto Pohl of the Bundesbank as well as myself."[33] "Exchequer Chancellor Lawson, who controlled U.K. monetary policy also supported Volcker, saying, 'that is was not a turf question, but the realization that on the merits it didn't stand up. Why? Because it is quite impossible to have exchange rate stability and interest rate stability. You can't peg both simultaneously.'"[34]

This exchange of views shows a clear position by those central bankers that domestic monetary policy is a separate decision from seeking to stabilize the dollar through intervention or through changing interest rates. However, this separation is difficult to maintain in the face of gross currency misalignments and huge trade imbalances. In 1988, upon the urging by Baker that the Fed lower the interest rate to help export sales, the Fed resisted, initially, because it felt that incipient inflation was brewing. But then the Fed intervened in both directions within a brief period. This lead to the following insightful comment after Fed efforts to arrest or reverse the dollar's rise then was forced to turn around and buy dollars to keep it from falling too much:

"We have been in on both sides of the market, which gives an impression that we know what the right exchange rate is", Hoskins exclaimed 'I don't feel comfortable that I know what the right exchange rate is, and I'm not sure anyone around this table does I think we run the risk of setting up the public and ourselves for a nice fall in the dollar simply based on expectations By doing this I think we continue to confuse the public as to what our policy is all about and divert attention from our long-term objective of stable prices. And secondly, I think we run the risk of confusing ourselves as to our abilities to influence exchange rates in an appropriate fashion '"[35]

This 'stand in the sand' approach to resisting favoring monetary emphasis on domestic price stability over any effort to change the dollar's exchange value weakened in the face of historic high trade deficits and an alarming national debt. Greenspan warned on November 16, 1988 that "deficit reduction" was crucial because our over reliance on foreign investors to buy U.S. government debt was putting the nation's finance in jeopardy.[36] Increased attention on the dollar's exchange value surfaced again when Secretary of the Treasury, Brady, stated that "he was not overly concerned" about the dollar's recent weakness and said he was opposed to high interest rates to support it.[37] This lead immediately to a rebuff by Volcker as narrated below:

"Brady's comments were very poorly received by already nervous financial markets, which detected a lack of commitment to support the dollar as well as the makings of a Fed-Treasury rift. Greenspan had just expressed concern about the dangers of a foreign loss of confidence in the dollar. Now here was the guy who would be running dollar policy for the next four years signaling he didn't much care. Once again, Fed officials felt forced to stress that they, at least, did care. 'A declining dollar can have adverse consequences for the rate of inflation and therefore can complicate the other major objective of U.S. macroeconomic policy--the preservation and consolidation of the gains made during the 1980s in the area of inflation and internal adjustments'. Johnson said later that day."[38] This did not reassure the market. Also, former comments on the inability to get the dollar's exchange value right and that one could not peg interest rates and exchange rates simultaneously seemed to be replaced by the attempt to join both in some coordinated way.

After the Crash of 1988, Greenspan continued to cautioned against lower interest rates as it might unsettle foreign investors' holdings of dollar-denominated securities and also discourage future holdings of U.S. securities.[39] He offered this frightening scenario: "There could be a 'flight from the future. At the moment, there is investment going on in the longer term of this country. In other words, people are buying longer term bonds, they are still buying stocks, and yields are not all that bad, the exchange rate is soft, but it's no falling on its face.' However, ' it is not all that difficult to imagine a less developed country scenario where what we had would have led to a dramatic collapse in the exchange rate, a huge rise in long-term bond rates or the effective disappearance of the long-term bond market....The stock market would fall away and everything would implode into the short term. And the bill rate would collapse, and we would have all these crazy, horrible events that none of us thinks can happen until we see them.' In that event, the Fed would be forced to raise the discount rate two or three percent, 'and then we would get into the types of problems that a historic monetary collapse always creates. We are far apart from that at this stage, but I suspect a lot nearer than we would like to believe .We could very readily see a major endeavor to shift portfolios out of the dollar-denominated securities into those denominated in other currencies.'"[40] A transcript from the December 16, 1987 meeting of the Fed revealed that "the dollar was a major factor in the decision to leave rates unchanged.") We had noted above that the Fed in 1990 had intervened first on behalf of a high dollar value, then intervened by selling dollars to bring its exchange rate down.[41]

        Given the policy choice of confining monetary efforts to domestic needs i.e. price stability and focusing on the value of the dollar which direction is the Fed presently taking? Interest rates to influence the domestic economy in a desired way or a heavy emphasis upon maintaining an appropriate exchange rate for the dollar? The headlines speak to both: Stimulating the economy and protecting the dollar. Again it seems that the Fed seeks to join both in some mutually compatible manner. We have shown the present controversy which threatens to rage over China's alleged artificially low Yuan which threatens export nations of Asia and is becoming an aggravation in the U.S. Perhaps the crisis which has seized the attention and response of our government is the unraveling of the financial markets and the accompanying financial institutions which threatened to contaminate the real economy and send it into a free fall. Reviewing the following litany of events and responses by the Fed betrays any notion that monetary policy is designed to revive an economy so distressed as ours. Rather than revive, it would seem that the most to be gained is a 'rescue' leaving the revival to more care for discrete matters such as great disparities in income and great imbalance in the structure of industry (too many service jobs-not enough manufacturing), and a new discipline to consumption which bears a more realistic relationship to personal debt. Nevertheless there is little talk of correcting these flaws; the headlines speak more and more to matters of currency and financial regulation. The opinion stated by David Malpass entitled "The Weak-Dollar Threat to Prosperity, Wall Street Journal, October 8, 2009. Basically, Malpass's argument is that a devaluated dollar (given a lower currency exchange rate) causes a flight of capital investment and imitates the plight of Third World nations. He remarked that "Investors have been playing this weak-dollar trade for years, diverting more and more dollars into commodities, foreign currencies and foreign stock markets. This is the Third World way of asset allocation."[42] With low interest rates, business and investors can borrow dollars cheaply and then use them to buy higher valued currency denominated assets. This parallels what low interest rates did in the securitization of financial markets--borrow cheaply to buy higher valued assets. (The difficulty with the financial strategy was the debt was short-term and the returns were long-term. Thus when cash flow become inadequate to pay short-term debts, the strategy collapsed.) We had encounter controversies surrounding the dollar before as early 1980s and then again during the Plaza Accord followed by the Louvre Agreement. But the dollar's value may be elevated into a higher concern by the European dollar crisis caused by the collapse of securitized financial instruments.

Without going into detail as to how securitization of financial securities led to a European dollar crisis, the following account provided by David Wessel will suffice to draw the parallel between the Fed's preoccupation with England's gold reserves and after the British abandoning the gold, with maintaining the proper gold reserves in the U.S. and in European nations as mandated by the gold standard and the Fed's attention being diverted to rescuing Europe from its scarcity of dollars:

"For years, there had been hand-wringing and nay saying about the U.S. dollar losing its status in the global economy to other currencies. But the value of securities issued outside the U.S. denominated in U.S. dollars-as opposed to home currencies of the countries in which the borrowers were located--rose from $322.5 billion in 2005 to $753.3 billion in 2006. That 134 percent increase far surpassed the 25 percent increase in euro-denominated issues. During the credit boom that preceded the Great Panic, the U.S. dollar was gaining market share in global finance, not losing it. With one hand, British and continental European banks were lending dollars to corporate customers and buying U.S. mortgage-linked securities. With the other, they were borrowing dollars in money markets to balance their positions. U.S. banks do the same thing but have one huge advantage: they have billions in ordinary deposits in dollars, so they don't have to borrow as much. European banks, especially those not large enough to have branches in New York or Chicago or Los Angeles, didn't have that option. So they had to rely almost exclusively on borrowing in the very wholesale markets for dollars that were suddenly seizing up."[43]

This "European lust for dollars" as Wessel coined it created a 'liquidity' problem for European banks when they were compelled to provide dollars to their customers instead of euros or other European currencies. David Wessel depicts this dilemma in the following narrative:

>"All this amounted to a classic liquidity shortage in Europe, the kind that 'the lender of last resort' can usually solve, but this time the problem had a twist. The ECB could print euros, the Swiss National Bank could print Swiss francs, but their banks didn't need those. They needed U.S. dollars. In ordinary times, the ECB would hand out euros and let the banks exchange them for dollars on global markets, but those markets weren't working normally. It was an early manifestation of the global nature of the Great Panic: many of the loans and securities that proved to be poisonous were grown in the United States, but they were consumed by banks and investors all over the world whose appetites appeared to be insatiable.

The solution was for the Fed to give dollars to the ECB and take euros in exchange. Then the ECB could lend dollars to its own banks. That was easily done mechanically, but egos and national pride interfered. Key players at the Fed and at the ECB, for different reasons, were reluctant to make what seemed the obvious move."[44]

Part of the problem was the tendency of the ECB to blame the Great Panic on the U.S. As reported by Wessel, when the Fed offered to exchange dollars for euros, the ECB replied, "It's a dollar problem, it's your problem"[45]

However, as the crisis intensified, "the dollar shortage was so acute that reluctance melted away. The swaps began, with the FOMC approving up to $20billion for the ECB-with only half that immediately available--and $4billion to the Swiss National Bank in December. The Fed got euros (and Swiss francs) in return, about as solid collateral as any available. The ECB and the SNB took the risk that banks might not be able to pay back the dollar loans.(From the Fed) Over the next year, the Fed expanded both the list of countries to which it was offering to swap dollars and the size of the swaps. In October 2008, it decided to lift altogether the cap on swaps with the European, British, Swiss, and Japanese central banks and provide as many dollars as their banks wanted."[46]

This may have been called a 'liquidity' problem for European banks, but the distinction between 'liquidity' and possible 'insolvency' for some banks was really a fine distinction without a difference. This is true because underlying any 'liquidity' problem was the fact that many investments made or offered by European banks were the flawed securitized securities of which many now could not be honored in full. The idea that the risk was spread so thin throughout the world in selling these innovative securities and that any risk was adequately insured through AID proved illusionary when AID bordered on bankruptcy. Claims would surfaced alleging that the originating banks and financial institutions of the securitized instruments should be held legally obligated to pay those who had purchased the investments. This liability could add to the already growing list of bankrupt or near bankrupt investment banks. So does the European banking crisis become one of 'liquidity' because the resulting insolvency will occur in the U.S. banking crisis? It is really too facile to treat the entire international banking crisis as one of 'liquidity' when so many banks were burden with unsound loans or investments. It would seem if a bank has acquired too many bad assets (loans or investments) it is merely 'accounting sleigh-of- hand to be able to convert it to one of 'liquidity'. However, in the U.S. 'pending insolvency' was converted into one of 'liquidity' through the U.S. government purchasing the 'tainted assets' of the investment banks. In the late 1929-1932 period, only intervention by major banks in efforts to rescue ailing banks was possible as the Fed did not have any 'veiled' authority to buy distressed assets of banks. As Paul Volcker pointed out in his Changing Fortunes;

> "As a matter of law, The Federal Reserve's authority to intervene is entirely independent of the Treasury's, and it is not too explicit, to put it mildly. Specially, the Federal Reserve has built its intervention practice and the whole swap network on language in the Federal Reserve Act of 1913 that says the Federal Reserve can buy and sell in the open market, at home or abroad, bankers' acceptances, bills of exchange and 'cable transfers'. In those days, money was traded internationally by cable, and a cable transfer usually meant a foreign exchange transaction."
> The explicit authority for the Treasury, and it too is a bit hazy about objectives came later in emergency legislation in 1933 when the United States went off the gold for a while. However, when Treasury intervention started in the early 1960s, the Treasury's own resources for intervention were interpreted as limited to the capital in the Exchange Stabilization Fund (funded in 1934 from the profits of the rise of the price of the government's gold holdings). To assure adequate capacity, Douglas Dillon and Bob Roosa wanted the Federal Reserve to join in, and it was all explained to and understood by the relevant congressional committees."[47] (While potential authority existed for currency intervention, this was not the point of focus in 1929-1931--maintaining the gold standard mandates

was the direction sought, internationally from which all currency exchange adjustments would flow. Also, absolutely no implied or other authority existed to buy 'distressed assets' of banks.--The Fed at its discount window could not legally accept anything but commercial paper and other 'real bills'.)

Today, the Fed has justified in a 'veiled manner' its authority to buy stressed assets of endangered financial institutions. Despite this extra ordinary intervention, the economic crisis in terms of lost jobs, of too many low-paying jobs, of too many part-time and temporary jobs, and of too much dependency upon low-priced imported goods has not abated. The efforts of the Fed have consisted, then, of swaps of dollars for euros and other currencies to avoid financial disaster in Europe and elsewhere, the buying of distressed assets of financial institutions to prevent their collapse, and in the very beginning efforts at coordinated interest rates changes by the major central banks.[48] In both 1929-1932 and in 2006-2008, the concern over international financial stability (first in gold reserves and today on dollar balances in European banks) could not remove an abiding difficulty---too many banks in the U.S. and elsewhere had made too many bad loans or investments and no 'accounting tricks' can cure this reality. Even if the Fed employs the 'trickery'. The distinction between 'liquidity 'and near 'insolvency 'will go far in determining another parallel-that of the credit crunch of 1930-31 and of today.

SO WHICH VOICE IS TO HEARD AND FOLLOWED: FED SHOULD EMBROIL ITSELF IN CURRENCY MISALIGNMENT SOLUTIONS AND ALSO USE 'EXTRA-MONETARY MEANS TO SAVE BANKS FROM INSOLVENCY.   OR   THE FED SHOULD CONFINE ITSELF TO ITS CONGRESSIONAL MANDATE--MAINTAIN PRICE STABILILTY WITH FULL EMPLOYMENT.

Perhaps a recitation of what outcomes currency exchange realignments have produced before will offer some assistance in evaluating the effectiveness and propriety of a Fed overly concerned and active about currency exchange alignments, trade balances, international imbalances in growth, financial markets, and monetary policy. Take this case study from developments of the late 1979-1981 period in assessing the following compelling question: WHAT IS THE PROPER MONETARY POLICY POSITION OF THE FED REGARDING FOREIGN FINANCIAL IMPACTS ON THE U.S. ECONOMY. DOES ALTERNATIVE RESPONSES SUCH AS IMPORT QUOTAS, HIGHER TARIFFS, DEVALUATION OF THE DOLLAR, AND COORDINATION AMONG MAJOR CENTRAL BANKS ON INTEREST RATES OR CURRENCY MISALIGNMENTS PROVIDE NECESSARY CORRECTIONS FOR THE U.S. DOMESTIC ECONOMY?

Which of the following newspaper accounts speak to the proper policy responses by the Fed to any perceived difficulty in the value of the dollar, to any trade imbalance, or any foreign financial distress such as the European need for dollars discussed above?

1. A Wall Street Journal, October 21, 2010 article, by David Wessel. In the article, Wessel cites the dilemma posed by Barry Eichengreen that while a lower exchange value for the dollar may rescue some domestic industries, an "exchange rate of 30 percent lower is not going to be of much help to an unskilled or semi-skilled worker in the U.S. competing head to head with Chinese labor." at page A6. Wessel, himself, places the currency-led solution to trade imbalance in this economic paradigm: "The U.S. government's recipe for stronger global economic growth has three ingredients. Big trade-surplus countries, notably China, should export less and rely more on their own consumers' spending. Big trade deficit countries, notably

the U.S. should export more and rely less on their consumers. For that to happen, the dollar needs to fall."[49] Wessel comments that Bernanke and Treasury Secretary, Geither, have discussed the first two but not the last. Both have acknowledge that "no country .can devaluate its way to prosperity and competitiveness. It is not a feasible strategy and we will not engage in it." quoting Geither.

Some nations are vulnerable on the trade issue as their domestic markets are inadequate to consume the mass-produced goods which modern technology permits. It is counterintuitive to sacrifice economies of scale which permit the manufacturing of low-cost goods in order to have a more independent, self-contained economy. Consequently, mass-produced goods available from industrial economies of scale must be sold through exporting. This is not the exact position of the U.S. which has an enormous continental consumer market capable of satisfying much of the manufactured goods produced. However, much of manufacturing has abandoned the U.S. (presumably under the principles of comparative advantage), leaving an economy consisting of 80 percent service jobs. (Some may be good in education and health industries) and as a consequence greater disparities in the distribution of income which compare to that entering the Great Depression. (Greenspan intimated as much in his Age of Turbulence.) Despite this natural foundation for a goods-producing dominated economy, blessed by resources of land, minerals, human, and entrepreneurship, the U.S. is caught in an "import trap" whereby our trade imbalance becomes tolerable due to the cheap imports sold at Wall Mart and other discount stores. The cheap imports permit this nation to accept the high number of low-paying jobs since low-income workers find economic salvation in the buying of low-priced imported goods. This is a Faustian bargain leading to the condemnation of future generations (also today's 20s and 30s) to be disposed of their human abilities which most service industry jobs do not require or encourage Wessel's recommendation of increased exports and less domestic consumption would contribute to an economic revival which would utilize many talents now neglected--but only if this reversal is founded upon exports which are human-resource utilization-led. But to have leading exports in manufactured goods or information technology, or life-sciences requires a domestic commitment for consumption at home. It would be an anomaly for advanced products/services in these industries be available in Asia but not in the U.S. This about-face must offer patience for the development of our human resources as they acquire necessary skills and knowledge in our colleges, universities, and technical schools. A transitional method would be to place great reliance upon internships where future employees learn their profession and trade while being educated at schools. This would provide a great release from businesses to depend upon immigrant workers. But until this or similar economic transformations are begun, helping increase exports through a lower exchange value of the dollar will not provide across the board economic security as would the whole-sale change advocated above. Restructuring of our economy has a greater capacity to distribute increased incomes across the board than would selective industries who benefit from increased exports. Without restructuring, the following are likely to occur over and over as patterns of responses by our domestic firms. Lower interest rates could assist this transformation, but as Keynes remarked -borrowing in the last calculation for businesses. They must have a product-related or service vision to pursue before acquiring debt becomes a consideration. Any revamping of the U.S. economy along the lines of life-science, biotech, and other risky adventures would not likely benefit from loans which offered low-interest rates. Higher risks demand higher interest rate-loans. So, it is problematic how even low-interest rates would assist such a revolutionary turn in the development of the U.S. economy. On the other hand, less consumption would offer more savings for capital investment. If savings and the money supply provided by the Fed reached such a surplus as to invite banks and others to lend to start-up firms in these fields, perhaps monetary policy could serve a role in facilitating this transformation. It is somewhat curious that one could argue that such a role was necessary in the 1920s when a great imbalance existed in that vital industries such as clothing merchandising, textiles, boots, coal for fuel and energy being tossed aside by emerging electricity fuels, agriculture still deprived of its natural rewards according to its contributions, excessive emphasis upon manufacturing given the great disparities in income and the fact that the same number of jobs existed in manufacturing in 1928 and in 1921. The 1920s economy contained breakthrough industries of radios, movies, consumer-friendly cars, and the airplane. Also, other high-tech products were in their infancy in terms of wide-spread application and use. Despite these imbalances the economy sped ahead on the wings of cheap credit and the fatal distraction of speculation which by its nature abhorred any long-term commitment to product-development. Similarly today, the entire Panic or Great Recession emanated from the notion that agility in paper transactions would provide immediate financial gain with the minimum of effort. This attitude has been of long-standing since the early 1980s when IRA accounts, pension funds, 401 (k) retirement accounts and other institutional funds provided the ammunition for 'shooting for the stars' through stock market short-term investing. (If quarterly returns of companies do not meet the anticipated returns envisioned by mutual fund managers, the company risks having their stock sold or 'dumped' in great quantities. This is adversity which companies seeking to raise capital through initial offerings cannot tolerate. Would lower interest rates through monetary policy help ward off this disadvantage by obtaining capital through loans rather than through the offering of company stock?).

  A. In any event, devaluation of the dollar in the early 1980s did not provide the textbook corrections. The following occurred instead:

    1. Japanese auto importers did not double their prices as the higher yen to dollar rate would dictate the consequences were as following almost occurring independently of currency exchange changes between the dollar and the yen.

    "A Nissan automobile that sold in the United States for $9,000 in 1984 and could have sold for $18,000 in 1987 according to changes in yen/dollar exchange rates, actually sold for only $11, 000. If it had really sold for $18,000, it might well have been priced out of the market. At $11,000... It was still highly competitive. In fact, Nissan's total U.S. car sales for 1987 fell only 3 percent from the prior year."[50]

    2. Take another example of an 'incorrect' response by American firms to the devaluated dollar in the mid-1980s.

    "Rather than raise prices to conform with post-Plaza rates, Japanese firms kept price increases modest, squeezed costs, and accepted lower profits to retain their share of U.S. markets. U.S. manufacturers, meanwhile, actually increased their prices to keep up with Japanese price increases. .'Studies by auto market research firm J.D. Powers confirm that while Japanese manufacturers were raising U.S. prices an average of 9-13 percent from 1985 to 1988, General Motors, Ford and Chrysler were raising prices by…..12-15 percent.'"[51]

    3. The following illustrate an important point often lost on economists who are more comfortable with linear models of prediction rather than on outcomes from policies which are more nonlinear- that is one change does not produce a straight-line result but more frequently results in a circular outcome.

    "Essentially, U.S. firms refused to take advantage of changing exchange rates. Rather than keep prices steady, which would have given U.S. automakers a price advantage vis-à-vis foreign car makers, U.S. firms raised their prices so they could make more money per car (rather than expand their production of cars) and swell profits, not increase their market share. U.S. firms emphasized short-term profits rather than increased market share because they wanted to increase stock prices and shareholder dividends.... They did this because the U.S. stock market plays a much greater role in corporate decision-making than it does in Japan, where firms do not seek to reward stockholders with dividends and instead concentrate on long-term investment strategies."[52]

It is noteworthy that another reason for U.S. automakers matching Japanese car prices is that firms in oligopolistic industries, such as autos, do not price compete. Experience teaches that price competition usually results with each firm retaining the same market share but now selling at the lower price. Instead, they compete through quality and style. This proved adverse to U.S. car companies.

"Faced with only modest price differentials between imported and domestic goods, differences that often disappeared when quality and brand loyalty were considered, U.S. consumers kept purchasing imported goods from Western Europe and Japan. Given a choice between a Honda Accord and a Chrysler K-car, cars close in price despite the dollar devaluation, American consumers kept buying Hondas."[53]
(Americans had been buying imports before the dollar devaluation. Thus a brand loyalty developed which could more readily be overcome only through price competition.)

Economists, hurting to explain why the U.S. trade deficit did not decline despite the devaluation of the dollar, attributed it to "hysteresis" meaning "resistance to change" in describing consumer and auto manufacturing responses illustrated above.

B. Currency exchange rate changes had not produced any desirable economic outcomes in the U.S. as reported by Tom Lauricella in the Wall Street Journal

He gives following reported exchange rate changes favorable to the dollar "The euro rose 11.5% against the dollar during the third quarter to $1.3634 while the dollar slumped 5.6% against the yen."

"For much of the first half of 2010, it was the euro that was in the worst shape as the European debt crisis had some investors wondering if Europe's common currency was going to survive. The euro hit a low against the dollar of $1.1917 on June 7 and for the first six months of the year was down almost 15% from where it had started 2010." As the principles discussed earlier regarding the long-term effect of currency exchange rate changes and how long it takes for a declining dollar, for example, to translate into increased exports, the declining dollar of 2010 against the euro and the yen had not contributed to any economic improved indicators. As Lauracella reported:

"Meanwhile, the environment took a turn for the worse in the U.S. as fears about a double-digit recession flared amid news of renewed weakness in the housing market and a stalling out of the recovery of the job market."

"These growth worries drove the Federal Reserve to not only maintain its easy money policy with rates near zero but also prompted it to alert markets that it stands ready to possibly engage in a new round of 'quantitative easing' that would pump more money into the system The dollar, already sagging before the Fed's pronouncement, sold off." Lauricella reported that the declining dollar plus the Fed's easy money pronouncement was not viewed favorably by foreign investors. This brings back to whether we should be concerned if the dollar declines to an exceptional low in light of Greenspan's and other's concern that an exceptionally weak dollar could led to the massive dumping by those holding dollar denominated securities, plus the fact that devaluation does not seem to produce lasting benefits. Both precautions argue for seeking solutions through currency and financial methods with a degree of moderation--- enough to maintain the dollar in some realistic alignment with major currencies. (those with whom we have extensive trade exchanges sufficient to establish some basis for targeting a realistic currency exchange rate)

C. Dollar devaluation began to accomplish stated goals in the 1990s as a long-term result of the Plaza Accords. However, as Professor Robert Schaeffer in his <u>Understanding Globalization</u> noted:

"But just when exchange rates fell to the point where they'd stem imports, reduce U.S. trade deficits, and redistribute manufacturing jobs, this time from Japan to the United States, policymakers in the United States and Japan reversed course. In mid-1995, monetary officials in the United States and Japan worked together to increase the value of the dollar, forcing it back up to Y114=$1 in 1996. It then stayed at about this level for the rest of the 1990s and into 2001."[54]

Two reasons for this reversal were a concern for the Japanese economy and a related possible consequences of the Japanese 'dumping' many of the dollar-denominated securities which they held. We felt, as Greenspan often cautioned, that the danger of the dollar becoming 'worthless' as a means of exchange or even international investment was too ominous.[55] So this currency exchange agreement had little to do with underlying economic factors such as productivity, research and development, price stability but simply because Japan depended too much upon exports for growth and a higher valued yen was hurting them. Rather than address internal disequilibrium, Japan sought to seek a rather facile, but artificial, means to reverse its fortune. (Greenspan had spoken of the potential flight from the dollar as a currency if our trade deficit kept growing.) [56]

D. The Internal Contradictions:

Other than unanticipated responses to devaluation as cited above, the exercise of monetary policy towards currency exchange goals invites contradictions.

For example, Greenspan raised federal funds rate to around 7 1/2 percent after the 1987 Crash. This of course would tend to raise the currency exchange rate of the dollar vis-à-vis other foreign currencies. This flew in the face of the desire of G-7 authorities of other major trading nations who were seeking through intervention to lower the currency exchange value of the dollar. This produced the following contradictory Fed policy targets. "The Fed, following the Treasury's directions, found itself trying to prevent the dollar from rising while simultaneously raising rates to prevent inflation.---a near impossible task. In contrast to earlier in the year when dollar weakness helped prompt rate hikes, the FOMC record from mid-year on suggests the Fed may have pulled its punches in raising rates out of concern with the rising dollar."[57] As in the late 1920s into 1933, the Fed attempted to serve two masters, domestic and foreign. Rather than focus upon its statutory mandate for domestic price stability, the Fed's attention was diverted to the currency dilemma faced primary by other nations.

"At the Fed, far from the dollar's appreciation being a problem, 'We're at a stage where it sort of gives you breathing room.' an official said. 'We're no longer bouncing along on the floor in a sense. It's absence of pressure.' The Fed's biggest concern was the pressure being brought on it to hold the dollar down, and not just from the Treasury. The Fed's fellow central banks did not like their currencies rising against the dollar because it made their imports of oil and other commodities more expensive. As much as the Fed might like to base monetary policy on domestic considerations alone, its fellow central banks could not because their economies were more trade-oriented."[58] Much of this conflict over currency exchange rates was attribute to the higher interest rates of the U.S. which drained capital funds from European banks.

2. Another seemingly path to contradictory policy efforts is contained in Bernanke's June 2008 remarks regarding the declining dollar.in the Wall Street Journal, June 4, 2008 Although the declining dollar had boosted U.S. exports, Bernanke revised his implied view of February 2008 in stating, "that the weak dollar has contributed to an unwelcome rise in import prices and consumer price inflation." He suggested that the Fed and the Treasury "continue to carefully monitor developments in foreign exchange markets."[59] and that the Fed would factor the impact of the currency into its interest rate deliberation to keep unemployment and inflation low." He called for "ensuring that the dollar remains a strong and stable currency."[60] Again, the Fed seemed to be drifting into efforts which would work at cross purposes. Stabilize the dollar with higher federal funds rates or through intervention with other central banks and yet promote economic recovery from the "Great Recession". The neglect of real economic policy efforts was perhaps sensed by Lisa Scott-Smith of Millennium Global Investments, a London currency trader, when she stated, "For the dollar to make a sharp turn upward, you need to have more of a turn in the real economy."[61] The determination to 'protect' the dollar as evidenced by Bernanke's remarks run counter to the insight offered by Greenspan in 1988 when he cited this objection to intervention for currency exchange rate change purposes: "Intervention, alone would only have a 'temporary influence.'"[62] "He agreed intervention unsupported by fundamental changes was ineffective, but said finance ministers did not realize that. 'There is an [adjective deleted] belief

now, particularly among the Japanese that, sterilized intervention can put the exchange rate where they want it.'"[63] Others had made essentially the same conclusion. Fed members, Hoskins and Angell felt that "if the Fed followed the right domestic policy, exchange rates will take care of themselves.[64] Angell believed that 'whatever was right policy domestically would also be right policy internationally.'[65] And "if the Fed was going to get inflation down it would have to settle for a stronger dollar and there was not a lot of point in trying to camouflage it with sterilized intervention in the currency market."[66] Regarding policy measures to take in 1988.) A sleight of hand effort by the Fed to do both, obtain currency exchange rate targets and domestic interest rate targets simultaneously could be 'effected' through 'sterilization'. Paul Volcker explained this method in his <u>Changing Fortunes;</u>"

> "The Japanese report dwelled at length on the distinction economists make between 'sterilized' and 'unspecialized' intervention. Unsterilized intervention means a central bank, when buying or selling a foreign currency, permit's the resulting change in its assets to work its way through to a change in the money supply and interest rates. Just as the textbooks say, if the Fed created dollars to buy marks, those dollars would, like any open market purchase, increase bank reserves and ultimately the amount of money in circulation by some multiple of that reserve increase; interest rates would tend to decline, other things being equal. That was what was supposed to happen in the classic gold standard when a central bank bought gold, it forced a change in monetary policy. Conversely, intervention is 'sterilized' if the initial purchase of foreign currency is offset by the central bank by the sale of another asset, say a Treasury bill, so that monetary reserves and monetary policy remain unchanged."[67]

Even though this technique seems to leave matters domestically the same, Volker cautioned that 'most central bankers do not frame their monetary policies in terms of the amount of its foreign exchange intervention."[68] If any intervention either enlarges or constricts the domestic money supply, sterilization would be employed in order to leave domestic monetary policy unchanged. [69] Volker reminds us that currency exchange markets can influence decisions on monetary policy, but the domestic decision "to ease or tighten is a separate one. It will be made on the basis of broader economic considerations, not because of the mechanical effects of intervention."[70] Volcker cited a communique," intervention can be useful to counter disorderly market conditions and to reduce short-term volatility......Intervention will normally be useful only when complementing and supporting other policies.-by which it meant mainly monetary policies."[71]

William Greider brought attention to this inner conflict between addressing domestic needs through monetary policies and the centrifugal force of international currency and financial markets pulling attention away from those domestic concerns. "Personal brilliance aside, currency speculators like Soros all operate on a fundamental insight about the great political distinction present in the global system: the national governments expected to guarantee stability were trapped between two worlds--their obligations to domestic economies and the new force of the global market. Central banks and elected governments were regularly compelled to choose between the two: either defending their home economy or yielding to the quick, disinterested judgment from the global traders. This was often a 'no win' choice for political leaders since yielding to the markets' idea of 'sound economic policy' frequently required them to depress their own economies, increasing unemployment or cutting social spending. Satisfying finance capital could be a formula for losing the next election."[72]

Written in the mid-1990s, Greider's observations hold for today and for the 1920s as during the latter period the proper flow of gold according to international trade balances was supposed to dictate any domestic policies. The fact that countries may have diverted from the gold standard on occasion did not remove this 'mandate from heaven' of the gold standard from policy-makers' measuring of policy decisions in not straying excessively from the standard. Criticism of the Fed during the period 1926-1931 stems from the Fed's indecisions on whether to be led by the gold standards requirements (making sure that Great Britain's proper share of gold was restored by the U.S. lower interest rates or to raise rates to discourage Wall Street speculation by making it more costly to borrow in order to buy stock despite any contradiction this may impose on gold flow requirements.) or to raise interest rates to ward off the outward flow or drain of U.S. gold reserves despite rising unemployment and a credit crunch.) Greider cited the Japanese crisis during the 1990s as another example of the Fed attempting to satisfy simultaneously domestic and foreign demands upon it.

> "The same sort of political-economic dilemmas regularly confronted the Federal Reserve and the Bank of Japan as those dominant central banks also attempted to manage the competing imperatives of domestic interest rates and international capital flows. Milton Friedman, the American apostle of free markets, had argued twenty years before that if governments would allow the global marketplace to determine currency values with a system of 'floating exchange rates,' then the central banks would be free to concentrate on their main function of controlling the money supply and domestic inflation. Roughly the opposite of Freidman's prediction has occurred, as global markets repeatedly trumped the domestic policy decisions of central banks-sometimes deliberately, sometimes randomly."[73]

Greider cites the deregulation of global finance, in particular of currencies from a fixed ratio, as the primary cause of this seemingly contradictory reoccurring policy choices between domestic needs concerning interest rates and what the international market may demand in order to realign currency exchange rates.[74]

A similar case occurred when in 1988, the Germans and the Japanese complained of the capital drain from their economies caused allegedly by the high interest rates maintained by the U.S. Fed. After attempting to accommodate the Germans and the Japanese through currency intervention, the Fed had only limited success in their intervention efforts. "The intervention had only limited success. By mid-July, the dollar had risen to a two-year high of nearly 149 yen and 2.03 marks, and the administration's effort to talk down the dollar and pressure the Fed into lowering rates became more desperate than ever.. Commerce secretary Robert Mosbacher, ordinarily under instruction not to talk about the dollar said, 'The recent strength of the dollar leads us to be concerned about the economy's ability to sustain the excellent (trade) trends so far.' On June 29, the Bundesbank again raised the discount and Lombard rates a half percent to 5 ad 7 percent, respectively." This attempt to accommodate the Commerce and the Treasury's demands regarding sustaining a trade export business caused consternation among some Federal Reserve members.[75]

> "Increasingly, Fed officials regarded this whole exchange rate rat race as a harmful distraction from the Fed's domestic goals. The Fed has been buying marks and yen covertly, using a commercial bank to make the transactions on its behalf, rather than intervene openly in the name of the central bank." Some saw the benefit of such surreptitious moves by the Fed, others were outraged at any such justification for covert movements. "'In operating more discreetly we have been able to kind of encourage the dollar down without appearing to try to take on the market in a direct way, ' Cross told the FOMC An outraged Angell pounced on Cross. 'I just do not agree that it's appropriate for us to act in ways that are intended to confuse the markets or mislead the markets…I just don't hold that these kinds of moves make that much difference. But even if they did, I do not believe it's appropriate for a government agency in a market society to be acting in such a manner.'"[76]

It is submitted that if changes occur in financial markets or commercial markets the real cause should be obvious and not disguised as a natural outcome of demand and supply dynamics of an unregulated market. Our experience in the currency debates suggests that any attempt at neutralizing any impact domestically through 'sterilization' has a similar disinformation effect. Recent headlines in November, 2010 show that nations are still insisting upon resolving trade and domestic difficulties through the expediency of changing currency exchange rates. From Wall Street 9, 2010 comes the headline, "FED GLOBAL BACKLASH GROWS" citing disagreements of the U.S. over China' currency policy. Also, the November 6-7, 2010 Wall Street Journal issue headline read, PEER PRESSURE SEEN AS CURRENCY WAR FIX" In a Wall Street Journal article, "Rescuing Dollar Raised Potential Policy Tug of War" of 2008, Craig Karmin cites a leading authority on this question of attempting to align domestic interest rates for both purposes of domestic price stability and the value of the dollar. "' I can't think of a time when the U.S. was simultaneously easing monetary policy and intervening in the currency markets,' said Jeffrey Frankel, a professor at the Kennedy School of Government at Harvard University. The confluence of those two government actions, he added, "would risk canceling each other. That could leave the dollar vulnerable to further declines." Moreover, the risk of failing to achieve the currency target could have unintended consequences as Karmin notes. "Analysts say any government intervention in the currency market that failed to achieve its goal of slowing the decline would be far worse than none at all. It would embolden speculators to increase their bets on the buck's fall, believing that governments couldn't stop them."

The application of Fed interventions to achieve proper international currency alignments and in the 1920s and beyond to achieve the proper flow of gold according to global commerce and capital national trade balances assume a certain symmetry, both logically and economically, which can be maintained through financial imperatives. This neat global model has been disturbed both in the late 1920s into the 1930s and today. The following narrative exposes any neatness of economic and financial order which the gold standard sought and presumed:

For example, many on the Federal Reserve debated whether they should raise interest rates to discourage domestic lending for stock market speculation. Raising interest rates would violate the mandates of the gold standard which did not incorporate any provisions concerning stock market speculation. Nevertheless, any orderly flow of gold from nation to nation according to authentic commercial and capital transactions was undermined by the independent effect upon the increased flow of gold to the U.S. as currencies fled to the U.S. seeking instant riches from Wall Street investing. Note the perverse effect this had upon any natural development of European economies.

"Perhaps the most perverse consequence of the bubble was that by the strange mechanics of international money, it helped to tip Germany over the edge into recession. For five years, hordes of American bankers had descended on Berlin to press loans upon German companies and municipalities. However much Schacht had tried to wean his country from this dependence on foreign capital, there was little he was able to do about it. Over the five years between 1924 and 1928, Germany borrowed some $600 million a year, or which half went to reparations, the remainder to sustain the rebound in consumption after the years of austerity."[77]

"In fact, Germany's appetite for foreign currency was so great that even the deluge of long-term loans from the U.S. bankers was not enough, and it was forced to supplement this with short-term borrowings in international markets close to home."[78] Much of the loans was 'hot money', short-term deposits attracted to German banks by high interest rates-- 7 percent in Berlin compared to 5 percent in New York-and subject to being pulled at any time."[79] This is exactly what the lure of high returns on the New York stock market did. "In the late 1928, as the U.S. stock market kept climbing and call money rates on Wall Street skyrocketed, American bankers mesmerized by the phenomenal returns at home suddenly stopped coming to Berlin."[80] Moreover, other investors pursued the Wall Street market with their currencies and again moved the corresponding gold in contradiction to the imperatives of the gold standard which did not really incorporate gold flows in accordance with how international movements for speculative purposes unrelated to capital investments in plant and equipment. This contradiction received this response from a leading member of the Fed.: "Should they respond to large increases in asset prices or confine their attention to prices, output, money, or foreign exchange rates."[81]

Any order remaining under the gold standard was dealt a fatal blow when the British abandoned the gold standard in 1931. Professor Donald Wells explains the crushing consequences of this decision:

> When Britain declared it would no longer redeem its pound Sterling in gold, there was a large increase in demand by Europeans for gold. Since the dollar was still redeemable in gold, there was a run on the dollar. Foreign central banks exchanged their dollar deposits at the New York Fed for gold. In six weeks, over $700 million of gold left the US for Europe. Governor Meyer did believe that the gold standard should be maintained; therefore, he agreed with the New York Fed that it should raise its discount rate and stop open market purchases of securities. The belief in the gold standard was very strong among financial leaders in not only this country but also in most European countries. But with central banks exercising discretion, the rules of the gold standard were often ignored, especially by the nation losing gold. This external pressure on banks from the loss of gold was matched by an internal drain by the public for more currency because people realized that many banks were failing. In 1931, a total of 2,293 banks failed. Banks losing reserves from the gold drain increased their borrowing from the Fed even though the discount rate was increased. Banks also dumped their commercial paper and government securities on the market to get needed reserves, but this caused the prices of these assets to fall and their yields to rise. By this dumping on the market, banks were only pulling reserves from one another.[82]

The above scenario exposes the fact that the movement of dollars, then gold, exceeded the ability of the Fed to impose any monetary corrections which the domestic economy needed in order to ward off deflation, unemployment, and a credit crunch. Similar disorder exists today in that the flow of dollars, foreign currencies, financial instruments, and other securities across the globe exceeds the ability of the Fed to achieve monetary targets. Greider noted this chaos in the 1990s and how such trading in financial markets produced wide swings in currency values, disturbing the natural conduct of commercial trading:

> "The dollar, the deutschemark and the yen, in descending order of importance, were the three main reserves currencies that served as anchors for global trade, but each was subject to its own continuing uncertainty and dramatic volatility. The monthly swings in exchange value between the dollar and the deutschemark, for instance, typically ran around 5 percent a month and frequently greater than 10 percent. In 1995, the dollar lost 20 percent of its value against the yen in three months. Then, as the three leading governments intervened to staunch the decline, the dollar lurched back upward and, three months later, was 20 percent stronger. How could the market be right about money values when it was always changing its mind?"[83]

Greider provided the answer to his own inquiry:

> "Across several years the market shifts in currency values were so extreme and contradictory they might be described as irrational. The dollar, for example, was said to be worth 260 yen in 1985, then marked down to 130 yen by 1987, then up to 160 yen in 1990, down again to 80 yen in early 1995, then up to 100 yen a few months later. Nothing in the economic reality corresponded to those violent swings in financial numbers. The United States did not suddenly become half as strong, then suddenly much more productive. Nor did Japan's underlying value as a national economy abruptly weaken, then surge. As Rob Johnson said, everyone runs to portside, then to starboard, but the boiling process of reallocations never achieve equilibrium"[84]

The current Panic is attributed to a great extent to the flood of capital which moved into the U.S. seeking instant profits/wealth in the U.S. housing market. "Ironically, the great credit freeze of 2007-2009 began with a condition in financial markets that was the exact opposite of a credit shortage. It was the huge flow of money from both domestic and foreign sources into U.S. real estate and other financial markets, especially after the stock market crash of 2000. Much of this capital flood came from foreign sources that were not subject to direct regulation by the Fed. So the Fed actually had less power to influence U.S. interest rates during the initial years of this capital flood that it had traditionally enjoyed."[85]

The Fed faced a similar dilemma in the late 1920s in any effort it might have made to curtail lending for speculative purposes as its reserves of government securities which it could sell to increase interest rates was far exceeded by the funds which corporate America could lend to counter any such Fed move. Today, central banks often confront a similar problem in attempting to realign currency exchange rates as their currency reserves are exceeded by those held by speculative funds. As Randy Epping has noted, "Unfortunately, it's not always possible to keep a currency from rising or falling precipitously on world markets. Currency crashes around the world, from Britain to Argentina to South East Asia in past years, attest to the power of speculators to bring down a currency by selling enormous amounts of that currency on the world's foreign exchange markets. The speculators often succeed because governments with weak currencies are limited in what they can do. If they don't have enough foreign reserves, they can't support the currency by buying it on the foreign exchange markets. And if they raise interest rates to attract investment in the country and the currency, it can bring the country's economy to a screeching halt."[86] Even the strongest currency can be faced with a contradictory choice in devaluating or strengthening it. Epping notes this conflict faced by the U.S. in any effort to manipulate the dollar for export purposes: "Since the world has gotten used to using the dollar as the primary reserve currency, any action on the part of the U.S. authorities to manipulate the value of the dollar can have far-reaching consequences. How can creditor nations continue to pay for the U.S. trade deficit by investing in dollar-denominated treasury bonds if they thought the United States was going to let the dollar fall on the world markets?"[87] Epping has recognized a more blanketing restriction on the Fed in addition to any irreconcilable conflict which currency issues may present to the Fed:

> "The growth of other financial instruments, such as derivatives and securitized loans like mortgage-backed securities, has made it almost impossible for central banks to effectively control the money and credit in modern economies. The Bank For International Settlements has estimated that the total value of outstanding derivative positions on the over-the-counter markets exceeded $400 trillion during the first years of the 21st century-when the entire U.S. economy, the world's largest, was estimated to be worth less than $15 trillion. The problem for central banks is that these new financial instruments give investors enormous amounts of nominal assets with a minimal outlay of cash. When the prices of these new financial instruments rise, investors can borrow against them--just as a homeowner can get a second mortgage on a home that has risen in value."[88]

How can a central bank address directly and immediately crisis such as the aftermath of the Crash of 1929 and the Great Recession of 2006-2010 in an economic landscape cluttered and disheveled by speculation, currency exchange manipulations, disharmony caused by one nation's high interest rates draining capital from other nations with lower interest rates--all compounded by electronic transmissions across the globe often in disregard of economic potentials needing time to develop? The following depicted trade patterns of various nations illustrates that one international currency rule cannot accommodate all:

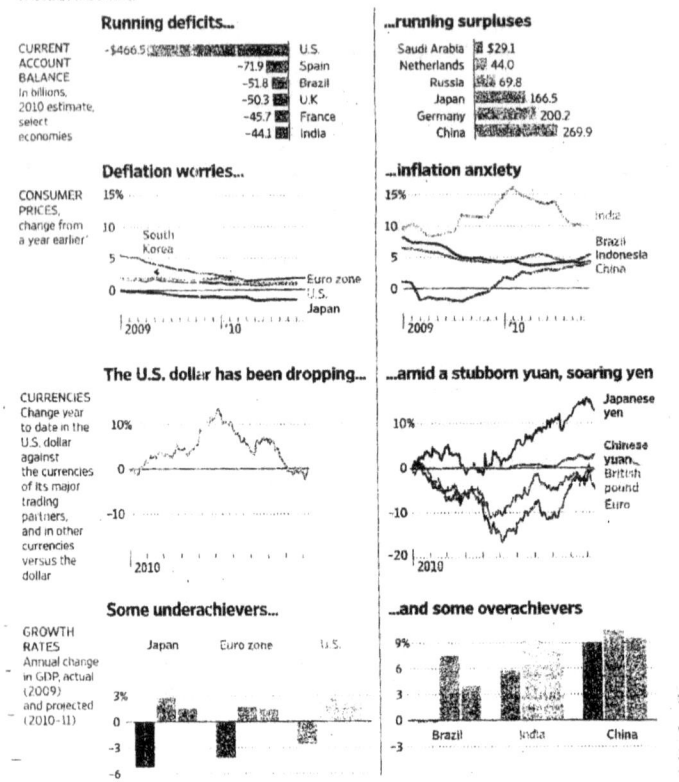

Paul Krugman places the modern dilemma faced by the Fed:

"There are three things that macroeconomic managers want for their economies. They want discretion in money policy so that they can fight recessions and curb inflation. They want stable exchange rates so that businesses are not faced with too much uncertainty. And they want to leave international business free--in particular, to allow people to exchange money however they like--in order to get out of the private sector's way.

What the story of the globo and its demise tells us is that countries cannot get all three wishes: at most, they can get two. They can give up on exchange rate stability: this means adopting a floating exchange rate, like the United States and Australia did They can give up on discretionary monetary policy: this means fixing the exchange rate: the way Argentina did in the 1990s, and possibly even giving up their own currency, like the nations of continental Europe did. Or they can give up on the principle of completely free markets and impose capital controls: this was what most countries did between 1940s and the 1960s, and what China does right now.

Which of these three imperfect answers is best? "There are some people who think that the gains from stable exchange rates are large, the benefits of independent monetary policy overrated. They like to point out that the United States, though spread over a continent, does very well with a single currency, and that some 300 million Europeans have adopted a common currency. So why not the world as a whole?"[90]

Krugman cites the continental features of the US and of Europe which favor a common currency for each, but that other nations are saddled by being smaller and having no contingency arrangement with neighboring countries in an effort to establish a common trade region.

Perhaps Robert Gilpin has cited the overriding factor which tends to pit one monetary policy choice against another:

> "The relationship of state and market, and especially the differences between these two organizing principles of social life, is a recurrent theme in scholarly discourse. On the other hand, the state is based on the concepts of territoriality, loyalty, and exclusivity, and it possesses a monopoly of the legitimate use of force. Although no state can long survive unless it assures the interests and gains the consent of the most powerful groups in society, states enjoy varying degrees of autonomy with respect to the societies of which they are a part. On the other hand, the market is based on the concepts of functional integration, contractual relationships, and expanding interdependence of buyers and sellers. It is a universe composed mainly of prices and quantities; the

autonomous economic agent responding to price signals provides the basis of decision. For the state, territorial boundaries are a necessary basis of national autonomy and political unity. For the market, the elimination of all political and other obstacles to the operation of the price mechanism is imperative. The tension between these two fundamentally different ways of ordering human relationships has profoundly shaped the course of modern history and constitutes the crucial problem in the study of political economy."[91]

Gilpin reduces the tension between the state and the market in this manner: "Whereas powerful market forces in the form of trade, money, and foreign investment tend to jump national boundaries, to escape political control, and to integrate societies, the tendency of government is to restrict, to channel, and to make economic activities serve the perceived interests of the state and of powerful groups within it. The logic of the market is to locate economic activities where they are most productive and profitable, the logic of the state is to capture and control the process of economic growth and capital accumulation"[92]

Compounding any attempt by the Fed to serve its national obligations under the law but also maintain necessary channels for international coordination on currency and other financial market matters is these colliding facts:

A. International trading is done through electronic transmission at speeds far in excess of the ability of one central bank to counter, correct, or modify. This requires coordinated efforts by the central banks of the major trading nations.

B. Any domestic monetary initiative by the Fed has a delayed fuse in achieving the target goal of economic growth. While the following findings may be somewhat discredited by the flood of capital into the U.S. seeking real estate investments and according to many observers disabling the Fed's efforts at monetary controls, it still serves, perhaps, as a guide in more normal economic times which do not experience the present calamity caused by capital moves. From the USA, August 22, 2001 page 2B, the following was provided as a guide on when to judge the effectiveness of lower interest rates established by the Fed:

> "Still, economists caution that it would be foolish to write off the power of the Fed. 'It's still too soon, historically,' to judge the effectiveness of the rate cuts, says Anthony Chan, chief economist for Banc One Investment Advisors. Chan and others note that rate cuts traditionally take from 6 months to a year or more to work The Fed began cutting rates in January. But some analysts say it wasn't until April that the cuts had gotten large enough to neutralize the Fed's earlier rate increases."

Given the dramatically altered financial and commercial landscape of today, it is problematic whether economists and the Fed could rely upon this time period for policy effectiveness. A last parallel to be drawn between the late 1920s and early 1930s and today would probably greatly alter any projections of 6 months to a year for lower rates to take effect-- that parallel is the credit crunch which is common to both periods.

Chapter Nine Notes

1. Sudeep Reddy and Peter Steit "Rising Currencies Bedevil World Economies" Wall Street Journal August 5, 2011.

2. All cited above are from Peter Coy "What Happens If The Dollar Crashes" Business Week October 26, 2009 page018

3. Ibid, page 018

4. Ibid, page 018

5. "New EuroWoe Carry Trade" Wall Street Journal May 25, 2010

6. Peter Coy, op. cit. page 020

7. Ibid, page 020

8. Ibid, page 020

9. Business Week, October 26, 2009

10. Indianapolis Star March 14, 2008

11. Ibid,

12. Steven Solomon Confidence Game cited in "Electronic Money and the Casino Economy" by Richard Barnett and John Cavanagh page 361

13. Ibid, page 362

14. Ibid, page 362

15. Ibid, page 367

16. Wall Street Journal October 8, 2010 at page C1

17. Ibid

18. Wall Street Journal June 22, 2010 at page A8

19. Wall Street Journal September 16, 2010

20. Tom Lauricella and John Lyons in Wall Street Journal September 29, 2010

21. Ibid at page C2

22. Ibid, page LC3

23. Alex Frangos "Push on Yen Aligns Japan With Neighbors" Wall Street Journal 17, 2010

24. Ibid, page A12

25. Samuelson and Nordhaus op. cit. pages 299-300

26. Ibid, page 301

27. Ibid, page 301

28. Ibid, pages 301-302

29. Ibid, page 303

30. Ibid, page 370

31. David Collander, Economics 2nd Ed. (   ) pages 365-375

32. Barnett and Cavanagh op. cit. page 308

33. Ibid, quote at page 307

34. Ibid, page 307

35. Steven K. Beckner Back From the Brink: The Greenspan Years (New York: Wiley, 1998) page 104

36. Ibid, page 107

37. Ibid, page 108

38. Ibid, page 108

39. Ibid, page 91

40. Ibid, page 91

41. Ibid, page 104

42. David Malpass "The Weak Dollar Threat to Prosperity" Wall Street Journal October 8, 2009

43. David Wessel In Fed We Trust (New York: 2009) page 140

44. Ibid, page 141

45. Ibid, page 141

46. Ibid, page 141

47. Paul Volker op. cit. page 233

48. David Wessel op. cit. page 231

49. David Wessel, "Weaker Dollar No Magic Elixir" Wall Street Journal October 21, 2010 page A6

50. Robert Schaeffer op. cit. page 45

51. Ibid, page 45

52. Ibid, page 45

53. Ibid, page 45

54. Ibid, page 53

55. Ibid, page 53

56. See Steven Beckner op. cit. page 91

57. Ibid, page 92

58. Ibid, page 92

59. Wall Street Journal June 4, 2008 at page A1

60. Ibid, page A18

61. Ibid, page A18

62. Steven Beckner op. cit. page 143

63. Ibid, page 141

64. Ibid, page 110

65. Ibid, page 94

66. Ibid, page 94

67. Paul Volker op. cit. page 236

68. Ibid, page 236

69. Ibid, page 236

70. Ibid, page 236

71. Ibid, page 237

72. William Grieder op. cit. page 242

73. Ibid page 243

74. Ibid, page 243

75. Steven Beckner op. cit. page 138

76. Ibid, page 138

77. Liaquat Hiram op, cit. page 324

78. Ibid, page 325

79. Ibid, page325

80. Ibid, page 325

81. Ibid, page 224

82. Donald Wells, op. cit. page52

83. William Grieder op. cit. page249

84. Ibid, page 249

85. Anthony Downs op. cit. page 124

86. Randy Eppins op. cit. page 70

87. Ibid, page 71

88. Ibid, page298

89. Ibid, page 298

90. Paul Krugman op. cit. page83

91. Robert Gilpin op. cit. pages 10-11

92. Ibid, page 11.

CHAPTER TEN

PARALLEL 8 THE CREDIT CRUNCH; PARALLEL 1930-32 AND 2006-2010.

The unwillingness or inability of banks to lend freely can be examined from both the demand side (creditworthy consumers and businesses) and from the supply side (solvent and solid-earnings banks and other financial institutions.). First, examining the demand side and the supply side, we may find that one side may be so weak that the disparities between its weakness and any strengthens of the other side may prohibit any meaningful lending as for example any easy supply of money may be unable to find sufficient creditworthy borrowers. Only the resorting to subprime lending may accomplish any target quantity of loans. With this comparison of demand and supply let us examine both periods, 1930-31 and 2006-2010 to see if one side is so weak as to render the other side inoperative.

Credit Crunch 1930-31

Examining the demand side of lending during this period, how strong is it in terms of creditworthy borrowers or even those who are somewhat creditworthy but would not rely upon loans for funds.

Repeating the various income classes in the 1920s, we find the following to be noncredit worthy before and after the Crash:

       1. White and black sharecroppers

       2. Textile workers

       3. Coal miners

       4. Farmers, especially those selling wheat

5. No equity loans for homeowners or effective refinancing. David Kennedy, in his <u>Freedom From Fear</u>, provides the credit conditions facing homebuyers in the 1920s: "Before the New Deal, only about four Americans in ten lived in their own homes. Homeowners in the 1920s typically paid full cash or very large down payments for their homes, usually not less than 30 percent. The standard mortgage was offered by a local institution with a highly limited service area, had only a five-to-ten-year maturity, bore interest as high as 8 percent, and required a large 'balloon' payment or refinancing at its termination. Not surprisingly, under such conditions, a majority of Americans were renters."[1] Thus, lower interest rates by the Fed would not offer the equity lending and refinancing stimulus for consumption as it did in the 2000s. The 5-to-10- year maturity of mortgages prohibited the long-term lending strategy which present mortgages supported under equity loans and under refinancing.

6. Real Estate developers were overextended in the 1920s and had a large unsold inventory of houses They represented huge liabilities to banks-not potential borrowers.

7. Even factory workers whose pay had supported installment buying were constrained by periodic unemployment before 1929 and many had exhausted their credit-buying capabilities by 1929. By the end of the decade, four out of five cars and two out of three radios were bought on credit. Personal indebtedness rose to an all-time high that could not be sustained.

8. Adult males reaching near age 40 were probably unable to continue to work in manufacturing. Their reduced physical strengths and skills made them vulnerable to dismissal, replaced by younger men. During the first years of the Roosevelt Administration, Harry Hopkins found that the typical unemployed urban worker on relief, "was a white man, thirty-eight years of age and the head of a household....{H}e had been more often than not an unskilled or semi-skilled worker in the manufacturing or mechanical industries. He had had some ten years'

experience at what he considered to be his usual occupation. He had not finished elementary school. He had been out of any kind of job lasting one month or more for two years, and had not been working at his usual occupation for over two and a half years." Hopkins stressed particularly the problem of the elderly, who, he concluded, 'through hardship, discouragement and sickness as well as advancing years, [have] gone into occupational oblivion from which they will never be rescued by private industry'"[2]

9. The manufacturing sector did not add new jobs during the 1920s and thereby deprived the mass produced durable goods of an expanding consumer market. (The total manufacturing jobs in 1929 was about the same as in 1921.) Automation undercut what might have otherwise been a self-fulfilling need of more workers providing more consumers for the products. (Many manufactures did provide their own financing for their employees to buy their products. However, total manufacturing workers did not increase during the decade.)

10. The extreme weakness of any demand for loans is exposed by the over-all limitation that at least one-third, and maybe 40 percent, of Americans lie in poverty.

11. Adding to the weakness of the demand side for loans is the absence of big business. Most had been self-financing through the sale of their stocks and bonds or even through the use of retained earnings. Commercial banks' only contact with corporate America was through their associate investment banks' underwriting of corporate stocks and bonds. Many were sold by investment banks without due diligence and ended up representing bad investments for many. Those victimized by the pooling of stock such as in RCA's case, or by the buying of unsound stocks and bonds would not be credit-worthy borrowers after the Crash.

Conclusion: From any close look at the American families, workers, and businesses one must be persuaded that the creditworthy demand side of lending was desperately weak and only the modern-like pursuit of subprime lending could stretch this demand to any accommodating reach for funds which might have been available for loans. Such a lack of due diligence in lending to subprime-like borrowers would be unlikely after the shock of the Crash. What about the supply side of lending- the commercial banks and private finance companies--- were they so solvent and profitable with many reserves as to be risk-seeking in their lending?

The supply side of lending in 1930-31

Bank Holdings: Toxic assets or merely a liquidity problem

1. Home mortgages totaled $3 billion by the middle of 1927.[3]

2. $8 billion call-loans to brokers for lending to stock speculators, (Ibid p. 182) When the stock became worth much less than it was originally sold, the banks would have to collect less than they loaned to the brokers.

3. Foreign bonds: $1 billion a year purchased in New York. Foreign loans averaged $500 million a year to Europe, $300 million a year to Latin America, and $200 million a year to Canada. Others included 36 investment banks seeking to loan to Budapest, 14 investment banks seeking to loan to Belgrade and $3 million actually loaned to Bavaria.[4] By 1929, the United States had accumulated over $15 billion in foreign investments, one-half in loans and the other half as direct investments by multinational corporations.[5]

4. In 1930, American banks held as assets some $1.5 billion in German and Austrian obligations.[6]

Nonmember banks (those not in the Federal Reserve System) equaled ½ of all banks, but only ¼ of all deposits. They were mostly local banks which were heavily invested in real estate mortgages. These banks suffered the heaviest blow after the Crash as their assets were mortgages which were not being paid or keep current. It is useful to repeat the declining economic conditions in the real estate industry which were provided previously:

The following would affect both Federal Reserve Banks and nonmember banks who pursued mortgage lending

(a) By the summer of 1929, there was a startling decline in building construction with net investment being over a billion dollars less than in 1928.[7]

(b) From 1926 to 1929, housing starts exceeded net household formation with subdividing producing vacant building lots.[8]

(c) Housing price increases were inadequate to provide incentives for increased investment by construction companies. A decline in residential construction from $5 billion in 1925 to $3 billion in 1929[9] reveals a declining market for mortgage lending for both member and nonmember banks. Nevertheless, during the 1920s real estate loans increased 179 percent with real estate loans represented 12.6 percent of all loans in 1928 compared with 6.5 percent of all loans in 1921.[10] "Banking unrest in Pittsburg, Philadelphia, and especially Chicago were directly related to depreciated real estate values in 1931."[11] Federal Reserve banks suffered losses too as federal legislation authorized mortgages as acceptable collateral at the discount window.[12]

Emus Wicker maintains that any banking panic in 1930-31 was contained in the rural areas serviced by the nonmember banks and that there was no nation-wide contagion in this period. Also, while some scholars assert that the collapse of the Bank of America as evidence of a wide-spread banking crisis, Wicker is persuasive in saying that the name was deceptive and the Fed successfully contained any banking crisis.

Even if one were to concede sound capital cushions for many Fed banks and adequate liquidity for some, problems remained insofar as banks being positioned to renew aggressive lending. We had listed numerous bad holdings by both fed member banks (through their associate investment banks) and others in the form of call-loans, foreclosed real estate mortgages, unsound foreign bonds and loans which all impair capital. Insofar as liquidity, the banks were victimized by their own lending practices as most holdings were ineligible as collateral at the discount window for loans from the Fed. Without any precise listing of balance sheet holdings and liabilities, it seems persuasive to state that any supply of credit was somewhat impaired and any efforts by the Fed through open-market activities to provide additional reserves to its member banks would be indecisive insofar as igniting aggressive lending. This conclusion seems warranted by the following responses of the banks who did receive infusions of money from the Fed.

(a) As Professor Leuchtenburg noted: "Although the RFC (Reconstruction Finance Corporation) helped shore up railroads on the verge of bankruptcy and cut down, at least for a time, bank closings, it did nothing to get the economy rolling again. Bankers viewed the RFC not as a way to expand the volume of credit but as a means of preserving their own and other institutions from bankruptcy "[13]

(b) Jane D'Arista in her The Evolution of U.S. Finance notes a 'new problem." Despite substantial additions to reserves, member banks were unwilling to either expand their loans or repay the borrowing to the system. The system's purchases created excess reserves held as cash balances by a majority of member banks who choose to protect their liquidity." The Fed had purchased millions of dollars of government securities which infused extra reserves for lending. However, this did not resulting in any noticeable resumption of lending.

(c) "Banks were going under in part because the assets they held on their books could not be used as collateral to borrow from the Fed. By the fall of 1931, the neat distinction between liquidity and solvency on which the Fed, following Bagehot, had placed so much emphasis, was becoming meaningless. Many banks experiencing withdrawals would have been fine under normal circumstances, but forced to call in loans and liquidate assets in a falling market at fire-sale prices, they were being driven into insolvency......"[14]

(d) A new fund created by larger and stronger private banks designed to provide funds to distressed banks folded after an initial funding because of the banks'" ultraconservatism and fear of losing money."[15]

One could argue that the banks retained a residual ability to restart the economy through aggressive lending if the Fed had been more aggressive in providing an infusion of money which would have created an easy money condition of lending. Even granted some remaining strength in banking, it is submitted that the weakness of creditworthy demand was so disproportionate to any strength existing on the supply side (banks) as to render credit a non-issue. The real link to financial distress can be attributed to the misalignment of capital investment of the 1920s coupled with a fatal disparity in the distribution of income.

Moving on to the recent/present credit crunch, is it attributed to similar economic disfunctioning? Beginning with the demand side of the present credit crunch, is the consumer/business demand for loans weak, moderate, or strong? Is it significant that the present credit crunch of 2006-2009 occurred during a period of historically low (zero) interest rates? Under Milton Friedman's and Bernanke's view this should restart the economy as they allege it would have in 1930-31. Yet, currently (December 2010) economists talk of only a "jobless recovery". Above, an effort was made to show that the demand side for credit during 1930-31 was so disproportionately weak due to extensive noncredit worthy workers/families as to be unresponsive to any strong supply side of credit--only the willingness of banks in 1930-31 to extend subprime loans would accommodate the lack of creditworthy borrowers. What is the situation today? Does it resemble that of the 1930-31 period in that it consists of so many uncreditworthy borrowers as to be also so disproportionately weak compared to the supply side of credit that only extensive subprime loans would accommodate most seeking loans? What does the demand side of people seeking loans consist of today, December 2010? Consider the following income categories and other financial constraints:

(a) Boomers--the largest generation until recently purchased nearly 70 percent of all electronic products during the 1990s. They were the dominant marketing target for decades as sellers attempted to exploit the largest consumer market in the U.S. Will this boomer generation continue to represent the largest consumer group and will it seek loans in order to pursue their buying? The unequivocal answer is NO!

The reasons are many: 1. Greatly reduced refinancing of mortgages due to their advanced age for purposes of seeking such lending. Refinancing does not reduce the principle of the mortgage but extends its maturity by reducing monthly payments. Boomers would more likely seek a reverse mortgage than refinancing their mortgage. Reverse mortgages provide more security but do not provide the extra spending power under refinancing. 2. As pointed out in a Wall Street Journal of August 16, 2010 entitled, "Another Threat to Economy: Boomers Cutting Back" which cites that declining returns on savings and bonds, declining asset values of homes, 401(k) plans, pensions, and other investments, a poor economy which is denying jobs to older workers has resulted in "2008, the latest data available, people aged 65 to 74 were spending 12.3 % less than they did ten years earlier…" The article provided this visual:

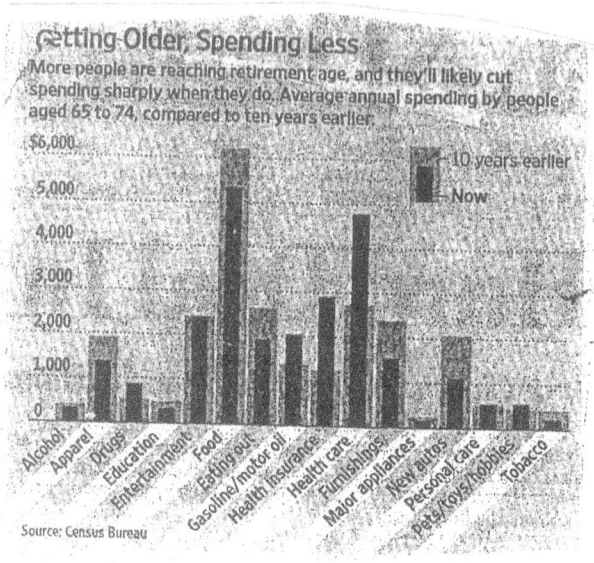

3. Another article in the Indianapolis Star, December 8, 2010 points out that some boomers "will suffer declining health which removes them substantial employment opportunities. Even those capable of working face a declining financial status: The Star cites these troubling facts for seniors which exclude them as meaningful consumers and borrowers: a. "For 20 percent of married retirees and 40 percent of single retirees, Social Security is 90 percent or more of their income." b. 'The search of jobs after age 50 can be excruciating. A Pew survey poll found that 30 percent of unemployed people 55 and older were jobless for a year or more. The number of discouraged older workers--those who have simply stopped looking for jobs--rose 14 percent in June (2010)......." c. The inability to find work compels many to have "to dip into their retirement savings early. About 67 percent of unemployed workers over 55 had to dip into retirement savings to make ends meet, according to a survey by the Boston College Sloan Center on Aging and Work....." While for some work during their later years can be rewarding, those

who must seek work to maintain present living standards face an economy which is not offering many jobs plus the disadvantage that "25 percent will have health problems or skills not matched to the existing jobs, and they will have a hard time working longer" quote from Alicia Munnell, director of the Center for Retirement Research at Boston College.

(b) The second income group/groups which are not likely candidates for substantial loans are those in their 20s and in their 30s. It was documented before how opportunities are being denied these workers in terms of skill-development and promotions to better jobs. As the Wall Street Journal Article above "Another Threat to Economy: Boomers Cutting Back", cited:

> "The impact isn't limited to people on the verge of retiring. Younger people, too, will have to reduce consumption now to save enough money to get by in retirement. That's one reason Richard Berner, chief U.S. economist at Morgan Stanley in New York, estimates that even after the economy recovers, consumer spending will grow at an annual, inflation-adjusted rate of about 2% to 2.5% in the long term, compared to an average of 3.6% in the ten years leading up to the last recession."

(c) Middle Class: This income groups often attains a middle class status through the earnings of both parents. It was cited above that child-care expenses can be as much as 20 percent of the second income, giving the effect of almost nullifying any financial gain from the second job. This group suffered generally the same as others with the great losses in mutual funds and 401(k) funds and with decreased equity in their homes caused by refinancing or by declining home prices. The surge in spending during the 2000s was based to a great extent on refinancing and equity loans. Also credit card debt contributed heavily to consumption. Even though the income of many in the middle class remained rather stable during the past year of 2009, 'households in the middle fifth of the population sliced their average annual spending to $41, 150 in 2009.....That was down 3.1 % from 2007 and 3.5% from 2008, the steepest one-year drop since record-keeping began in 1984[17] However, the poorest Americans 'spent more as prices for necessities such as food and rental housing climbed. Spending rose 5.6 % from 2007 to 2009 for the poorest fifth of consumers, the most of any other income group, despite a 5.5 % drop in after-tax income to an average $9,856 a household."[18] The Journal provided this breakdown of spending patterns for all income groups:

Making Do With Less | How the recession has changed Americans' spending patterns

Change from 2007 to 2009 for the following income groups:

	INCOME AFTER TAXES	FOOD AT HOME	ALCOHOLIC BEVERAGES	APPAREL AND SERVICES	ENTERTAINMENT
All consumers	-0.17%	8.31%	-4.81%	-8.29%	-0.19%
Highest 20% (ABOVE $91,290)	-0.85%	6.91%	-3.71%	-13.25%	
Next 20% ($57,944-$91,289)	1.70	8.44	6.92	-11.66	-7.55%
Middle 20% ($36,070-$57,943)	0.04	9.66	-20.10	15.24	7.21
Next 20% ($19,301-$36,069)	-0.53	9.41	-8.09	11.42	-2.05
Lowest 20% (BELOW $19,301)	-5.49	22.21	-3.41	14.22	10.83 / 9.61

	AVG. ANNUAL SPENDING	FOOD AWAY FROM HOME	HOUSING	HEALTH INSURANCE	EDUCATION
All consumers	-1.15%	-1.84%	-0.15%	15.53%	13.02%
Highest 20% (ABOVE $91,290)	-2.55%	-0.54%	-4.71%	18.57	16.73%
Next 20% ($57,944-$91,289)	-0.71	-1.72	-0.82	17.45	27.81
Middle 20% ($36,070-$57,943)	-3.06	-9.45	2.90	18.66	3.01
Next 20% ($19,301-$36,069)	0.74	3.29	3.85	9.09	6.65

[19]

Finally, as cited in the Wall Street Journal, June 30, 2010, 'Middle-age workers-50 to 64 years old--are most likely to have taken a hit in the last 30 months of the downturn, a group normally at the peak of its earning potential, according to a report being released Wednesday by the nonpartisan Pew Research Center."[20]

Even where spending may increase as during the Christmas season, consumers are using less credit cards and more cash or debt cards in their purchasing. The Indianapolis Star provided a visual in its article of December 2, 2010 "THIS YEAR, CASH IS KING AT STORES."

      Paying for Purchases.

      (d) OVER-ALL RESTRAINTS ON LENDING/BORROWERING

1. Referring again to the Wall Street Journal article above of June 30, 2010, the most restricting adverse condition for credit-lending (in addition, I would argue, to the great disparities in income) is the continuing recessionary condition. "Out of the 13 recessions the U.S. has endured since the Great Depression of 1929-1933, 'none has presented a more punishing combination of length, breadth and depth than this one' write the report's authors. (Pew Research Center). Unemployment data 'don't fully convey the scope of the employment crisis that has unfolded during the recession." As reported in the article, the recession has cut a swath across all income sectors, low, middle, and upper middle class.

The effect of income reduction on spending and borrowing is substantiated by the Wall Street Journal in its article of September 18-19 page A6 where it provides a chart showing 1.household net worth 2. Reduced consumer borrowing 3.stalled bank lending 4. And corporate hoarding of their own cash:

Significantly in this article is cited the following which provide disincentives for seeking or even granting loans:

"Despite the frugality of households and companies, total U.S. debt edged up 1.2% as state, local and federal governments borrowed to finance massive deficits." (This could have a 'crowding out' effect in taking funds which would otherwise be available for lending, but instead is absorbed by either taxes or the buying of government securities by banks.) With respect to consumer borrowing becoming more active, the article cites discouraging facts: "Households pared down their debts for the ninth-straight quarter, largely by defaulting on mortgages and credit-card debts. Total household debt outstanding fell $77 billion to $13.5

trillion in the second quarter. That's close to the value of mortgage and credit-card debt that banks and other investors wrote off after borrowers defaulted. Commercial-bank records suggest such write-off amounted to more than $70 billion."[22]

"At 119% of annual disposable income, household debt has fallen from its peak of 130$ in September 2007. Economists believe a sustainable level would be closer to 100% or even lower. Other measures of consumers' debt burden suggest they're closer to the point where consumers can start spending again."[23] (However, by start spending again does not mean seeking loans as before but rather savings are more likely to begin as the rest of the article shows as does a Wall Street Journal article of November 26, 2010 "Facing A World Without Credit" page A6. This last article shows greatly reduced use of credit after families/individuals filed bankruptcy. The bankruptcy freed them of excessive accumulated debt, but did not result in the subsequent pursuit of loans. The article cites that {t}here years after filing for bankruptcy, just 3.4% of debtors obtained a mortgage, according to an early survey of debtors by Deborah Thorne, an Ohio University sociologist.. Of those who didn't own homes, 41% had leased an apartment. Those who didn't rent lived with family or friends or were homeless."

Any temptation to resume consumption based on excessive debt should become reacquainted with that past as recited in <u>Secrets of Economic Indicators</u>:

> "By 2005 and 2006, personal savings fell into negative territory as households routinely spent more than their income. So in addition to spending their entire paycheck, Americans borrowed more money and even dug into savings they had accumulated from past years to finance all that shopping. One of the most startling illustrations of how hooked consumers have become on living beyond their means can be seen by doing a simple calculation from this table. ....Back in 1980, wages and salaries paid for nearly 80% of all spending, with the rest (20%) being financed by debt and from withdrawing from past savings. By the summer of 2006, wages and salaries financed barely 65% of all expenditures, which meant consumers had to borrow more than ever before as well as tap some savings to fill the gap between income and spending."[24]

The gap between income and spending was filled and continued to be fed by refinancing, equity loans, and then subprime loans. Mortgage refinancing in 2003 reached 72 % of all mortgage originations of $4 trillion.[25] Subprime lending reached 32% of all mortgages in 2004 and 24% in 2005.[26] This was a weak foundation then and would be today as a way of curing the credit crunch.

BUSINESS LOANS AS PART OF THE DEMAND SIDE

Just as in the 1920s, commercial banks are being deprived of business customers due to the independence of major corporations from bank lending. Several articles in recent years have noted the huge stashes of cash accumulated by large businesses. The following reported accumulated earnings of major corporations is being put to non-economic expansionary purposes. Instead, the cash holdings are used to pay dividends or to make merger and acquisition deals.

1. Business Week article of July 1, 2005, page 80 reveals an early disposition by corporate America to avoid risk-taking. In its article captioned, "Too Much Cash, Too Little Innovation". Business Week cited the following examples of the idling of capital:

a. "But mostly chief executives are deciding that the best thing they can do with their mountains of cash is turn them over to shareholders. Tech companies are paying out more in dividends and buying back more stock than ever before. It's not just Microsoft Corp. which dispersed about $35billion over the past year in special and regular dividends to whittle down its cash hoard to a mere $38billion. Hewlett-Packard, IBM, Qualcomm, and many others are also handing out more cash back to investors."[27] The article notes the importance in this development.

"This is a huge change for the tech industry. For years the makers of computers, chips, software, cell phones, and other tech gear devoured chunks of capital because they could put it to productive use. Now some economists see the industry's accumulation of cash and the handouts to shareholders as an admission that the sector is slowing". Economist Milton Harris suggested that 'maybe there aren't good growth opportunities out there."

2. Even prior to the above article, Business Week in its article of December 27, 2004 captioned, "Making a Pile of Cash-Rich Companies, pp122-123 The article's author, Dean Faust suggested, for example, that Bristol-Myers' $725 billion cash sitting on the company's balance sheet was predicted to be used for high dividend payments or for acquisitions. Other similar situated companies are cited to intend the same disposition of their accumulated cash.

3. Again, the Chicago Tribune in an article of June 23, 2005 by Bill Barnhart reported reasons for this corporate disposition:

"First, 'companies like having the increased financial flexibility, given the increased interest rate environment.' quoting Newman.

"Caution has persisted well into the current economic expansion," Newman said. Other reasons cited for hording of cash were a. company's sense that we were in a slowing economy b. slower growth usually leads to more mergers and acquisitions. c and if you have cash, 'you don't have to borrow as much at higher rates to make acquisitions' Newman said. d more growth companies are reconsidering distributing dividends as opposed to seeking more growth. From "Companies sitting on big cash piles in need of a plan"[28]

4. Again Business Week in its September 12, 2005 cited the following largest holdings of cash:

STOCKS

U.S. CORPORATIONS get brownie points for having so much cash on their balance sheets, and that is often cited as reason to be bullish on the stock market. But the truth is that the money is in relatively few hands (table). According to Banc of America Securities chief equity strategist Thomas McManus, just 10 companies hold 25% of all the cash held by companies in the Standard & Poor's 1500-stock index (excluding financial firms).

The Largest Cash Holdings

COMPANY	CASH BALANCE (BILLIONS)
Microsoft	37.8
ExxonMobil	30.3
Aetna	16.4
Pfizer	14.6

Data: Banc of America Securities

The Largest Cash Holdings

5. Wall Street Journal article of December 7, 2009 p. C8 shows a continuation of this reluctance of big companies to unleash their cash holdings for productive, innovative, or any other risk-taking use. The options cited for disposing of their cash holdings of almost $2 trillion include buybacks, dividends, and mergers. This type of corporate retained earnings is not designed to bring economic growth. All of the usages cited in this article are merely financial arrangements not conducive to building new plants/facilities, introducing new products, new process engineering research and application, or any other productive usage. This use of corporate retained earnings bears an eerie resemblance to the use of earnings in the 1920s which saw about one-thousand companies disappear each year as a result of merger activities.

6. Wall Street Journal article of April 20, 2010, captioned, "Tech Firms Bulk Up With Debt" shows a start in technology companies to selling their bonds instead of relying on selling their stock in raising needed capital. Again, businesses are not part of the demand side

for credit. Nor are they a source of investment capital and therefore are absent from the supply side of credit lending.

7. From the USA Today, July 28, 2010 Matt Krantz reported the continued absence of corporate capital from being made available for productive purposes. The caption of the article is provocative, given the plight of many Americans:

"Companies are sitting of a pile of cash" Enough to pay 2.4 Million workers $70, 000 salaries for 5 years--yet they're not hiring." As the author notes, the consequences for the economy could be severe. "Rather than investing in their future, companies are piling up cash and collecting practically zero interest on the money, hoping there will be a better time to invest." Krantz continued:

The stockpiling of cash is troubling to some, who say that if companies keep hoarding money instead of investing in new facilities and products, it will put a lid on what the economy really needs to get going: new jobs." Many profits were earned through cost-cutting measures such as downsizing and therefore the hoarded cash does not represent the efforts of growth seeking which normally adds jobs to the payroll. The USA Today article provided a list of companies who had the most cash:

In summarizing the demand side for loans, we see boomers with declining income and consumption, generation Xs and Yers with poor credit and jobs, a middle class which for many is a misnomer due to the need for two-parent incomes which is reduced severely by child-care costs and businesses with huge cash hoards and no need to borrow. Technology companies are beginning to offer their company bonds instead of selling stock or seeking loans. There is little doubt that the unavailability of easy credit terms has hurt a number of business attempts at start-up projects and also has impacted severely on some infrastructure needs. However, in terms of assisting consumption to resume its past component of GDP at 70 percent, the demand is decidedly saturated with poor credit risks and only a renewal of subprime-type lending could aspire to regain a consumption level of 70 percent of GDP.

THE SUPPLY SIDE OF CREDIT CRUNCH

Is the supply side of lending (amount of money available for credit on low-interest rate terms) strong enough to overcome the gravitation pull downward of consumer debt exceeding disposable income, of the declining financial strength of the boomers who were the biggest consumers of the 1990s, the debt-ridden, poor employed generations of the 20s and the 30s, and the adversely impacted middle class? It is submitted that the present circumstances bear close proximity to those of the late 1920s and that regardless of the solvency or liquidity status of most banks, lending for consumer purposes would not be high on the banks' lending strategy. Again, profits will demand that banks steer away from commercial lending for consumption and/or building facilities or buying equipment. Unless our industrial structure is revamped toward product-making, research and development, and public goods which bring back jobs of middle class and above incomes, no strong banking system can accommodate a working population which consists of too many low-paying jobs and a business sector more inclined to 'manufacture' profits through mergers, acquisitions, and cost-cutting measures. Nevertheless, a balance presentation of the credit crisis requires a close examination of the present condition of banks and other financial institutions which represent the supply side (suppliers of) of credit.

The reader can revisit the previous chapter concerning the imposition of stress tests on several major financial institutions and the government's requiring that banks shore up their capital to the point that they could absorb any losses without inviting insolvency. Also, we have noted the rescue efforts of the Fed and the U.S. Treasury Department with Congressional authorization buying 'toxic' assets of the banks and investment banks and also buying their corporate stock. Adding to these disparate measures is the troubling source of bank and investment bank profits prior to the financial meltdown--securitizing mortgages, credit card debt, auto loan debt, and other financial innovation which bore no direct relationship with commercial lending for building business facilities or equipment. This plagued banks in the 1920s when corporate sell of stocks and bonds practically eliminated the need to seek bank loans.

The collapse of Lehman Brothers, an historic brokerage, plus the cliff-hanger bailouts of other investment banks are highly suggestive that the financial markets are merely being repaired , not activated for aggressive commercial lending. While the Federal government has been adequately compensated for taking over the 'toxic' assets, the label 'socialism capitalism' as coined by the Chinese is not reassuring that the banks will resume any time soon as an active participant in offering capital funds for new ventures which are much riskier than conventional financial deals.

Recently, the Fed has order a second round of stress tests as reported in the Wall Street Journal, [29] Wall Street Journal reported the following: "The Fed, in guidance issued Wednesday, said the 19 largest bank-holding companies must submit capital plans by early next year showing their ability to withstand losses under a set of conditions to be determined by the central bank, including 'adverse' economic conditions and continuing real-estate-related woes."

The article cites the reason for the first imposition of stress tests in 2009.

"In 2009, U.S. regulators tested the resilience of the same 19 companies. Regulators made the first round public in large part to help assuage investor fears about the extent of losses at the nation's largest financial firms. The tests, which showed banks faced a total of $599 billion in losses over two years, directed 10 banks to add altogether nearly $75 billion to their capital buffers...."

While the stress tests are purportedly just precautionary, Wall Street Journal reported: "Concerns about the health of most large institutions have decreased, though investors remain nervous about the extent of losses banks face if they are required to repurchase flawed mortgages and mortgage-related investments. As part of is review, the Fed will require banks to assess their exposure to so-called 'put-backs' of mortgages."

The banks' profits are returning, but are still cautious about making loans as reported in the USA Today, September 15, 2010 page1B-2B. The following possible adverse contingencies intimate aggressive bank lending:

(a) any sharp decline in U.S. housing prices or in commercial real estate could weaken bank balance sheets on which these properties secure listed loans.

(b) Aftershocks from any European banking collapse could affect U.S. banks' balance sheets.

(c) A double-digit recession in America would require banks to raise an additional $80 billion in capital-as concluded by the International Monetary Fund. IMF stated that "Stability is tenuous... Bank balance sheets remain fragile, and capital buffers may still be inadequate in the face of further increases in non-performing loans." quoted in USA Today,

September 15, 2010 page B2.

      (d) Another reason for little lending is, as was cited above, very little interest in many companies to seek loans. "With existing factories operating far below capacity, there is little reason for many businesses to expand. Demand for new commercial and industrial loans was roughly unchanged in the most recent quarter, after having dropped during the three months that ended I April, the Fed said."[30] The article did state that more loans are becoming available for small businesses.

      Any hope that your 'friendly' local banker will be available for loans is on shaky grounds for many areas of the country. The USA Today in the article above cited a troublesome finding by both the IMF and FDIC: The IMF offered this finding: It noted " a rising gap between the number of home foreclosures and 'seriously delinquent loans; at regional and community banks, suggesting additional loan losses for these institutions." Large banks are protected somewhat by diversified holdings that can absorb some losses, but smaller banks tend to rise and fall with the local economy, especially with respect to the real estate market.

      The FDIC's listed problem banks as 829 mostly smaller lending institutions, up from 775 in March. In another eerily similarity, it was the small banks in rural and small town America in the late 1920 that suffered initially According to Elmus Wicker, there was no nation-wide panic until around 1933 and that the Fed had contained any panic-occurrence in New York City from the Bank of America crisis. Even granted some restored banking ability to provide financial stimuli for renew economic growth, three persistent barriers remain to any banking-led recovery: (a) a demand side of credit which is so disproportionately weak compared to any strong supply of lending as to make only a renewed sub-prime type lending able to achieve an equilibrium of demand and supply for loans. (b) secondly, the industrial sector is not one capable of wholesale expansion through lending as even those cash-cow companies see no growth opportunities which accounts for their hoarding of cash. (3) the great disparities in income which an unbalance economy has created by the excessive emphasis upon finance, real estate, and insurance among others which contained very few middle class rung jobs. It would seem only intervention by the national government in subsidizing the industries which should have been receiving more capital would provide any immediate hope of 5 to 10 years of achieving a satisfactory economy. We will be drawing conclusions like this in the final chapters as we seek to explore any lessons contained in the 1920s experience which are instructed today.

Chapter Ten Notes:

1. David Kennedy op. cit. p 370

2. Ibid, page 165

3. Ibid, page 182

4. Jeffrey Frieden op. cit. page 141

5. Ibid, page 140

6. David Kennedy op. cit. page 76 (paperback ed.)

7. Harvey Green op. cit. pages 76-77

8.   The Great Bull Market   page 25

9 William Leuchenberg op. cit. page 245

10. Elmus Wicker op. cit. page 16

11. Ibid, page 16

12. Ibid, page 16

13 William Leuchenberg op. cit. 258

14. Liaquat Hiram op. cit. page 37

15. Ibid, page 437

16.   "Another Threat to Economy: Boomers Cutting Back" Wall Street Journal August 16, 2010

17.   "Middle Class Slams Brakes on Spending" Wall Street Journal October 6, 2910

18. Ibid, page A4

20.   "Recession Strikes Deep Into Work Force" Wall Street Journal June 10, 2010

21. Ibid, page

22. Wall Street Journal September 18-19, 2007

23. Ibid, pageA6

24. Ibid, page A6

25. Bernard Baumohl op. cit.page651

26. Anothony Downs op. cit. page 19

27. Ibid, page 18

28. "Too Much Cash, Too Little Innovation" Business Week July 1, 2005

29. Bill Barnett "Companies sitting on big cash piles in need of a plan" Chicago Tribune June 21, 2005.

30. November 18, 2010 page C1

31. USA Today September 15, 2010

CHAPTER ELEVIN

BURDEN OF PROOF--WHO HAS OFFERED MORE PERSUASIVE CASE, THE MONETARISTS WHO MAINTAIN THAT THE FED COULD HAVE PREVENTED THE GREAT DEPRESSION WITH A MORE AGGESSIVE POLICY OF INCREASING THE QUANTITY OF MONEY AND THEREFORE ESTABLISHING LOWER INTEREST RATE OR ARE YOU CONVINCED THAT LOWER INTEREST RATES CANNOT COMPENSATE FOR GREAT DISPARTIES IN INCOMES IN WHICH AT LEAST ONE-THIRD OF THE PEOPLE ARE IN POVERTY. DOES THE CHAPTER OF BANKING POLICIES OF THE 1920S AND RECENTLY SUPPORT BANKING PRACTICES WHICH ARE DESIGNED TO HELP COMPANIES AND WORKERS OR DO THEY REALLY SHOW AN EMPHASIS BY FINANCIAL INSTITUTIONS OF GENERATING INCOMES WITHIN THROUGH FEES AND COMMISSIONS AND IN THE LAST DECADE THROUGH SECURITIZATION OF MORTGAGES AND OTHER DEBTS? DOES THE CHAPTER OF CONSUMER LENDING SHOW CONSUMER DEBT BASED ON SOLID EMPLOYMENT OR OVER-RELIANCE UPON ASSETS CONTINUING TO RISE IN VALUES, SUCH AS HOMES. IN ORDER TO UNRAVEL THIS WEB OF INTRICATE INTERPLAY OF VARIOUS ECONOMIC FACTORS SUCH AS INCOMES, CONSUMER DEBT, HOME VALUES, INTEREST RATES, CAPITAL INVESTMENTS, AND OPPORTUNITY COSTS ASSOCIATED WITH EXCESSIVE SPECULATION, WE BEGIN WITH A SIMPLIFIED EXPLANATION AND ILLUSTRATION OF HOW THE FEDERAL RESERVE SYSTEM WORKS IN ITS EFFORTS TO LOWER INTEREST RATES (OR INCREASE INTEREST RATES).

STUDY THIS SIMPLIFIED BANK'S BALANCE SHEET:

ASSETS		LIABILITIES
CASH	$30,000	DEMAND DEPOSITS $100,00
US.TREASURY BONDS	$50,000	
CORPORATE BONDS	$30,000	
EQUIPMENT	$70,000	
LOANS (ACCOUNTS RECEIVABLE)	$90,000	

CAPITAL ACCOUNT

STOCK (IN ITS OWN BANK)

RETAINED EARNINGS

The Federal Reserve Bank has two primary methods of influencing the economy either in raising the fed fund rate (what one bank charges another bank for over-night loans) or in lower the fed fund rate. The Fed can establish a reserve requirement in which a bank must keep on hand cash or cash balances with the Federal Reserve Bank equal to a designated percentage of demand deposits. Thus, if in the above example, the reserve requirement is 10 %, this bank must keep cash balance of $10,000 (10%x $100,000). So, how much cash in this bank is available for lending? Pick an answer from the following: (a) $10,000 (b) $20,000, or © $70,000? Ans. $20,000 or $30,000 - $10,000 (the reserve required amount) only cash can be loaned. What if the Fed wanted to allow more of this banks' cash to be available for lending? It could lower the reserve requirement to , say, 8%. Under a 8% requirement, the bank is now required to keep on hand in reserve only $8,000 or 8%x 100,000) The bank can now lend $22, 000 instead of only $20,000 of its cash on hand. This ability to lend more creates a larger money supply as the loans are spent by depositors and received by other banks in which the merchants deposit checks spent by the original borrowers of our bank above. While no single bank can increase the money supply, it's loans are spent and deposited in other banks, thereby increasing the amount of money available for lending or spending. In the example above where the bank can lend up to $20,000, this $20,000 has the potential to increase the money supply to $200,000. How is this possible? The reserve requirement creates the multiplier by which amount lending can potentially enlarge the supply of money in circulation. Thus, a reserve requirement of 10% creates a multiplier of 10. What if the Fed feels that this potential increase of money to $200,000 will not trigger a sufficient lower interest rate to encourage capital loans, consumer loans, or real estate lending? Does the Fed have an alternative method of lowering interest rates which would increase the money supply beyond the potential $200, 000 which our bank above can do under the reserve requirement of 10%? Yes, the Fed can pursue open-market activities in which it can buy U.S. Treasury bonds from the banks or depositors. In the case of our bank above, the Fed could buy our bank's holdings of $50,000 in an effort to increase the amount of money available for lending. How does this improve our bank's lending capacity? Examine our bank's balance sheet after the Fed has purchased our bank's Treasury Bonds.

ASSETS	LIABILITIES
CASH $80,000 ($30,000+ $50,000 FROM SALE)	$100,000 DEMAND DEPOSITS (ASSUMING NO DEPOSITORS MAKE OTHER DEPOSITS.)
CORPORATE BONDS $30,000	
EQUIPMENT $70,000	
LOANS $90,000	

With the same reserve requirement of 10%, our bank is still required to maintain cash on hand of only $10,000. This gives the bank the ability to loan up to $70,000 which is $50,000 more than before and even $48,000 more if the reserve requirement were reduced to 8% without any Fed's buying of U.S Treasury bonds. Whereas the multiplier effect before was $220,000 with a reserve requirement of 8%, the multiplier effect can now potentially create a money supply of $700,000 (10 x $70,000) or if the reserve requirement were 8% a money supply of ($72,000x 8%) or $576,000. Obviously, the Fed can activate the economy much quicker through its open-market buying of bank U.S. Treasury bonds.(If the Fed wished to 'cool' the economy by increasing interest rates, it would sell its U.S. Treasury bonds to banks or individuals. This would take money out of the hands of banks (and of individuals) and reduce lending and spending.)

A similar multiplier effect would result if the Fed purchased U.S. Treasury bonds from individuals who would then substitute any bonds which they had in their bank safe-deposit boxes for cash deposits in their banks. Thus, if the Fed purchased $70,000 from our bank above from the bank's customers, demand deposits could increase from $100,000 to $170,000. In depositing their cash received from their sales to the Fed, depositors would increase the bank' cash holdings from $30,000 to $100,000. With a reserve requirement of 10%, the bank would be required to maintain cash reserves of $17,000, leaving $153,000 of the bank's cash eligible for lending. Essentially, buying the bank's U.S. Treasury bonds or the bonds of individuals has the same effect in increasing the money supply. The following excerpt from the Wall Street Journal illustrates the reaction of market indicators to the Fed's buying of securities, called Quantitative Assessment:

Journal article of June 30, 2011 provided

A Quantitative Assessment

The Federal Reserve's second round of so-called quantitative easing comes to an end today, after $600 billion in Treasury-bond purchases over the past eight months.

Chairman Ben Bernanke's stated goals: lower mortgage rates to boost housing, reduce corporate bond rates to encourage investment and raise stock prices to increase confidence and spending. Markets responded soon after the program was first hinted at by Mr. Bernanke in an Aug. 27 speech in Jackson Hole, Wyo. But the end goals proved more elusive.
—*Matt Phillips and Stephen Grocer*

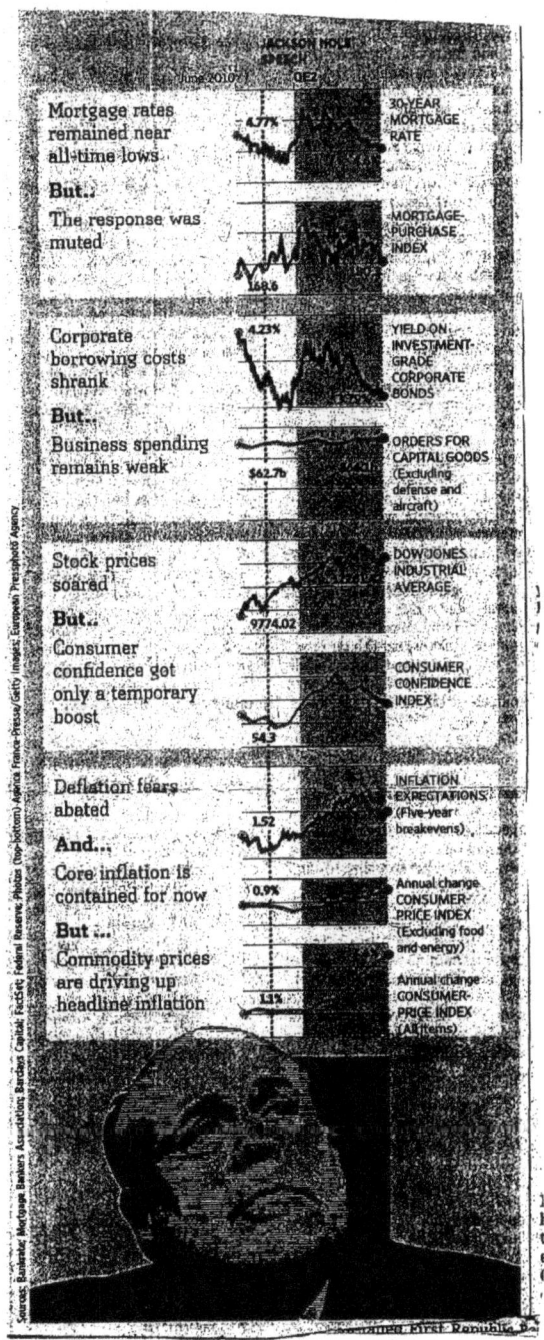

Time Magazine provided this easy to understand example of how the money supply is expanded through bank lending:

HOW THE FED WORKS

The Federal Reserve System, created to head off periodic bank panics and add flexibility to the financial system, is one of the nation's most watched—yet least understood—institutions How the Banking System Creates Wealth

(1) A saver deposits
$100 in a bank; a
Federal guarantee
Ensures that he can
Withdraw it later

(2) The bank holds $10
In reserve and lends the
Other $90 to a borrower,
Collecting interest on the loan

(3) The borrower's $90 is spent and gets
Deposited in another bank, which then
Lends out $81 of it.
(4) Eventually, the original $100
Deposit expands to $1,000 with $100 now held in reserve

In this system of fractional-reserve banking, too many withdrawals at once could cause a crisis. The Fed was created to minimize that risk[2]

Finally, the Fed has another tool--lending to distressed banks through the Fed's 'discount window'. Historically, banks have avoided the 'discount window' loans as it is regarded as a sign of the bank's severe financial distressed condition.

GOING BEYOND ORDINARY MEASURES AND ORTHODOX FEDERAL POLICIES:

During the past decade of the 2000s, the Fed has resorted to extraordinary measures beyond open market buying, or changing the reserve requirement, or even relying upon the discount window as a rescue of distressed banks. Consider the following narrative of the Fed's responses to the emerging and on-going financial chaos:

A Cascade of Federal Responses

Lending markets were experiencing a virtual meltdown, not only concerning housing and other real estate but also concerning housing and other real estate but also concerning the provision of credit to all other business. This threatened to bring the entire U.S. economy to a halt. In response, the federal government made several dramatic moves to shore up the financial sector:

It seized the government-sponsored enterprises Fannie Mae and Freddie Mac, fired the chief executives, and guaranteed that all their securities would be backed by the federal government.

It refused to provide funds to prevent the investment banking house Lehman Brothers from going into bankruptcy, which it shortly did.

It seized control of the nation's largest insurance company—AIG, provided it with $125million with which to stay in business, and controlled a majority of AIG stock. It fired the top executives and replaced them with its own appointees, but it did not fully nationalize AIG.

It opened up its lending window to provide credit to other financial institutions in dire need of funds to stay in business.

Then Treasury Secretary Henry Paulson and Federal Reserve Chairman Ben Bernanke proposed a massive program of buying up so-called bad assets from banks and investment banks with federal funds. The goal was to get those assets off the books of major lenders, replace them with usable cash, and free lenders to start supplying credit again to the U.S. economy.

The estimated overall gross outlay was $700 billion, to be paid for by enlarging the U.S. national debt. This proposal required action by Congress, which President George W. Bush promoted in a nationally broadcast speech in September 2008. The proposal set off an intense legislative effort by both houses of Congress to get something done before members recessed to participate in the national election in November. On September 29, the 'bailout bill' was voted on by the House of Representatives and defeated 228-205; the Dow Jones Industrial Average fell 777 points.

On October1, the Senate passed an expanded version of the same bill by a vote of 74 to 25. This version contained $107 billion in earmarks mostly unrelated to the financial crisis but added to persuade many Senate and House members to support the bill.

Two days later, on October 3, the House of Representatives passed the same bill that the Senate had supported, this time by a vote of 263-171. The president immediately signed the bill into law. The Dow Jones Industrial Average fell anyway, but by a much smaller amount than on September 29.

On October 13, the U.S. Treasury convened a meeting of nine of the nation's largest banks and announced that it would spend $125 billion to buy preferred stock and warrants in all those banks to shore up their capital. These infusions would amount to an average increase of 20 percent in the total capital of the nine banks. Treasury Secretary Paulson demanded that all nine banks agree to accept such capital infusions immediately, and they all did. He also announced that another S125 billion in such capital infusions would be made available to other smaller banks in the near future. The preferred stock would pay a dividend rate of 5 percent, rising to 9 percent after 5 years. The government would give up half of its warrants if the banks got private capital infusions matching the public investment before 2010. This second major federal approach to attacking the credit crunch followed a policy that the Bank of England had already suggested and carried out.

On October 29, the Federal Reserve Board lowered its target for the federal funds rate to 1 percent, the lowest since 2003.

Despite the credit squeeze, investors were still making about $5 billion in transactions of REIT stocks every day on the New York Stock Exchange, according to NAREIT. On November 25, the Federal Reserves and the Treasury announce $800billion in new lending programs to help consumers and mortgage borrowers. These programs were designed to free up more private lending and put downward pressure on interest rates for households. Up to $600billion of that was to be used to purchase debt issued by Fannie Mae, Freddie Mac, Ginnie Mae, and Federal Home Loan Banks 9 ($100billion) or debt tied to mortgages issued by Fannie Mae, Freddie Mac, and Ginnie Mae ($500bilion Another $200 billion was to be used to support credit for consumers and small businesses.

According to the New York Times of November 26, 2008, the federal government has advanced or promised to advance a total of $7.7 trillion to aid banks and other firms in difficulty. That included $3.1trillion to insure against private default, of which $97billion had already been spent; $3.0 trillion to invest in private banks and other companies, of which $649 billion had already been spent. Thus, $1.363 trillion of federal funds had already been spent to shore up the financial sector of the economy and ameliorate the likely recession.[3]

The unconventional programs utilized by the Fed during this period may be reviewed in the following narrative from Mark Zandi's Financial S Hook:

With the banking system increasingly cash-strapped and discount-window borrowing at a standstill, the Fed became creative. In mid-December, the central bank unveiled an alternative to the discount window, which it called the Term Auction Facility (TAF). It enabled institutions to bid for short-term funds by putting up a wide range of securities, including mortgage-related instruments, as collateral (see Table 12.1) In a TAF auction, the bids begin at a rate above the federal funds rate but well below the discount rate, thus providing institutions with at least the cover of a reason to borrow funds from the Fed other than potential stress. It worked: Because no apparent stigma was attached to borrowing from the TAF, response was strong, beginning with the first auction. Although money markets were still not functioning normally by mid-2008, worries that the banking system might grind to a halt for lack of cash had faded. [4]

Perhaps the greatest indicator of severity of the financial crisis is exposed by the Fed's buying the troubled assets of banks under TARP (Troubled Asset Recovery Program) or even buying the capital stock of the distressed banks. David Wessel provided a chart showing the Fed's portfolio holdings as of December 2011 see his article in the Wall Street Journal, December 7, 2011 page A4.[5]

The Fed's TARP acquisitions actually represent loans using the troubled assets as collateral with the hope that government possession of these assets will increase their value for resale. Nevertheless, despite this Fed intervention into bank asset holdings and even capital stock, the Fed has imposed stress tests on many major and small banks. These stress tests evaluate the current liquidity and solvency conditions of these banks. In the next section on the banks' response to Fed's policies, we will examine more thoroughly the stress test problem. It is still with us as shown by a recent Wall Street Journal article. [6]

The article by Alan Zibel and Victoria McGrane begins "Banks will be tested on their ability to withstand a severe recession-including a sharp slowdown in China-as part of a new round of 'stress tests' to be completed next year, the Federal Reserve said."

As the article states the stress tests have been applied to determine a bank's ability to pay dividends or buy back shares. The focus of the tests are to determine the ability of various banks' capital to survive economic reversals.--Liquidity or cash ability to lend seems to be collateral concern of the government regarding many banks.

Another object of the Fed's lower interest rate strategy is to restore the peoples' asset values as announced in September 16, 2012 issue of a local Indiana issue of The Anderson Herald Bulletins entitled, "Fed seeking to create wealth, not just cut rates."

"The idea is for the Fed's $40 billion-a-month in bond purchases to lower interest rates and cause stock and home prices to rise, creating a 'wealth effect' that would boost the economy' Ands 'if people feel that their financial situation is better because their 401(k) looks better or for whatever reason--their house is worth more, they're more willing to go out and spend' Chairman Ben Bernanke told reporters."

What about the needed increases in disposable income required for many workers in order to repay their prior debt and to establish a reasonable relationship between consumer debt and disposable incomes? Bernanke, it is submitted, has it backwards when he surmised that peoples' increased assets values will lead to increased consumption. How, through equity loans and refinancing? Nevertheless, we are left with that presumption when he stated, "That's (increased wealth) going to provide the demand that firms need in order to be willing to hire and to invest." This is highly problematic or uncertain if one reviews the following efforts of the Federal Government to restore the housing market:

1 The Home Affordable Refinancing Program (HARP) As of 2011, this program has fallen short of its intended number of applicants. President Obama has announced an

intention to renew this effort in 2012.

2. Mortgage Modification under HARP. Again, this program has been a disappointment both for home owners and the government.

3. Reverse Mortgages- Really only an option for the elderly who are not likely to be great consumers.

4. A tax credit for the purchase of new homes has had success during the period of eligibility.(The tax season.) But home buying slacks off after the tax season.

5. The Mortgage Assistance Program. Recent media coverage during the 2011 year shows a significant percentage of defaults under this program.

Will Bernanke prove that a sense of resorted wealth will trigger enough consumption which the economy has come to expect (70% of GDP) to overcome considerable negative equity, accumulated credit card debt, high unemployed and about one-third of workers employed in part-time, temp-postions, and other nonstandard jobs.? That is what really remains as the ultimate proof. Meanwhile, in reaching for this final proof we must examine if lower rates have provided the needed incentives for banks and investors to seek capital loans for plant and equipment.

Chapter 11 Notes:

1. June 30, 2011

2. Time Magazine   December 28-January 4th, 2010 page 311

3. Anthony Downs op. cit. pages 28-30

4. Mark Zandi op. cit. pages 194, 202, 214, 218

5.

6. Alan Zibel and Victoria McGrane "Fed Details Stress Test Scenarios" Wall Street Journal November16, 2012

7.   Hutt, The Keynesian Episode   page

8. August 28, 2013

9, Ibid page A2

10. Peter Coy et al "The Disposable Worker" Business Week

11. Donald Peck op. cit. page 64

12. Ibid, page 64

13. Ibid, page 64

14. Ibid page 65

15. Ibid, page 65

16. Ibid, page66

17. Wall Street Journal March 20, 2013

18. Ibid at page A5

19. Historical Abstract of U.S: Colonial Times to 1970 Part 1 Bicentennial Series F 144-162 page 234

20. Ibid, page 234

21. Ibid, page 235

CHAPTER TWELVE

THE MANDATE FOR CHANGE

Any economic policies or system which fails to satisfy the Four Freedoms cited by Franklin Roosevelt among which he included "Freedom from Want" and seek economic security for those who occupy the lower social rings of society cannot call itself a policy "of the people." We cannot ignore those today who are similarly situated as were the coal miners, textile workers, sharecroppers, tenant farmers, and the disabled and the elderly during the 1920s and call ourselves a free and caring people. It is easy to remain content while living in ignorance of the plight of others. Even with the knowledge of others' poverty, some remain indifferent, relying upon the doctrine of self-reliance or even Social Darwinism to justify their political isolation from the fate of the nation.

It is easy to ignore the existence of extensive poverty or unfair disadvantages when the final yearly accounting in our GDP shows economic growth and rising corporate profits. Many have spoken to this deception. Among them is Nobel Prize winner, Joseph Stiglitz, who wrote in his column entitled, "Good Numbers Gone Bad" Why relying on GDP accounting can lead to poor decision-making." in Fortune, October 2, 2006 page 68. This article addresses the failure of GDP accounting to allow for an adjustment for the depletion of resources needed to achieve the GDP. Also, even a robust increase in GDP often fails to reflect the great disparities in earnings as in the 1920s and today. Even more, GDP accounting fails to note the lessening of the middle class, due primarily to the decline of middle class type jobs. The failure to detect such weaknesses in the GDP result from the tendency to apply observations and examinations from the top or coarse grain applications which fail to show in more enlightening detail the composition of how this particular GDP was obtained through the various earnings of workers. The latter would apply a 'fine grain' study to the earnings distribution which occurred. The tendency to rely upon 'macroeconomic results' for policy-making purposes is that it offers a more straight forward policy-one which does not question microeconomic policies of employers, investors, or product-making decisions such as the failure of car makers in the late 1970s to abandoned the large cars which required low gas mileage as compared to the high fuel efficient cars emerging from Japan. Macroeconomics does not concern itself insofar as government spending, taxation, and monetary policies are concerned. Only an intrusion policy under microeconomic tools would concern itself initially with this fuel problem.

A rather conservative economist, Hutt in his The Keynesian Episode wrote,

"The modern emphasis on macroeconomics, the validity of which depends-as few writers in the field seem to realize- upon its reconciliation with microeconomics, aggravates the situation. For macroeconomics, which is particularly amendable to mathematical enunciation, is now being taught at an early stage in the typical curriculum, and the young student tends, I fear, to spend more time grappling with mathematics than with economics, the difficulties of which are not mathematical. His attention is diverted from rigorous thought about the phenomena of scarcity and price and the stabilizing and coordinative role of the price system, to the study of complex truisms. When he graduates, he may have learned very little of basic economic science." He went on the say that the ground-level business decision-makers have more day to day insight as to the workings of the economy than do those who occupy higher public positions."

Today, macroeconomic derived accounting results conceal the decline of the middle class, the growing scarcity of standard jobs consisting of good pay and a 40 hour work week, and finally any measurement of GDP in recent decades will reflect how financial earnings have outperformed those who make products and provide essential services. We cannot be so enamored of our growing successes in electronics, biotech, and even medical research as to be blinded to how the earnings of all endeavors are being distributed. We, as a people, should not celebrate our apparent achievements like the reasonably affordable car, radio, appliances, and other consumer goods which were made more available in the 1920s to ordinary people than in history. This so-called Jazz Age ignore at least one-third who laid in poverty and disease. In forgetting that if these people had received decent pay and working conditions their purchasing of goods and services then perhaps the economy would have been buoyed sufficiently in 1929-1930 to ward off the Great Depression since only marginal adjustment by industry, banks, and government would have been more likely to suffice to begin an economic recovery.

We must correct those practices which inure to the benefit of only the few. We must regard today's injustices as requiring an urgent and steadfast pursuit of these corrections which must precede any solutions. This bottom-up, grass-roots support has always been important in those measures which have endured to the benefit of the general welfare. It is true because politicians are cautious people who only follow where the people lead when it comes to momentous and defining moments in history.

Among the realizations to await the people is that it makes a difference what goods are made and enjoyed. Too many play- full gadgets bring leisurely enjoyment at the expense of long-term investments for vital goods and services. The failure to enjoy some vital needs because of excessive speculation and trading in financial instruments is known as "opportunity costs" and cannot be ignored indefinitely. A good example of the failure of capitalist to take risks in a vital product because of 'easy' profits on Wall Street and excessive luxury spending by the rich is the failure to pursue the life-saving drug, penicillin, whose discovery in the early 1920s made marketing possible. When did the drug finally become available?---at the end of World War II in an effort to save lives of wounded and diseased soldiers. How many 'opportunities' have we lost in the past 3 decades in medicine due to the diversions of Wall Street speculation and of institutional holdings impatience with quarterly returns of companies who otherwise would undertake risky R&D. Sure, computers and its by-product industries have been celebrated in the past few decades. However, it was government initiatives in data processing and computers which set up a foundation for the future of the industry. Have we missed pursing a "New Frontier" in medicine, education, agriculture, and energy because of a risk-adverse model being pursued over the past decades? Much of engineering has been devoted to process engineering-how to make products better and cheaper. Computer industry has been a true ally to this type of engineering. However, product-making engineering results in more jobs as process engineering usually seeks the need for less workers. In the early 2000-2004 period, low interest rates led to mainly cost-reducing equipment investments-not plants and equipment which needed many operators. So, as we re-examine these parallels, one must constantly ask 'was this the result or cause of opportunity costs?" We begin with perhaps the most dominant variable an economy must deal with--the distribution of incomes and wealth. Does inequality matter? Nobel Prize winner, Joseph Stiglitz states it causes great social instability. Also, one might add that as in the 1920s, the inability of one-third of the households to buy essential food, clothing, and shelter products adversely impacts on those industries. This failure of so many people to buy adequate food supplies, adequate clothing, and adequate shelter reduces the demand for these products and thereby deprives these companies of sales and possibly the production economy of scales which allows the least cost per unit to be achieved. Ask yourself in reviewing the following, "Does it matter for the financial security of the future of these young people who the following shows a general lack of opportunities in their chosen or allied fields or do the cited material represent only a 'bump' in the road to success which almost everyone has experienced. Or are these 'bumps' different in kind and scope from any obstacles the boomers faced in the late 1950s and the 1960s and for many the 1970s and 1980s. Did college graduates of the 60s, 70s, 80s, or even the 90s suffer the accumulated college debt of today's students who generally average over $25,000 debt? Did the generations of the 1950s, 1960s, 1970s, and beyond faced the limited professional and occupational opportunities which today's skilled and educated young age's 25-35 face. Those readers who are in those age groups of former decades must be honest with themselves and rise above generational bias that typically the old have against the young. Let the facts speak to all and motivate them to somehow register a concern, if not complaint to our government and their policy-makers. This will require an act of courage for many boomers who have suffered recent losses in their retirement funds and have been forced into the labor market rather than enjoying retirement. Their loss is our loss, especially for the future of our economy. The boomers were responsible for much of the consumer purchasers in electronics, for example, during the 1990s and cannot expected to sustain that pace of consumerism which would become unnatural for those in a retirement age group. Who will be the next consumers of homes, cars, appliances, computers, etc. in sufficient numbers to compensate for the decline of buyers by boomers-to the tune that consumption represented 70 percent of GDP for many past decades-with the help of easy credit during the past decades? Again, do the following recitation of facts concerning employment of the young adults represent a crisis brewing in America? Does it matter if an aspiring teacher cannot afford to be one because of her/his accumulated debt of $25, 000 which he/she could not reasonably maintain monthly payments and also a quality of life. Does it matter that for many such conditions will not improve but will become an ordinary situation since taking any job just to live tarnishes that college grads reputation as to his/her qualifications for even the fields they initially studied and sought. Or do these employment denials for college grads reach even non-professional types in denying any good-paying jobs for those who have only a high school education or an incomplete college education. What about those who seek only certification in skilled occupations? They may fare better as a rule but in terms of the future of an educated, innovative, expert leader, will skilled employment as plumber, heating and cooling tech, and similar skilled necessary employees compensate for the denial of opportunities in education, the sciences, medicine, engineering, and law. A law graduate now faces a three year law school debt of over $100,000 with diminishing opportunities in traditional fields of law. So in evaluating whether the following which reflect the results of the great disparities in income, ask yourself can low interest rates solve this problem.

Let us begin by showing a personal effect suffered by the age group 25-35 -an effect which is embarrassing and humiliating as time goes on. Young people may be maligned by living with their parents after achieving a college education, but I know of very few this age who would willingly give up an independence which they felt during their college years. Consider two related circumstances impacting young adults, having to live at home and suffering from working at nonstandard jobs often times trying to pay a college debt of $25,000 or more:

Exhibit no 1: From Wall Street Journal article entitled, "More Young Adults Live With Parents" by Neil Shah August 28, 2013 page A2 where these findings are cited: "In a report on the status of families, the Census Bureau on Tuesday said 13.6% of Americans ages 25-34 were living with their parents in 2012, up slightly from 13.4 % in 2011. Though the trend began before the recession, it accelerated sharply during the downturn. In the early 2000s, about 10% of the people in this age group lived at home.

"The figures are the last evidence of the recession's continuing impact on young Americans who are finding it harder to land jobs and take on the costs of setting up their own homes."

Older people might debunk any reasons offered by the young and others for this trend, but consider the profound economic implications down the road:

"The last findings have important implications for the nation's housing market and broader recovery, since they suggest fewer young Americans are buying houses, furniture and appliances- purchases that fuel much of the country's economic growth." Ibid, page A2.

Will there be any relief for this age group in terms of being able to buy those items which represent a quality of life within the reasonable expectations of not only college grads but anyone occupying the middle class.? Not if you examine the composition of the workplace offerings:

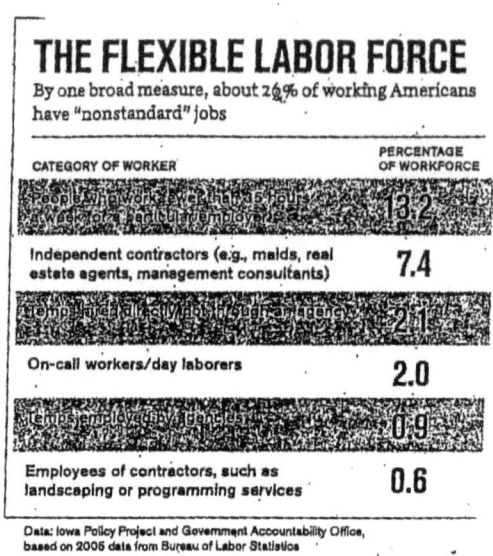

Flexible Labor Force

With respect for those seeking a middle class status, it is undeniable that the middle class today is shrinking-thus denying entry for others in any age group. In order to achieve middle class status, we have seen how often a family must have two income-earners. Any advantage from a two-parent working family is diminished by the cost of child care and work-related expenses. Any ordinary non-college grad or uncertified skilled worker cannot rely upon the job opportunities provided by those shown above. For the college grad, limitations exist beyond the nonstandard jobs shown above. College grads suffer from a peculiar pattern of opportunities which become available. They are exposed to an unnatural demand system for their positions. We must correct the unnatural results imposed on college graduates that occur primarily due to the timing of their graduation. Those who graduate in good economic times will have a lifetime earnings advantage over those who graduate during down times-without regard to any respective abilities of the graduates. Don Peck recites these consequences facing college graduates who graduate in differ economic times:

(a) "The earnings gap between college graduates benefiting from good economic times at graduation and those not so lucky seems to persist. It persists to the point that 'five, ten, fifteen years after graduation, after untold promotions and career changes spanning booms and busts, the unlucky graduate never closes the gap." Pinched, page 64.

(b) The unlucky graduates at mid-career "were significantly less likely to work in professional occupations or other prestigious spheres." Ibid, page64.

(c) They "clung more tightly to their jobs: average job tenure was unusually long. People who entered the workforce during the recession "did switch jobs as much, and particularly for young workers, that's how you increase wages." (by finding a new job which is a better match for your education, training , and skills-that part of unemployment which is to be encouraged so as to establish a better alignment of skills with jobs throughout the country.)" Ibid, page 64.

(d) A bad start in a profession can be a persistent barrier to upward mobility. Peck quotes Lisa Kahn from her study, "when you're forced to start work in a particular low level job or unsexy career, it's easy for other employers to dismiss you as having low potential. Moving up or moving on to something different and better, becomes more difficult." Ibid, page65.

(e) Any bad start by a college graduate can have a permanent effect on their financial well-being. "Recent research suggests that as much as two-thirds of real life-time wage growth typically occurs in the first ten years of a career. After that, as people start families and their career paths lengthen and solidify, jumping the tracks becomes harder." Ibid, page 65

      The final verdict becomes often times like the following path:

      The longer college graduates go without finding suitable jobs as their degree and training would warrant, the greater they become 'damaged' or different people. Krysia Mosskowski, a sociologist at the University of Miami, has "found that in young adults, long bouts of unemployment provoke long, lasting changes in behavior and mental health." Ibid page 66. She cites such behavior changes in drinking problems or depression symptoms unrelated to a person's past. These changes persist even after the person finds steady work. Ibid, page 66. The result for many, then, is as found and foreseen in an article by Ben Casselman entitled, "College Grads May Be Stuck in Low-Skilled Jobs," March 20, 2013 He reported that "The recession left millions of college-educated Americans working in coffee shops and retail stores. Now, new research suggests their job prospects may not improve much when the economy rebounds."

He continued, "Underemployment-skilled workers doing jobs that don't require their level of education-has been one of the hallmarks of the slow recovery. By some measures, nearly half of employed college graduates are in jobs that don't traditionally require a college degree."

Casselman ends on a foreboding note: "Economists have generally assumed the problem was temporary. As the economy improved, companies need more highly educated employees. But in a paper released Monday by the National Breau of Economoc Research, a team of Canadian economists argues that the U. S. faces a long-term problem. They found that unlike the 1990s, when companies needed hundreds of thousands of skilled workers to develop, build and install high tech systems everything from corporate intranets to manufacturing robots demand for such skills has fallen in recent years, even as young people continue to flock to programs that taught them." Ibid page A5

It is submitted that the economic evidence of 1932-33 supports at most a 'jobless recovery'. The following economic 'brief' is persuasive that very little, if any, recovery had begun by 1933-a recovery consisting of appropriate marginal adjustments by most American industries upon which low-interest rates could build or assist. (Would low interest rates in 1930 have started a recovery? Is monetary policy designed to ignite economic recovery? How, through increase in consumption via loans? By increase in industrial capital investment encouraged by low interest rates? What households would qualify for consumer loans from distressed banks or from installment buying? Why would companies with idle capacity resulting from declining sales want to obtain loans to expand their facilities?

1. National Income Statistics for 1930, 1931, 1932, and 1933 fail to support any argument that aggressive Federal Reserve action in 1929-1931 would have averted the great depression. Has much greater Fed actions in 2008-2010 restored economic growth today under much more favorable atmosphere in terms of what the Fed is permitted to do now that it could not do in 1929-1931?

1930	75.4
1931	59.7
1932	42.5
1933	40.3
1934	49.5

(From Historical Statistical Abstract of U.S.: Colonial Times to 1970, Part I Bicentennial Series F144-162, page 234.)

2. Even disposable income declined from 1932 to 1933, Ibid page 234.

3. Private wages and salaries declined from $30.5 billion in 1932 to $29.0 billion in 1933, Ibid, page 235.

4. Per capita disposable income declined from $390 in 1932 to $362 in 1933. Ibid Series F17-30, page 225. (Although per capita consumption went from $389 in 1932 to $364 in 1933 which exceeded per capita disposable income of $362 in 1933, this anomaly could be explained by an increase in credit-lending or distortions caused by luxury spending by the wealthy.)

5. Any recovery in 1932-33 through marginal adjustments occurred without any general re-employment of American workers. Note the number of workers in the following industries in 1932 and in 1933:

	1932	1933
Total (in thousands	23, 628	23,711

(This slight increase reflects the following industries which added workers to their force; (in thousands)

Mining: from 731 to 744

Manufacturing: 6,931 to 7, 397

Wholesale Trade and Retail: 4, 683 to 4, 755 Ibid, Series D-127-141

Any suggestion of great improvement in the financial conditions of workers is allayed by the following conditions of pay and employment:

All manufacturing:	average Weekly Hours	:Average Weekly Earnings
1932	38.1	$16.89
1933	38.1	$16.65

Hours and weekly earnings increased in durable goods manufacturing--weekly hours went from 32.5 to 34.7 from 1932 to 1933 and weekly earnings went from $15.00 to $16.20 Ibid, Series D 802-810. While this may suggest improving times for workers, it obscures the reality of the fate of full-time workers as shown below:

	1932	1933
Average Annual Earnings		
Wholesale and Retail	$1,315	$1,183
Finance, Insurance, Real Estate	$1652	$1,555
Services in General	$ 918	$ 854
Agriculture	$ 250	$ 232

Manufacturing	$1,150	$ 1.086
Mining	$1.016	$ 990
Construction	$ 907	$ 869
Transportation	$1,333	$1,334 (Ibid, Series D739-

764 pages 166-167)

The above statistics provide only a coarse-grain view of the economic trends from 1932 to 1033. A fine-grain view will not only confirm the implications which the above figures offer but will provide the needed reality of every-day working and earning conditions of most Americans from 1932 to 1933.

By 1932, "the automobile industry was operating at only one-fifth of its 1929 capacity…….By the summer of 1932, steel plants operated at 12 per cent of capacity and output of pig iron was the lowest since 1896…..Between 1929 and 1932, freight shipments were cut in half…." Leuchtenburg, op. cit. page248. "Prices of wheat fell from $1.05 a bushel in 1929 to 39 cents in 1932, corn from 81 cents a bushel to 33 cents a bushel, cotton from 17 cents to 6 cents a pound, tobacco from 19 cents to 10 cents a pound." Ibid, page 248. These generally declining prices and output would translate into the following generally deteriorating conditions for Americans:

"The depression touched every area of American life. Bergdorf Goodman slashed sables 40 per cent, Marcus and Company offered a $50,000 emerald ring for $37, 500, and the Pullman Company cut rates on upper berths 20 per cent. The Yankees mailed Babe Ruth a contract for the 1932 season with a $10,000 salary cut, and the Giants offered their star first baseman, Bill Terry, 40 per cent less. The United Hospital Fund reported that donors not only reneged on pledges but even asked that the previous year's contributions be returned to them……Ibid, page 249.

"Three years after the Crash, factory wages shrank $12bilion to $7billion: Ibid, page 254. Others also suffered cutbacks after the initial 'honeymoon' by employers.

"On September 22, 1931, U.S Steel announced a 10 per cent wage cut. General Motors, Bethlehem Steel, and other corporations immediately followed. The wage front was broken. Within a year, sweatshops had mushroomed all throughout the East. In one factory, 13-year old packing girls were paid 50 cents a day. In another plant, apron girls received a daily wage of 20 cents." Ibid, page 254.

Employment practices of wage cutting often resulting in formerly higher paid skilled workers receiving nearly the same pay as unskilled workers. From The Lean Years, page 320. Use of part-time workers, pay cuts, speed-ups on production, and other employment practices permitted some companies from being in the red. Some had returned to profitability like G.M. by selling luxury cars which was a niche market requiring less production output and sells at higher prices per unit. Some companies remained solvent by "rather than dismiss workers with experience and skills would keep them at reduced hours and pay. The rubber industry experimented with six-hour daily shifts and thirty-hour work week as a substitute for the eight-hour shift and forty-hour workweek. Rubber workers held on to their jobs, but with no hourly wage increase pay-checks shrunk by 25 percent" Daily Life in the United States: 1920-1940 page 222.

Use of part-time workers would allow companies to survive, perhaps profit, as illustrated by the Edgar Thomson Works of United Steel at Braddock, Pennsylvania in January 1932:

"There were 424 full-time employees out of a 'normal' force of 5,235. Moreover, while 3,292 others were listed as part-time, only 800 of them found work on a given day." The Lean Years, op. cit. page 317.

Other similar practices flourished in industries as evidenced by the fact that "at the height of the season in men's clothing industry in January 1932, according to Sidney Hillman of the Clothing Workers, only 10 percent of the New York manufacturing was employed." Ibid, page 317.

Despite improved profits by Chrysler, G.M. in its luxury car sales, and others, 1933 does not hold up as a year of wide-spread economic recovery consisting of significant increases in the sale of durable goods, housing, steel, lumber, and other 'commanding heights' of the economy. The fact that some of the best engineered cars in history offered at lowered prices in 1933-34 failed to achieve significant increases in sales is proof that cars and other durable goods were naturally linked more to changes in incomes rather than changes in prices or even interest rates. Only excessive extension of credit in the 1920s supported sales of cars and other durable goods. Credit became a substitute for earnings.

The above summarized narrative of conditions during the 1920s reveal parallels between then and today. Again, any listing of these conditions could apply to the 1920s and 2000-2010:

1. Employment practices of wage cuts.

2. Employment practices of hiring part-time workers or temps.

3. Increasing profits but no increase in the number of job.

4. Employment practice of outsourcing of jobs.

5. A number of skilled workers receiving low pay as would an unskilled worker.

6. Great disparities in earnings due to in great part an unbalanced industrial structure favoring financial markets and real estate.

7. Consumption which is artificially supported by easy credit not justified by the consumers' income

8. Spending and investments motivated excessively by a sense of one's increased wealth-wealth which has not actually been converted into cash or its equivalent.

9. Several banks in financial difficulty due in great part to ill-advised lending and investing.

10. Investment banks generated too much income internally through fees and commissions as opposed to serving the interest of their clients.

11. While several companies enjoy accumulated retained earnings, others are in industries which required dramatic changes in management policies-changes which represent high-risk taking. Many of these companies which represent high risks make new

products and are regarded as high-tech type firms. One period had new pioneering products like T.V. (1920s) while the other period witnessed the emergence of bio-tech firms.

12. Both periods were overly concerned with international finance whether it be the gold standard or the exchange value of the dollar.

How could monetary policies address all of these issues? Minsky, the late economist stated that great disparities in earnings and the need to restructure the economy could not be addressed through market solutions-solutions which monetary policy favors excessively. Lower interest rates only provided incentives for speculation, excessive consumer credit, mergers, and the advent of questionable securities such a securitized mortgages. In other words, in addition to it intended positive effects, low-interest rates also introduced added volatility to the economy as security prices bounced up and down with bubbles created by the monetary policy eventually crash. The peril is that financial 'innovations' will return with financial institutions and brokers again pursuing securitizations, derivatives, mergers, and currency manipulations in the quest for short-term profits. There is growing evidence that these practices are returning as reflected below:

financial deepening' in its September 2008 issue which feature this graphic display to illustrate the 'deepening':

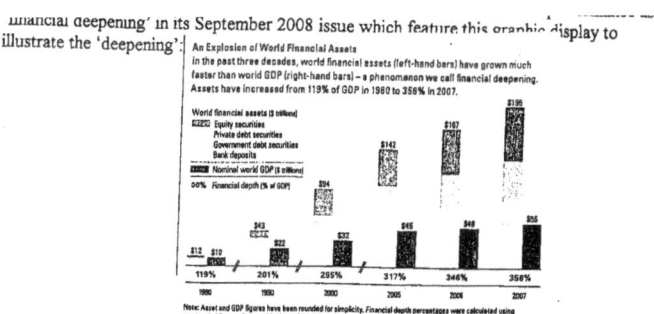

(From New Thinking for a New Financial Order" by Diana Farrell page 26, at 27.

Despite increasing evidence of a need for a redirection of capital investing and trading, recent articles have shown a propensity for banks and other financial institutions to resume the practices listed above. Consider this report from the Wall Street Journal in September 2013:

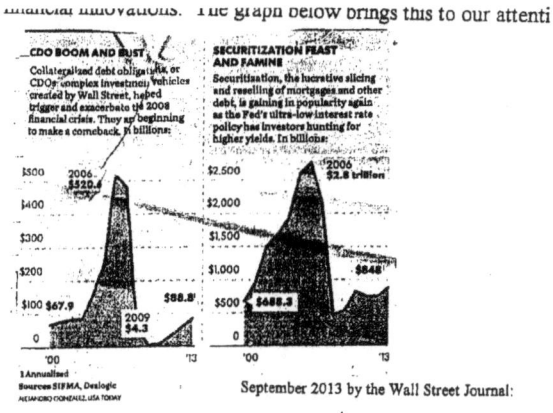

September 2013 by the Wall Street Journal.

Instead of adhering to the risk adverse model of investing, firms, governments, and individuals must pursue worthy projects such as infrastructure, which are of a long-term nature. A shift of capital investment towards human and technological advancements must occur.

"That shift (into the next new industry) never happened. At the beginning of the second decade of the third American plutocratic era, finance preferred to invest in old technologies located in new regions rather than in new technologies located in old regions. Finance's conception of risk management makes it most comfortable with incremental changes within established investment fields (portfolio diversification): short-term profit horizons (quarterly or yearly balance sheets) and 'financial engineering' thanks to the supposed predictive accuracy of complex computer models based on data drawn from only the past ten to twenty years. Investing in new industrial sectors such as biotechnology and clean energy did not conform to any of these conceptions of good risk management. What did conform, and conform perfectly, was real estate." American Interest, "The Foreign Policy of Plutocracies" by James Kurth November/December 2011 pages 5 thru 17, at page 15.

One could summarize the 'effective' cause of this misalignment in capital investments—it is the temptations for quick financial profits offered to 'investors' by the historical low interest rates. Accompanying this misallocation of capital is an economic landscape which harmonizes with the dominance of finance over the real economy of goods and services. This landscape consists of the following:

      1. Employment practices of wage cuts.

      2. Employment practices of hiring part-time workers or temps.

      3. Increasing corporate profits but no increase in the number of jobs.

      4. Employment practices of outsourcing work

      5. A number of skilled and educated workers receiving the low pay of unskilled workers. See the graph below:

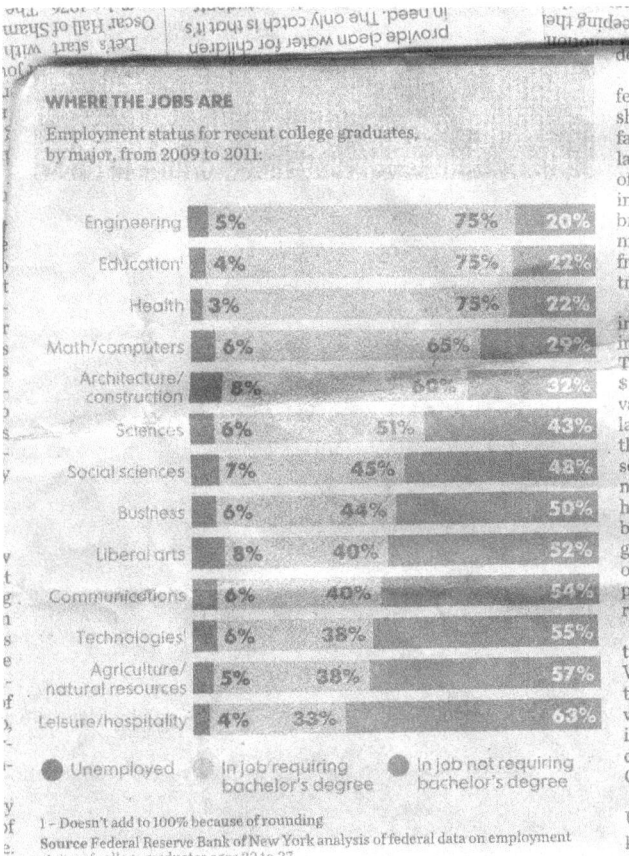

6. Great disparities in earnings due in great part to an unbalanced economy in which industries such as finance, real estate, and insurance lack middle income positions.

7. Consumption is artificially supported by consumer debt-not increase in disposable income.

8. Consumption is provided incentives by a sense of increased wealth or well-being produced by rising prices of real estate.

9. Several banks became financially distressed due to improper lending and investment practices.

10. Investment banks generated too much income internally through fees and commissions with almost complete indifference as to the advisability of both.

11. A credit crunch occurred as a result of wide-spread indebtedness of banks, households, and businesses. The credit-crunch lingered as banks used cash infusions from the Fed to shore up their balance sheets and corporations hoarded their earnings.

SUMMING UP

Our country has been guided, more or less, in its history by two documents, The Declaration of Independence and Adam Smith's Wealth of Nations.-the former emphasizing equality and the latter emphasizing freedom of individual pursuit of self-interest in achieving economic wealth and prosperity. H. W. Brands has given the following warning in his book, American Colossus:

"Yet the dual manifestos of 1776 were also dueling manifestos. The visions limned by Jefferson and Smith were in some ways complementary, with each claiming to maximize personal freedom, the first in politics, the second in economics. But in other respects they were antagonistic. Democracy depends on equality, capitalism on inequality. Citizens in a democracy come to the public square with one-vote each: participants in a capitalist economy arrives at the marketplace with unequal rewards. Nor is inequality simply a side effect of capitalism. A capitalist economy can't operate without it. The differing talents and resources of individuals are recruited and sorted by the differential rewards, which reinforce the original differences. Inequality drives the engine of capitalism as surely as unequal temperatures drive heat engines— including the steam engines that were the signature devices of industrial capitalism." Page 5 of Anchor 2011 paperback ed.

One lesson to be gained from this narrative is that the condition of the economy cannot be reduced to the matter of growth in GD P. Many have commented on the need for a fair distribution of the earnings which compose GDP. "Affluence can be shared, or hoarded". Steven Stoll, "The Mis-measure of All Things" Orion September/October 2012, pages 67-71 at page 68 only through the instrument of the peoples' government can sufficient energy and resources by brought to bear on the need to restructure our economy towards a long-term destiny of an economy "for the people, of the people, and by the people".

www.ingramcontent.com/pod-product-compliance
Lightning Source LLC
Chambersburg PA
CBHW051759170526
45167CB00005B/1812